THE DISCRIMINATING MIND

Steven J. Hendlin, Ph.D., is a clinical psychologist in the full-time private practice of psychotherapy in Irvine, California. He has published over thirty five professional and popular articles, reviews and book chapters in various areas of psychotherapy, personal growth, Eastern philosophy and forms of meditation.

Dr Hendlin is a Diplomate in Psychotherapy, American Board of Psychotherapy and a Diplomate in Behavioral Medicine, International Academy of Behavioral Medicine. He is an adjunct faculty member of the California Graduate Institute and holds membership in a dozen professional associations. He has been a student of Eastern philosophy and various forms of meditation for the past twenty years. He lives with his wife, Deborah, also a psychologist, in Laguna Beach.

M
A
N
D
A
L
A

THE
DISCRIMINATING MIND

A Guide to Deepening Insight and Clarifying Outlook

STEVEN J. HENDLIN, Ph.D.

M A N D A L A

UNWIN PAPERBACKS

London   Boston   Sydney   Wellington

First published by Unwin ® Paperbacks, an imprint of Unwin Hyman Limited, in 1989.

Unwin Hyman Limited
15–17 Broadwick Street
London W1V 1FP

Unwin Hyman Inc.
9 Winchester Terrace, Winchester, Massachusetts 01890, USA

Allen & Unwin Australia Pty Ltd
8 Napier Street, North Sydney, NSW 2060, Australia

Allen & Unwin New Zealand Pty Ltd
with the Port Nicholson Press
Compusales Building, 75 Ghuznee Street, Wellington, New Zealand

---

British Library Cataloguing in Publication Data

Hendlin, Stephen J.
    The discriminating mind: a guide to deepening
insight and clarifying outlook.
1. Self-development
I. Title
158'.1
ISBN 0-04-440501-4

Phototypeset in Palatino by Computape (Pickering) Ltd.,
North Yorkshire
Printed and bound in Great Britain by
The Guernsey Press Co. Ltd., Guernsey, Channel Islands.

*Dedicated with love to
my mother,
Susan Selma Hendlin Phillips*

CONTENTS

PREFACE

I wrote this book because I believe there are certain basic concepts with which all educated, self-reflective people interested in personal growth ought to be familiar. My attempt has been to bring together selected ideas from Western psychology and psychotherapy and tie them to Eastern spiritual concepts.

I have tried to keep this book as simple as possible, while at the same time, not sacrificing the essence of the concepts. Because my intended audience is psychotherapists and teachers in the field of psychology, as well as the greater educated public, the book will most likely be too simple for some and not simple enough for others. The challenge has been to take what are not-so-easy to explain ideas and make them intelligible for larger numbers of people.

What are called the Eastern 'consciousness disciplines' have much of value to offer traditional Western psychology and psychotherapy. And much to offer the larger public, who want to use whatever is available, in thought and practice, to improve their minds and deepen the meaning of their lives. The practical maps of the mind these disciplines have offered for over two thousand years, and the disciplined practices that go with them, are only now beginning to be discovered, used and abused by growing numbers in the Western culture.

Because I spend most of my time practicing psychotherapy as a psychologist in private practice, I also wanted to share case examples which I felt would be instructive in illustrating certain concepts. All of the case examples given are composites of over a thousand patients I have seen over the last fifteen years. As they used to say at the end of the TV show, *Dragnet*, 'the names have been changed to protect the innocent.'

Additionally, I wanted to offer some basic exercises which related to the concepts being presented, to make them more meaningful for the reader. But, as you will see, I promise no simple solutions, no easy answers. I have witnessed far too many people delude themselves over the years in their search for easy answers.

So, this was my combination plate: Western psychology, Eastern philosophy and clinical experiences, sprinkled with some practical experiments. I hope this recipe is neither too spicy nor too bland. I will be satisfied if this book offers something to both those who are just beginning on the road to self-discovery as well as those who are already some distance down the path.

I am grateful to all the patients I have had the privilege of working with and learning about the intricacies of the mind from over the past fifteen years. In sharing their struggles with me, they have helped me discover something profound about the resiliency of the human spirit.

I thank Apple Computer for bringing us the simplicity of the Macintosh SE, which makes writing and editing fun and creative instead of drudgery. Writing became literally 'word-play,' and the play has been very satisfying.

I thank and deeply honor all those who have been my spiritual, philosophical and psychological teachers and therapists, both living and dead, through direct encounter and through written word, who have contributed to my growth and understanding.

I thank my editor at Unwin Hyman, Marion Russell, for her honesty, level-headedness and flexibility during our numerous trans-Atlantic phone calls and letters, and her support of my work. In my writing she saw something she liked and, based on only three chapters, was not afraid to take a chance with it.

Most of all, I thank my devoted and loving wife, Deborah Hendlin, PhD for tolerantly accepting the role of 'computer widow' over the year of three-day weekends it took me to write this book and for her unrelenting confidence in and support of my writing. I thank her as well for reading each chapter as it was hot off the printer and her many constructive comments. To balance my soaring flights of fantasy, she would always gently bring me and the manuscript back down to earth.

Steven Hendlin
November, 1988
Laguna Beach, California

Introduction

SITTING IN THE CABOOSE: OUR PREDICAMENT

Much of the common suffering that we experience we bring upon ourselves. While it is true that we are sometimes 'victims of circumstances' seemingly beyond our control, much more of the time, we are simply 'victims' of the chatter of our own minds and the stories we tell ourselves about the nature of our personal world. There are so many conflicting voices we hear that it becomes, quite often, extremely difficult to slow down this 'chatter' and these various voices long enough to hear clearly what we need for ourselves. We need to learn to be on 'speaking terms' with ourselves.

There are certain ways we may work with the chattering 'monkey-mind,' which we will work with as 'experiments' in the following chapters. For now, it is only important that we see that the nature of our predicament includes each of us being 'issued' a chattering 'monkey-mind' with which we are continually having to come to terms. Our attempts to come to terms with this out of control mind will be the focus of much that follows.

The nature of our predicament includes some very basic facts about ourselves. It includes the fact that we are forced to live our lives facing great contradictions about the nature of life itself. One aspect of this nature is that we strive to find meaning and satisfaction knowing that we don't have forever, that someday we will die. How do we deal with this knowledge? How does it add or subtract from the meaning of our lives?

We are biological animals with very real biological needs; we are continually having, in one way or another, to relate to our needs for food, shelter, stimulation, rest and metabolic homeostasis. In addition we face the fact that we must relate in some way to the social world in which we find ourselves.

1

Much of our identity, of who we feel ourselves to be, rests on exactly *how* we relate to the significant others in our world, and the kind of reactions we receive from these important people. Part of our personal identity and self-image rests on how we 'process' the reactions and direct feedback we receive from others. We cannot escape this social world in which we are embedded, although, from time to time, there are always those who try. 'Just the facts, ma'am!'

Among the other contradictory facts of our existence is the need to both 'fit in with the herd' and, at the same time, to in some way stand out and establish our own, unique identity. We are constantly forced to play a balancing game (actually one of many balancing games), in which we must attempt to satisfy contradictory felt needs for being included and yet standing uniquely apart.

Not so surprisingly, we end up at times very confused! Very confused as to who we think we are, as to what the meaning of our lives 'should' be, and as to how to make choices which will bring us satisfaction and a sense of well-being in our lives.

Nor is it so surprising that we reach out in every direction to 'experts' in all areas to guide us and help us make the 'correct' choices when we are unsure which path to take. So much of the time, it feels like there is no guaranteed way to know that the choices we are making will work out to be the 'best' ones when we look back and try to judge. You have probably read all kinds of 'self-help' books which will try to make the whole business of knowing one's mind seem easier than it actually is.

And because we are in such a hurry to get it all NOW, we are easily taken in by promises of instant change, instant cure, instant happiness, gobbling up all the 'one-minute manager,' 'one-minute lover' and 'one-minute parent' books we can get our hands on. Not so surprisingly, much of this material is swallowed whole and is not of much real use to us.

Anyone who ends up being a 'one-minute' anything is not going to do a very good job at it and will most likely spend a lot more minutes making up for the sloppy consequences their 'one-minute' mentality has led to. And we partially understand this, as we realize that simply reading a book about controlling one's mind isn't the same as actually being able to do it.

The truth is, no matter what the books tell you about being able to control your own mind, the greater realization is that this is probably the single most difficult thing for a human being to do!! Think about it – can you think of *anything* more difficult than controlling your own mind?

So while I don't want to discourage you from reading 'self-help' books, I do think that you must be very wary of *any* book that makes it sound too easy. And, of course, that's what makes these books sell – authors and publishers would like you to believe that just reading their book on guilt, anxiety, sex, relationships, or anything else is enough to do the job. And even when we realize it isn't, do you think this stops us from buying and reading more of them? Of course not!

I can forewarn you right here, at the very start, it is highly unlikely that you are going to be psychologically 'transformed' or spiritually 'enlightened' when you finish this book! It is more likely that you will have acquired some good ideas with which to think about yourself and some good exercises with which to experiment, if you choose.

But, please, don't believe my book is going to take the place of psychotherapy (if you need it), or spiritual guidance by a 'qualified' guru or member of the clergy, if this is what you need. This is your warning or, what in my profession of clinical psychology, we call getting 'informed consent.' To paraphrase Ram Dass (1971):

Paper Cakes Don't Satisfy Hunger!!

This means that all the reading of psychology books in the world, including this one, is not the same as satisfying the hunger to understand through **personal experience**. But let us do the best we can to gain some cognitive understanding that points to the experience. That is what we will do in this book.

Now that you have been 'informed,' I shall assume if you continue to read you are giving your 'consent' to be responsible for however this book may affect you. I hope, if nothing else, it gives you something valuable to think about. If the concepts, examples, or experiments help change your thinking and behavior then you will

3

have gotten a lot. But this 'a lot' will have been because you *experienced* the truth of what you were reading about. We will talk more about our hunger for experience in Chapter 10.

SITTING IN THE CABOOSE

Back to the issue of controlling this mind. One image and metaphor that seems to be helpful in conveying this out of control feeling and lack of direction as we go through our lives is that of riding on a train chugging down the track of our life. It is as if we find ourselves sitting at the back of the caboose, only able to watch the scenery pass by as we feel the whiz of the motion of our time passing.

We feel unable to control the direction of the train, and even unable to look in the same direction (forward) that the train is going. Only as events go by do we seem, through reflection, to make meaning of them. As they unfold, we are only able to be as present as possible and yet, so much of the time, we don't allow ourselves to be fully present or don't even *want* to be fully present.

So, the feeling is more that we know we are living by the experience of time passing, just as watching the scenery go by as we sit facing where we have come from lets us know the train of our lives is moving in some direction. If we could just catch up to the present, maybe we could get a grasp on where we are going, but – wait a minute – first we have to make sense of where we just came from!

This seems to be the nature of our predicament, not something we ask for, but just part of what comes by being alive. We need to be honest with ourselves about some of these things – it is easy to pretend that these things aren't true, that our 'real' predicament is not so complicated or so demanding of us.

But when we begin to pay close attention to the nature of our own mind, to our thoughts which form our persistent attitudes, we see some things about this chattering mind that just aren't very pleasant. We could try to make it sound prettier than it is – but, in the end, we always will have to come back to facing this mind; there's just no getting away from ourselves!

The alternative becomes to get to know this chattering mind and learn methods for controlling its incessant chatter. This is not easy, but can be learned with persistent practice, and slowly, we can begin to feel some control over this mind – a mind that we call 'ours' but which is not about to be dictated to by any part of us. The truth is, this mind we call 'ours' is controlling us – we are not controlling it. Again, we like to pretend that this isn't true to avoid the anxiety of feeling out of control.

'BRING ME YOUR MIND!'

And where is this mind we are attempting to control? There is an old Zen story about the monk who, after intense meditation practice, is frustrated because he can't still his mind and can't find any peace. He runs to his teacher and begs him to do something to help him still his mind. The teacher says to his student, 'Bring me your mind and I will still it.'

And this request – 'bring me your mind' – is enough to send the student into a deep understanding. He realizes there is no substantial 'thing' of a mind to bring to his teacher. He can't 'find' his mind to give to his teacher.

So, as we talk throughout this book about 'knowing your own mind,' and various other references to our minds, you might want (in the back of your mind) to gently ask yourself: 'Where is my mind?' Yes, we will assume we all know what we are talking about when we refer to one's own mind, but don't pass up a good opportunity to ask at a deeper level what it really means to have a mind.

IDENTIFYING THE CONTRADICTIONS

Let's go back and examine more closely some of the contradictions which face us – contradictions and facts of our existence which we are loosely calling our 'predicament.'

For example, the most astounding contradiction of all is that on the one hand, we are aware of ourselves as unique individuals, and this gives us a feeling of overwhelming importance. But on the other hand, we are also aware of our mortality, and this gives us a feeling of fear and frustration. Working with this contradiction is perhaps the central problem in our lives, and how we relate to it determines largely what meaning and satisfaction we experience in our lives.

A second contradiction is that while we must honor the physical body and attend to its needs, we are much more than the physical body. We spend much attention caring for the body, trying to keep it functioning without pain, and do our best to experience pleasant physical sensations through the body.

And yet, we watch this physical body change continuously, and are always alert as to what disease process may be taking place, and what could happen to this body to make us experience pain and suffering. We do our best to deny that this physical body is slowly deteriorating and that having a body means we are going to suffer. And the more we identify with the body as being solely who we think we are, the more suffering we have to bear.

An ancient inquiry goes like this: 'What is the most amazing characteristic of human beings?' Answer: 'That although fellow humans grow old and die all around them, they delude themselves it will never really happen to them.'

A third contradiction is that we are torn between the parts of us that are capable of the most insensitive, cruel and unbelievably horrid behavior on the one hand and the most compassionate, loving and altruistic behavior on the other. We are capable of the most stupid, foolish, petty and destructive impulses and behavior and also the most thoughtful, brilliant and creative projects which may elevate us next to God.

We have all of it within us, individually and collectively. And, as we know, it's not always so easy to live with – our psychological stew can get quite spicy!

We also live with the contradiction of needing to establish an identity which distinguishes us from others where we can value our personal, idiosyncratic relationship to our self and yet also obtain the gratifications which can only come from connecting to others.

Each of us is a subject to ourselves and an object to all others. We do our best to bridge this objective gap by sharing ourselves with others as intimately as we are able. And yet if we get too close we fear we will lose ourselves in the other, unable to remain separate and unique. We wonder 'If I get lost in you, what will become of me?'

A final contradiction is the problem related to the above issue of uniqueness. While each of us needs to build a strong sense of individual identity, develop positive self-images and, as psychologists like to say, 'heighten ego strength and self-esteem,' at a certain point of our individual growth, self-assertion needs to give way to self-transcendence.

6

TOWARD SELF-TRANSCENDENCE

By self-transcendence I mean identifying with something beyond ourselves, something that relates to our spiritual nature of being part of all existence – not just a puny brain and a slowly deteriorating body. This brain that we possess is truly amazing as to what it is capable of doing.

We all know the wonders of our own minds – our capacity to visualize 'in the mind's eye,' to imagine our futures, to plan, remember, think creatively and think about our thinking. This mind that we have is so powerful, so capable, so astounding in its power and depth. And yet, it is actually rather 'puny' compared to the vaster realities in life that our minds are unable to comprehend.

So, when I speak of identifying with something larger than our mind, it is this 'larger than' that I am calling 'spiritual.' It is of spirit because it is not of the material world we live in. It is not a reality we can touch, although it is a reality that is possible to experience. It is the ground of all realities and our natural state before we divide up our world into subject and object. In Chapter 3, following Zen terminology, we call it 'Absolute self.'

While it is important that we try to paint as realistic a picture as possible of our predicament, my intent is not to make it sound like we are 'doomed.' We must remember how much real satisfaction, joy and growth is possible, even with all of the limitations and constrictions we must face. How sublime, poetic, meaningful and poignant our lives are! And, of course, how fragile and delicate life itself is and therefore, how much it must be taken seriously and sincerely for all it is worth.

In writing this book, I have purposely introduced certain topics which are touched on in one chapter, and then again in a subsequent chapter or chapters. I believe this 'hammering it in' method will help the reader understand and assimilate the material presented as well as help tie the chapters together. One task in writing has been to present what I believe are important concepts in clear, coherent and readable terms without overly simplifying them or watering them down. In line with this, I have purposely kept references and citations of other works to a minimum: you will see only a few in the text.

The purpose of this introduction has been to briefly and in very broad strokes paint a picture of some of what we all face as human beings. Now, let us look more closely at some of these issues.

=== 1 ===

CONFRONTING THE
MONKEY-MIND

Why do I refer to the mind as a 'monkey-mind'? Because, just as the monkeys at the zoo never stop moving, never stop chattering, our minds react normally in this same agitated way. This is not my own symbol for the mind – the chattering monkey is the symbol used in Hindu philosophy to represent the mind. We all understand how hard it can be to simply stay focused long enough to pay attention to the free flow of our own thoughts.

As I write this, for example, of all the thoughts which may pass through my mind, I am forced to choose one from the stream and somehow focus on it, instead of simply allowing it to come and go. To make this more real for yourself, stop reading for a moment and try the following simple experiment.

Experiment
Notice the fragments of thought which pass through your mind for two minutes. Simply watch one thought and how quickly it associates to a second, related thought. Watch what happens when you interrupt the free flow of thought and choose one to focus on. What happens next?

How much does it feel like your thoughts come on their own and how much does it feel like *you* are consciously able to will what thought will next appear? Spend another minute just watching what thoughts come up which are associated to your answering of these questions. Notice any tangents your thoughts may take before you come back to this writing. Also notice any resistance you may experience to trying this experiment with your thoughts.

*

The purpose of the above experiment (one, of course, which you may try again at any time when you are interested in turning toward your thoughts), is to help us understand how so much of what we are thinking is really quite out of our control. We fight 'tooth and nail', not wanting to believe this is the actual state of affairs with which we are continually confronted. But, like it or not, this is just part of what it means to have a 'monkey-mind.'

And what is important to understand about this is that we *resist* letting this awareness stay with us for very long because we can't tolerate the feeling of being out of control of our own minds . . . we just can't stand it! So, we prefer to pretend that we are very much in control of our minds, and that we can make orderly, rational decisions to help satisfy our needs on all levels. How true is this when we are honest with ourselves?

Of course, we *are* able to think rationally with our minds and we *are* able to focus our minds to a high degree to be able to organize our thinking and produce all kinds of theoretical and practical projects through the power of our thought. But (and this is what I'm driving at), no matter what focused thinking we are able to do, our *unconscious* feeling is that *basically we can't control our own minds*. For many of us, this may be painfully conscious.

But being able to think rationally doesn't mean we're 'in control.' To 'think rationally' means we know how to use the cognitive functions we have developed over a lifetime. And, to whatever degree we are able to think clearly and logically, our rational thinking will actually *be* rational, linear, orderly and help us solve daily problems.

But to have this rational process available does not mean we are able to control the welter of thoughts which are bubbling up continuously just below the surface of awareness. There is a vast inner universe of quasi-logical and non-logical chatter of which we are totally out of control. The truth is, we don't know what thought may pop up next! We experience it as more true that 'a thought just occurred to me' (which is how we most often verbalize it), than that 'I just had this thought.'

Now, even though we could say that someone who is more mentally healthy will be more able to identify with their own thoughts and express them accordingly (for example, 'I just had this thought . . .'), the actual *experience* of it is not so much of being the agent producing the thought as much as being the passive recipient of what thought makes itself 'heard' inside. Isn't this true?

This can get tricky because when we use our minds to think rationally and critically in a focused manner, it *does* feel like we are more the agent producing the thought. Our own ambivalence as to who is doing the thinking shows up in our way of expressing ownership of our thoughts.

In my work with patients in psychotherapy, this is many times expressed by people as the fear of losing control of their minds, or of 'going crazy.' Many understand how little control they have over strong impulses which come up repeatedly and how futile is the effort to control these impulses simply by 'will power,' compared to the strength of the impulses themselves. It is as if the impulses have a mind of their own. And, in a certain sense, they indeed do!

THE 'MIND' OF IMPULSES

What do we mean by saying 'impulses have a "mind" of their own'? What we mean is that sometimes even with our greatest exertion of will power and good intention, the desires which come up crying for attention and satisfaction are many times more powerful than we can possibly control. And, of course, this is part of the story of human-kind from the very beginning – how civilized (rational) versus how primitive (impulsively driven by strong emotion) we are toward each other.

How quickly do we befriend each other and treat each other in 'civilized' ways versus how fast do we feel threatened by and attack each other? How fast, to put it bluntly, do we attack or kill the other when faced by threat? And how are we to control the powerful drives which make themselves felt beyond our ability to mentally contain them?

When our impulses feel so powerful and our desires are so strong, what chance does the mind have of being able to temper the storm? How, in other words, can we use our minds to keep these impulses in check? Or at least learn to satisfy these impulses in safe and moderate ways? Can we really gain control of our feelings of sexual desire, rage, anger, jealousy and emotional pain?

Yes, we can – at least to some extent. But, as Sigmund Freud showed, we pay a price for the 'civilization' of our impulses. And part of that price is that a lot gets held in and turned back against ourselves. This is the defense mechanism called 'retroflection,' which we will go into in more detail in Chapter 3.

In addition to stronger impulses, we have more subtle impulses which are more commonly thought of as everyday desires. Desire plays such a powerful role in our daily life that it seems at times like we are simply being dragged through our lives in the pursuit of satisfying one desire after another. If it is not the desire to make ourselves comfortable and feel at least neutral and, at best, pleasant physical sensations, it is our emotional and psychological needs and desires that clamor for attention.

We spend a lot of time simply putting mental checks or controls on our desires, especially the ones related to immediate psychological and emotional desires. And even our powerful physical desires we are continually needing to hold in check, even though we may not be aware of it.

Because of the battle to keep all of these desires in check, Sigmund Freud was not very optimistic about our chances for finding much deep satisfaction in our lives. He thought that the best we could do was to find meaningful work and be able to have loving relationships. He did not see much value in anything of a religious or spiritual nature being of much help to us.

This is because he felt that our strong desires were needing constant attention just to be kept in control – otherwise, he thought, we would simply stop being 'civilized' and do nothing but spend our time pursuing satisfaction of these desires. Sex and aggression were the two most powerful, he believed. So the best he thought we could do was to 'sublimate' (refine, purify and externalize) these strong urges into some productive work projects.

In other words, although he thought we really might want to be indulging in sexual pleasure all day, instead we learn to go to work, play sports, build tall buildings, watch erotic movies and watch men beat each other to a pulp in a boxing ring, and do all kinds of other things just to keep these desires under control. We learn, in other words, to compromise and find 'socially acceptable' outlets for these impulses. To the degree we don't we face the wrath of the civil and criminal law system and social ostracism.

Eastern philosophy, and Buddhism in particular, teaches that the reason for this predicament is that we keep wanting something that really can't be had. That is, we want to create a state of continual satisfaction – a state of satisfaction that doesn't stop, so we are in continual bliss. Yet this is not possible, no matter how much we wish it were. And so, as our satisfaction changes into the awareness of a new desire, we keep trying to get back to a state of satisfaction.

According to Buddhist thinking, this is one of the things that has to be understood: as long as we keep trying to keep some permanent state of satisfaction we are going to suffer because *things are changing from moment to moment, and we need to be able to allow things to change without holding on too tightly to our satisfactions or temporary states of pleasant consciousness.* We will come back again to this theme of needing to learn how and when to let go in our lives.

BEING ON SPEAKING TERMS WITH ONESELF

The nature of the chattering 'monkey-mind' is that with so much noise taking place, it is often impossible to sort out the various parts of ourselves which are clamoring for attention. If we can assume that the various voices we hear inside, especially those which are in conflict, represent different parts of our personality, it becomes crucial to greater self-awareness to be able to *hear* our different voices and appreciate the messages they are trying to give us on their own behalf.

But how can we distinguish between these competing voices? Don't they all, much of the time, just sound like nonsensical chatter? To be 'on speaking terms' with oneself means to be able to hear the individual interests being represented by each voice. We can hear the different voices by listening closely for a particular tone or manner with which they present themselves.

For example, we may hear a nagging, whining, complaining tone which is always the tone used by Mother. Or we may hear the stern, commanding and intimidating tone reserved for Father and Other Authority Figures. Or maybe we hear the teasing, cajoling and enticing tone of an old lover. We can, with some close listening, get a good idea of what part of ourself a specific voice represents by listening for its distinctive tone.

Another good way to learn more about these different parts of ourself, as represented by our different inner voices, is to give each of our inner voices an outer voice. To speak out loud, in other words, exactly what we hear from the inner voice. This is actually a very powerful technique used in psychotherapy, especially in Gestalt therapy, to help one get in touch with parts of oneself on more 'intimate' terms. Let's try to make this more concrete.

Experiment

Sit quietly for a minute and wait until you hear an inner voice which comes through 'loud and clear.' Perhaps it will come through only as a 'one liner,' just one short phrase or sentence or maybe more than a sentence will be heard. Whatever you hear, take it seriously by staying with it for a few moments. Now say what you hear inside *out loud*, just to hear what it sounds like.

Don't worry what the content is for now – just get the feel of hearing yourself voice out loud your inner chattering. (Don't be bothered by the word 'chattering' – this is simply what it is – not to be taken as a negative judgement about our inner voice contents, although, much of the time, it is not all that useful.)

In psychotherapy, the technique made popular by Gestalt therapists involves asking the client to have a conversation between two different inner voices representing two different and usually conflicting parts of oneself. Thus was born the famous 'empty chair' method, popularized by Fritz Perls in his demonstrations in the 1960s.

Now, we are talking about not just a phrase or sentence that comes through but entire dialogues which make up our different 'sub-personalities.' Usually, we are much more aware of and in touch with one side of the polarity (two opposite sides) than the other. So, in playing both parts, one purpose is to help us become more aware of the part with which we have lost touch.

For example, I may have one part coming through (the 'Unrelenting Taskmaster'), who tells me to write something every day, with no excuses. Another part of me (let's call it 'All in Good Time'), coming through in a very different, more understanding and supportive voice, reminds me that while 'Taskmaster' has good intentions, it is not always possible or even desirable to live up to his expectations. A fragment of the dialogue may go like this:

> **Taskmaster** *Come on, get with it! If you want to get the writing done you must stay with it and write something every single day. Stop trying to drag the thing out forever . . . Let's get going and*

really pour yourself into this project. You're getting older and still no book. What are you waiting for? The sky to fall?

All in Good Time   Stop pressuring me, Taskmaster, I really don't always feel like writing and certainly am not going to commit to writing every single day! You know very well that I don't have the luxury to sit down every day and write unless we were willing to wake up very early to write before going to the office or late at night, after a full day's work. What's the hurry, anyway?

Taskmaster   *Look, I don't care when you want to do it, but I insist that you take the writing of this book more seriously and stop giving yourself excuses for not persevering. I know you well enough to know that you will always have a 'good excuse' to put this writing aside. I will hound you continually, reminding you of your inability to sustain your effort, if I must . . . And don't give me that sour grapes bit about resisting writing because you don't want the book to be lumped with all the other simplistic psycho-babble!*

All in Good Time   You may try to make me feel guilty if you must, but don't expect that to do the trick. You know we have been quite productive with our writing the last ten years – just because we haven't punched out the book for the public yet is no reason to use these 'strong-arm' tactics. Have some trust in me that the writing will be done as it gets done – there is no reason to pressure me as you do.

So, there you have a short example of two conflicting parts of me, represented by two different voices, each making itself heard. These conflicting or polar opposite voices can, when they are out in the open, learn to respect and even appreciate each other and realize that they may co-exist with each other in relative harmony. They may also, when less threatened by each other, begin to compromise. Instead of being just 'chatter,' each voice may contribute to a fuller sense of my diversity. But the first step is to acknowledge them.

WHAT IS THE DISCRIMINATING MIND?

We can't over-emphasize the importance of paying attention to these internal voices as a tool for gaining more control over the 'monkey-mind.' Unless we are able to decipher exactly what is going on with our internal chatter, we have little chance of gaining any control over it. And the control that we gain in hearing our internal voices is a control which allows us to think more clearly and to slowly develop what I call the *discriminating mind*.

The discriminating mind is the mind that is able to make distinctions and to see subtle differences between ideas, relationships and forms. It is the mind that keeps things where they belong, understanding that 'apples are apples and oranges are oranges.'

The discriminating mind is the mind that we develop as we get to know who we are and what matters to us, that is, what we value and what gets priority.

The discriminating mind is the mind that doesn't confuse one thing with another and the mind that produces our best judgement after considered thought. It is the mind which is capable of razor-sharp clarity in noticing subtle changes in the ongoing flow of life experience. It is the highest use and respect for the rational mind along with emotion and intuition. We will come back and focus on the discriminating mind in a later chapter.

For now, let us stay with the chattering monkey-mind. It is from the chaos of the monkey-mind that we develop the disciplined thinking which becomes the discriminating mind. And the discriminating mind is always having to deal with the internal chatter, although it becomes less predominate and chaotic as we learn to 'turn down the dial' so that this chatter is not so loud.

You will probably realize (if you haven't already), as you begin to pay attention to sorting out your internal voices, that it is not always so easy to hear one voice come through very clearly. What we don't often consciously realize is that most of the time there is actually one chain of thought going on behind another.

Perhaps you've had the experience of listening to music with part of your attention and noticing a chain of thought associated to what the music brings up in you. Then you will notice there may be a whole other level of associations commenting on the first chain of associations.

OUR THOUGHT IS LIKE CHINESE BOXES

To put it more simply, it appears, when we pay *very close attention* to the nature of our internal monkey-mind chatter, that there are simultaneous *levels upon levels of thought*. Some are much more subtle than others and only begin to come through clearly as we are able to direct our awareness precisely through a focusing device such as meditation.

It is nothing short of an amazing awakening to hear, for the first time, this whole other level of thought which is always there but out of our usual awareness. It can be initially difficult to even believe that this more subtle level of chatter is actually always taking place (not just when we happen to tune into it). It is, in fact, the existence of this phenomenon which (among other things) makes it so hard for us to hear ourselves clearly. And when I call it 'subtle', I mean it only in the sense of the elusiveness of this hidden layer. Actually, when we hear it, it is quite loud and irritating.

It is this level of internal speech which I believe very disturbed schizophrenics and paranoid people are tuning into when they complain of overwhelming voices which laugh at them, command them to do certain things and torture them to no end. They are unable to keep out of awareness what most of us have learned to keep out of 'earshot.' If we can't hear it, we think it doesn't exist.

But it does, and it is continually affecting our motivation, attitude formation and sense of identity. This is what is meant by 'unconscious motivation.' What we don't know certainly can affect us and sometimes can even hurt us!

So, we are talking about first being able to hear our internal voices clearly, as distinct from the low rumble of ordinary indecipherable chatter. Next, we are talking about being able to hear the layers upon layers of underlying chatter beneath this initial layer. A reasonable question here is: Why don't we normally have access to this under-lying chatter?

The answer is that there is simply too much noise going on to be able to notice it. Much like trying to hear a radio signal apart from the background static interference, there is just too much 'static inter-ference' for us to hear all of what the mind is producing. These underlying levels seem to make themselves known only after we are able to slow down the chatter enough to hear underlying 'signals.'

One powerful way to do this is to go a significant period of time (at least a few days) without speaking to anyone. When we do this, more of our attention may be focused on internal speech instead of our normal external speech. Obviously, this requires special circum-stances and is not likely to be possible for most people, without

17

special motivation and preparation, such as some time away from people, where your not speaking will not be misinterpreted as rudeness.

Sitting quietly, with eyes closed and with attention focused on the in and out of the breath will be another powerful tool and one which is more possible to do without any special circumstances. When we sit quietly and do nothing with our attention but focus on the breath, we can begin to hear the ongoing chatter going on inside.

Experiment

Sit in a comfortable chair with your feet flat on the floor. Let your arms rest calmly on the arms of the chair or in your lap. See if you can sit very still, without any movement for at least five minutes. As you sit without moving, let your eyes close gently and simply focus your attention on your breathing. Specifically, notice the rise and fall of your abdomen as you continue to sit still.

Notice any impulse to move. Resist the temptation to scratch or move in any way. Just pay attention to your breath, the in and out sensation of your abdomen. If you notice that your mind wanders off to some fantasy, gently and without judging bring it back and again focus on the sensations of your breath. Do this experiment for at least five minutes, to give yourself adequate time to adjust to not making any movement. **Resist the temptation to move!**

This form of meditation is an important tool in helping us learn to control the business of the mind. How? By calming the mind as we consciously calm the body. So that our attention may stay focused on our breath, we purposely try not to make even the slightest movement. What we discover as we practice this for a while is that we do have a certain ability to slow down the rapidity of our thought and that the method is to still the body. *Stilling the body helps still the mind.*

BODY 'CHATTER'

Just as we need to accept how out of control we are with regard to controlling our own thoughts, we also need to accept that much of the time we are only peripherally aware of the ongoing movements of the body. For the most part, we don't really think about movements before we make them nor do we notice our initiation of movement. If you pay attention to your own movement, this will quickly become obvious. One benefit of a quieting method such as meditation is that it allows us to begin to become more aware of just how often we are making gross and subtle body movements seemingly out of conscious control.

As you are reading at this moment, for example, you may notice how there is ongoing body 'chatter' taking place. You may move every few seconds to find a more comfortable position in your chair, scratch your head, uncross your legs, or stretch to grab a pencil – all with little or no awareness being given these movements.

And the amazing thing is that we don't even realize certain movements have been made until *after* we make them! Much like the ongoing flow of internal chatter in the form of thoughts, the body represents the vehicle for the expression of the *outward* chatter in the form of continual movements to find temporary physical comfort and rid ourselves of discomfort.

There is a Buddhist style of meditation called *Vipassana* in which a large part of what is focused on is this ongoing desire to reposition ourselves to feel physically at ease. Again, this is simply one of those things we take for granted, not really noticing how often we are stretching, squirming, reaching, twisting and making all kinds of other movements in the service of finding a temporary sense of physical comfort. Much wasted energy goes into these movements, in addition to the stirring up of the mind which takes place when we are unable to control these movements.

In Vipassana meditation, the purpose for paying attention to our ongoing desire to reposition ourselves is to understand how basically our bodies are always signaling us to keep moving to keep us from experiencing discomfort. In the practice of watching these movements, we may come to understand at a deeper level that having a body means we're in for continual discomfort.

For the Buddhists, a body which continually needs to be repositioned to rid us of pain and discomfort (not to mention the effects of disease, injury and age), is not something with which we want to exclusively identify our sense of self. Of course, we also may experience great pleasure from the body. But the point is that *all* of these passing sensations of pleasure and pain are not to be taken as more than transitory states, arising and passing away.

In this chapter, we have just begun to confront the nature of the monkey-mind. We have tried three experiments. One helps us pay closer attention to our thoughts; the second was offered to help us hear internal speech which, we said, represents parts of ourself wanting to be heard; and a third experiment gave us a tool for focusing our attention on our breath as we still the body.

We pointed out that there are layers of thought built upon each other that, for the most part, we are unaware of and which we recognize only when the mind is slowed to a great enough degree to permit us to hear these subtle layers of internal speech.

=== 2 ===

MIND IN MOTION:
THOUGHTS, DESIRES AND TIME

It all begins with our thoughts. Our cherished attitudes, deepest held beliefs and even our sense of identity ultimately rest on the foundation of our own thought. One of the realizations we make as we begin to pay close attention to our thoughts is how powerful they are in shaping and maintaining our world. We don't usually appreciate the degree to which our whole internal world and our perceptions of the external world are shaped just by our thought.

The major lasting changes which take place in the process of psychotherapy are due to radically different ways of thinking about ourselves and our relations with others. If one learns to become more emotionally expressive, this follows a change in one's thinking which allows for this greater emotional openness. And the major changes leading to growth outside of psychotherapy also come about as a result of changes in our thinking about our world in altered ways, which may then lead to changes in behavior.

Although strong emotional experiences may be long remembered as influencing us, behind these experiences are the memories we hold on to which continue to make the experiences themselves important. And what do you think these memories are made of? Good old thought! It is what we *tell ourselves* about these experiences that makes them so important and deserving of being considered 'cherished memories.' But we would prefer to believe that our memories are how it 'really' happened and not just what story we decided to tell ourselves about a particular experience in our life. In simple language, we prefer to delude ourselves.

The reason we find it easy to forget the central role of our thoughts in constructing our psychological worlds was intimated in Chapter 1. If the mind acts like a 'scattered monkey,' climbing from branch to branch (or from one mental association to another) and like a 'chattering monkey,' in which it is hard to clearly hear one thought as distinguished from another, it is not so surprising we are going to be reluctant to give such central importance to a process in which we feel so little control.

What I have termed the *discriminating mind* is the mind that has learned to clearly distinguish the power of its thought and therefore is more willing and able to give thought its due importance. As well, it is the mind that knows *when* and *how* to let go of thought and experience itself as calm and clear, before thought has broken the world into subject and object.

It is the mind that realizes that all separation, all discriminations, no matter how profound, come originally from Absolute mind, the mind we have before the *discriminating mind*. When this mind is achieved, it is as if the monkey has been temporarily put to sleep. We will focus on the discriminating mind in a different chapter. We will also look more closely at Absolute mind. For now, let's stay with thoughts and desires.

TURNING CHERISHED BELIEFS INTO STONE

Consider for a moment how reified or crystalized our beliefs tend to become. To 'reify' something is to make a 'thing' out of what is essentially a process. As applied to our beliefs, it is not uncommon for us to have a number of 'cherished beliefs' which we no longer think of as just beliefs but hold to be as dear to us as life itself. We think we *are* our beliefs. We become so identified with certain beliefs they lose their status as just beliefs and become our very ground of self-existence. 'What's a man without his beliefs?'

Our beliefs become like 'hardened arteries,' where little or nothing flows through easily. They have become so hardened they are no longer open for question. For example, we are quick to believe in and defend the values of our country.

'My country – right or wrong!' 'Love it or leave it!' We would put our 'bodies on the line' for those deeply held beliefs which we have accepted to be the very embodiment of all that is worth living for.

Perhaps we cherish other beliefs, like the need to resist all wars, feed all hungry children, or fight against all racial injustice. Or maybe we know for absolute sure which God is the 'true' God, what beauty is the 'real' beauty, or what political cause is the 'most righteous.'

Could we consider living under communism? Of course not! So we develop the belief that we will fight and defend our country 'to the death.' Could we consider going to Vietnam if we were a Berkeley radical? Of course not! So we think of fleeing to Canada, becoming a conscientious objector, or going to jail.

How did we get these positions so firmly in place that we are willing to go out on a limb for them? In the name of 'belief' and 'conviction' we do the strangest things!

After a lifetime of repeated thoughts, leading to repeated assumptions and repeated actions, combined with early emotional experiences to reinforce these assumptions and early learning, we end up with a hardened belief that is no longer open for question.

'My country – right or wrong!' To question this belief would be to question everything one 'stands for.' It is to question 'the very fabric of our being.' And, of course, this is exactly what happens in psychotherapy practiced at an intensive level. Are we really ready for this? It takes courage and a firm resolve to question our beliefs.

Some are willing to question the rightness of their country but, much deeper, they have patriotic feelings which will make them honor the flag, sing the National Anthem, and even shed a tear when their country makes them proud by winning all the gold medals in the Olympics. Does any 'real' patriotic American watch the raising of the American flag while American athletes receive gold medals without being sentimentally touched?

My point is not to argue the rightness or wrongness of our country's ideology but to emphasize that the whole foundation of our emotional attachment to our patriotism (whatever form it takes) is founded upon elaborations of thought. And a belief worth dying for or going to jail for is certainly a belief worthy of serious consideration!

Another example would be how some patients in psychotherapy are initially reluctant to explore beyond the surface in talking about their relationships to parents. Parents are given a special place in the internal world for most of us, even if in the outer world we may have occasional difficulties in relating to them.

23

We want to think of our parents as basically good and loving people. And because of this, we are reluctant to confront this belief with any evidence that may contradict this pleasant picture and conflict-free picture.

This position is really not so surprising. To begin with, they did bring us into the world, didn't they? Without Mommy and Daddy we would have no life! So we are rightly appreciative of this basic fact, even if, as we sometimes think (and perhaps say) in moments of frustration with life (and parents), 'I didn't ask to be born!'

With this in mind, we further strengthen our positive picture by remembering all the (hopefully) countless times they were there for us, taking care of us when we were helpless and absolutely dependent on them. We don't want to remember all the times they may *not* have been there for us.

And this is the job of the psychotherapist – to help one get back in touch with the whole picture – not just the pleasant part that keeps us safe from conflict. We want to feel loved by them. And we want to remember having had a 'happy childhood,' even if this means 'forgetting' large chunks of our past that may not have been so pleasant because Mommy and Daddy weren't there, or didn't take care of us very well if they were.

What about all the times they frustrated us by not giving us just what we wanted when we wanted it? I am always suspicious when a patient tells me they had a 'happy childhood' but then can't recall much about growing up and has not much to say about their relationship to their parents.

Again, my point in using this example is to indicate how our need to 'carve our beliefs in stone' may prevent us from realizing that the whole foundation of our story rests on what thoughts we repeat to ourselves.

And, we must remember, we are *not even aware* of how we are repeating a great many of these thoughts. We may be aware that we have a basic 'story line' we want to put forth to others, an image we wish to project, but we are not able to notice how we repeat this story line to ourselves on a perpetual basis below the level of awareness. In other words, we are not aware of our not being aware!

It is the same formula for most of our rigid beliefs: early thoughts reinforced by learning from parents, teachers, friends and culture combined with emotional experiences to further solidify the beliefs.

And then a 'cooling' process for years, in which the beliefs simply become part of who we think we are and act as the psychological 'glue' which helps to hold our identity together. But in holding tightly to our limited beliefs we pay a burdensome price. Let me give an example of the effects this may have.

Hypnotized by Father: the Story of Janice

A new patient, Janice, comes in and tells me she 'looks like everyone else' and can't attract men. She goes on to say that although she had a boyfriend for two years, the whole time she was with him, she never really felt very attractive to him. And, she claims, even though he would tell her that he was very attracted to her and showed her, through ongoing affectionate playfulness and continual interest in her sexually, Janice just wouldn't believe him. She knew 'it couldn't be true.'

She thought he was 'just saying this' to make her happy and get her to return the affection. Or that he was 'just wanting sex' but not really wanting *her*. I ask her to tell me what evidence she had that she was unattractive to men.

Certainly, I pointed out, her boyfriend's behavior with her was only evidence to the contrary. Janice says, yes, it is evidence to the contrary, and this adds to her confusion. Then she tells me that other men look at her but she rarely interprets their glances as indications of physical interest. How *does* she interpret their looks, I inquire.

Janice says, 'I think they are just playing with me, not really interested. They want to make eye contact or give me the "once over" but they're not really attracted to me.'

Now, it happens that Janice, age 28, is quite attractive. She has a wide, open smile and shapely figure. Her voice has a natural earthiness that adds to her appeal. She is bright, alive and struggling to realize her own skills and talents. She projects an inner intensity, and tends to emotionally 'suck in' those she interacts with, needing a lot of attention, and usually getting it. In many subtle non-verbal and not-so-subtle over behaviors, none of which I have chosen to point out to her at this early stage in our work, Janice has been seductive with me.

We have been working together for a few months now. But from the very start, Janice made it clear she was physically attracted to me.

Most women do not verbalize these feelings early in the therapy relationship, if at all. So she is aware of her femininity and sexuality and quite willing to talk about it. But she just won't trust it. She won't trust herself, so how can she trust her attractiveness?

For example, Janice tells me how a girlfriend whom she shared a hotel room with during a work-related conference saw her undressed for the first time. Her girlfriend had complimented Janice on the size of her breasts. Her manner of relating this to me was to complain that perhaps her breasts were *too* large, not being able to allow for her friend's compliment, needing to turn it into nagging doubt. Janice then wanted me to be the referee: Were her breasts 'big enough' or 'too large'? I was silent.

My response, after about a half minute of silence (time for Janice to think about the meaning of her question to me), was to point out her inability to take her friend's compliment *as* a compliment and how it seemed necessary to indirectly (by way of referring to her friend's comment) 'fish' for a compliment from me regarding her breasts.

She was wanting me to 'take the bait' and indicate whether her breasts were to my liking. My point in sharing this incident is to show that Janice was quite provocative when she wished to be and not at all unaware (at least a part of her) that she was an attractive, vivacious woman. But she could only deal with this in a backhanded, indirect and doubting manner.

But did this attention from her boyfriend or female friend help Janice overcome her belief in her own unattractiveness? Not for a minute! And the reason for this was that she basically could not allow herself to change a lifetime hypnotic-like program initiated with her father that basically went like this:

'You will *never* be attractive enough for me, and because of this, I will not love you unconditionally. Even though you will never be enough, you may try as hard as you like to please me. But you must remember, I will *never* be satisfied. And if you are not ever going to be beautiful enough for me, you must never believe what any other man may tell you about your looks. They will be lying to you, no matter what they tell you. And never believe what you see in the mirror. Remember only what I tell you.'

With this information, it is reasonable to interpret her wanting my opinion regarding her breasts as a hope that I could counter her father's negative program regarding her not being attractive enough to be loved. As a substitute father-figure, I had (she hoped) the power to 'undo' his assessment of her.

Janice was not aware that she was continuing to respond to this program. Where was it coming from? From unconscious repetition of some basic beliefs that were having a powerful effect on Janice's self-esteem, ability to see herself as she actually appeared to others, and on her attitude regarding the possibility of ever believing a man, especially regarding her appearance.

On one level (the surface), Janice used her acknowledged physical attributes to tease and be seductive. But she would then refuse to believe that her intentional seductiveness was able to have an effect! In her strict enforcement of her unconscious program, Janice needed to deny what was patently obvious: that her efforts to attract men were indeed successful, no matter what her father had told her. This program also allowed her to disown her own sexual curiosity in men and instead see them always looking at her.

Janice is a good example of this dynamic: what we repeat at an unconscious level can make us disregard our actual experience in the world. It can be so powerful in shaping our beliefs and perceptions that we may severely distort the truth and 'convince' parts of ourself that should 'know better,' parts which make up what I have labeled the *discriminating mind*.

These parts are our reality-testing faculties which we rely on to make sense of our world. And when we can no longer count on them for valid information, we have lost one of our 'rudders' in finding our way in the process of discrimination.

EXPERIMENTING WITH BELIEFS

Sit back and close your eyes for a minute, letting your mind wander. Just let go of trying to direct your thoughts. Now gently ask this question, just to stimulate any thoughts:

What beliefs really matter to me? What is the single most important belief in my life?

Now let go and see if any one belief surfaces. If one does, simply be aware of it without judgement. If one doesn't, carry this question with you for a while and gently ask it from time to time. So if you're standing in a line at the bank: 'What beliefs really matter to me?' Or walking through a park, or sitting on a bench – whatever time you have to let your mind wander to this question. See over a period of two or three days, if your beliefs change in answer to this question. Do they stay the same?

Imagine now holding the exact *opposite* belief to the one you consider the most important. How would you see yourself differently if you actually held this opposite belief? Could you imagine living with this opposite belief if you had to?

Could you imagine making *no* belief worth giving up your life for? Consider what adjustments you might make in your feelings about yourself if you 'really believed' this opposite belief. Now come back to your original 'true' belief and see how it feels to be back with what is so familiar. Who wants to give up such a 'comfortable' belief?

Consider a personality trait that you identify with strongly. A trait is an 'enduring tendency to behave in a certain way,' something which we believe is relatively stable over time. Pick only one and take a moment to see how firmly you believe this trait to be an accurate trait of yours.

Now that you have chosen this trait, consider how you came to believe this trait to be true in describing you. Did others tell you that you were this way? Or is it a desirable trait that you believe enhances your self-image but is not necessarily an accurate picture?

Can you identify with the *opposite* trait to the one you have chosen? For example, if you think of yourself as generous with gift-giving or with money, can you identify at all with a more 'stingy' or possessive part of yourself? Or if you think of yourself as compassionate to the suffering of others, can you identify with your own callousness or lack of interest in the plight of others?

The purpose of the above mental experiment is to gauge how rigid your beliefs are and your perceptions of personal traits. When we identify with only one end of a polarity and believe, for example, that we are generous but never stingy, we lose touch with a fuller picture of personality functioning which allows for us to accept *both* ends of the polarity. So we can accept that at times we will be generous and at other times we may be stingy and withholding. We don't need to box ourselves in to just one end of the polarity. We will come back to examine polarities in more detail in Chapter 7.

At higher levels of psychological health we can allow for all of our

different traits and tendencies to be owned and exhibited appropriately – to this degree we will be psychologically integrated and
possess a wide range of flexible behaviors to make our way through
the world. Then when someone says to us, 'You are generous,' we
say, 'Yes, you're right. Thank you.' And when someone else says,
'You're stingy,' we say, 'Yes, you're right. Thank you.'

The way to tell that this is working, is simple. Just notice when you
feel defensive when someone accuses you of having a certain trait or
behaving in a certain manner. If you are defensive, you know you
have not accepted that they are seeing something that is probably
true about you but that you have not yet owned (identified with).
When this defensiveness slows down, you know you're beginning to
accept that, yes, sometimes you can be stingy, cruel, tender, loving,
withholding, passive, domineering, quiet, loud, etc.

THOUGHTS IN MOTION

Again, the truth is, we do not like to admit how out of control our
thoughts really are. Disturbing thoughts can torture us to such a
degree that we are unable to take our minds off them. Or maybe
they're not so disturbing but just won't leave us.

We begin to hear a certain commercial jingle, or theme song of a
show, one we may have heard so many times on television: '"Have
gun will travel" reads the card of a man – a knight without armor in a
savage land. Paladin, Paladin, where do you roam? Far, far from
home . . .'

Or, 'Use Ajax, and away go troubles down the drain!'

Or what about this annoying one (which very few of you reading
this will be familiar with): 'Stanley, Stanley – two blocks off the Santa
Ana Freeway – 11401 East Firestone – Stanley Chevrolet!'

And over and over again you hear the same jingle just as you
remember it from twenty five years ago, when you first heard it as a
kid. Do you ask for this jingle to come up and begin playing? No. Can
you simply will it to go away when you're tired of hearing it? Not so
easy for most of us! We can even go to sleep with the jingle playing in
our head and wake up eight hours later with it going right back on!

The example of being 'temporarily obsessed' given above is
such an obvious and common one. I use it to point out this 'out of
control' aspect of our thoughts. It is also an example of how early

'programming' by television can be remembered and available to pop into awareness at any time.

Everything that has been 'imprinted' in memory is potentially available to surface once again. Such methods as hypnosis and meditation are effective in bringing these 'lost' memories back into awareness. Unfortunately, most of the time we are too 'asleep' to be able to recover large chunks of our past that have been unwittingly 'forgotten' without these and similar techniques.

Thoughts, old tunes, associations, mental pictures – all come and go of their own accord. How much control over our thoughts do we really have? How many of us wish we could just control these thoughts which appear and then pass away?

Or make one thought come rather than another? Or get rid of one thought rather than another? Or just concentrate better so there wouldn't be so many intrusive, distracting thoughts and more could be accomplished?

How creative we could all be if only we could control our own minds! Then we wouldn't talk so much about 'writer's block,' being 'out of control' of our impulses, 'procrastination,' or an inability to 'discipline' ourselves. We would never feel like we have been 'floundering' or regret having spent our years in certain activities. These are all consequences of something more fundamental – the inability to control our own minds.

And yet, how much effort do we spend learning how to control this mind or learning how it works? Going to schools and filling the mind with information, concepts and the ability to think in a linear or logical manner is *not* the same as really understanding the nature of our own thoughts and desires. We don't seem to really work very hard at wanting to know what makes this mind 'tick.'

As I mentioned in the Introduction, in the process of psychotherapy, it is common for patients to be fearful of 'losing control of their minds.' What they mean by this is that they are unsure what possible craziness may surface should they allow themselves to explore certain topics or dangerous areas that they have long since learned how to push out of consciousness. They might have to confront all kinds of thoughts that are unpleasant, disgusting, horrible, or guilt-producing.

It's like jumping into a boiling cauldron of 'God only knows what' and not knowing what will be discovered but believing that whatever it is, it will probably cause pain. And not only that they must also *pay* for the experience! Pay – a lot of money to have a (hopefully) qualified professional help them explore all the deep, dark places that they want to avoid.

No wonder so many of those entering psychotherapy don't make it very far! Staying in psychotherapy beyond the surface requires a degree of courage and willingness to tolerate frustration at not receiving immediate relief and realizing that growth takes time.

EXPERIMENTING WITH THOUGHTS

Take a moment to consider what you commonly do to avoid unpleasant thoughts. How often, just as an unpleasant thought trickles into awareness, do you quickly distract your thoughts off somewhere else as fast as possible? Many times, there is an anxious body movement that accompanies an unpleasant thought.

In psychotherapy work, for example, patients many times bend forward, start scratching their heads, screw up their mouths, or make some other sudden movement as they reach a place of discomfort in their thought processes. And the interesting thing is that many times they are totally unaware that their movement has anything whatsoever to do with their unpleasant thoughts.

Come back now to your own thoughts. What are you avoiding? If you need to walk around asking yourself one question all day, this would be a good one to walk with.

'**What am I avoiding now?**' *Just asking the question* periodically during the day can help develop the capacity to 'tune into' thoughts leading to an answer. *Just asking the question* stimulates certain mental associations which can lead you to an answer. See what you are willing at this moment to allow into awareness.

The trick here is to allow your concentration to stay with your mental associations long enough (without being distracted) to see what you are avoiding. This process of 'thought-avoidance' is occurring repeatedly. The more we have developed our *discriminating mind* the more we are able to become conscious of more of our thought-avoidance of unpleasantness.

THE SWIRLS OF DESIRE

We mentioned in Chapter 1 how our everyday desires play such a powerful role in our daily life. We said that we seem to want a state of perfection that is impossible to achieve: we want all our desires satisfied NOW and we want them satisfied **COMPLETELY**. We want each and every desire, as it comes to our attention to be magically fulfilled – nothing less than that. And yet we said that we are going to continue to suffer as long as we continue to be attached to our desires.

To be 'attached' to our desires means not to be able to let go of them when they rear their powerful heads. At their worst, our desires seem to be so strong we can't control them. They are much more powerful than our mental chatter because many times our desires relate to some kind of pleasant sense stimulation. And for most of us, the satisfaction of our sense desires is more captivating and re-inforcing than even the most sublime thought.

When we begin to look at the nature of desire, the easiest way to work with it is to look at all the material things that we want. We need to look at what the accumulation of material things, like clothes, furnishings, cars, homes, possessions, has to do with our sense of identity. The real issue here is how we relate to our desires, not so much that we have them.

When we are unable to satisfy our desires for material things it is easy to begin to feel sorry for ourselves and to resent others who have more 'stuff' than we do. We become envious of others who we think are doing a better job of satisfying their desires through accumulation of things than we are.

BIG ICE CREAM CONE FANTASY

We may begin to believe empty slogans like 'He who dies with the most toys wins,' or 'Living well is the best revenge.' Or this clever one: 'The person who thinks money can't buy happiness doesn't know where to shop!' We believe that if only all our desires were satisfied we could be *so* happy.

There is no question that the satisfaction of basic desires, and even many desires that are not basic, can make us feel good about life and propel us to work very hard just for the 'pay-off.' We know how good it can feel when a strongly desired object (no matter what it might be) is finally earned and possessed after a long wait and hard work.

And yet, for most of us, the state of satisfaction just doesn't last. And before long, we begin to seek something new, something usually bigger and better than what we had before. We grow tired of the old and want new stimulation. Or our ego tells us, 'Yes, that last one was nice, but see if you can make it just a *little bit nicer* this time.' Things can always be just a little better, can't they? For some, they could be *a lot* better.

What happens (as we all know from experience) is that the satisfaction and belief that we will 'finally be happy' and contented is shown to be nothing but wishful thinking. We can call this belief in the magic of accumulation as the 'savior' of our contentment, the 'Big Ice Cream Cone in the Sky Fantasy.' If only (we tell ourselves), we could have the 'Big Ice Cream Cone in the Sky' everything would be perfectly heavenly!

Eastern philosophy, and Buddhism in particular, teaches that the reason for this predicament is that we keep wanting something that really isn't possible. We want to create a state of continual satisfaction that won't stop, a lasting state that won't throw us back into another desire that needs attention. We know satisfaction won't last very long, no matter how badly we wish it would. And with each new desire, we keep trying to get back to that state of satisfaction and hope it will last.

MOMENT TO MOMENT CHANGE

The Buddhists tell us that as long as we keep trying to grasp some permanent state of satisfaction we are going to suffer because things are constantly changing from moment to moment. And if they are changing from moment to moment, we need to allow things to come and go, without holding too tightly to our quickly passing states of pleasant (or unpleasant) consciousness.

You might think this is obvious, that everyone understands that things are always changing. We have clichés like 'The only constant in life is change itself.' But, again, we are hypnotized, out of the need to create a certain sense of stability in our psychological world, to pretend that things are more stable than they really are.

The truth is, because most of the time we are *not* present-centered, we have difficulty appreciating the new opportunities for change that come with each new moment. Instead, we would prefer to believe that we are set in certain patterns which make change impossible, at least deeper personality change. And, because of the strength of some of our early mental programming, it does, indeed, seem like certain changes in our thinking and behaving are not possible to make.

And yet, when we assume this kind of position, we lose touch with the possibilities inherent in the meaning of the present. We lose touch with an awareness of our many options to experiment with our beliefs, our emotions and the ongoing decision-making of how we wish to spend our next moments, minutes, hours, day, months and years. Let's examine our ways of perceiving time.

EXPERIMENTING WITH 'MENTAL TIME ZONES'

For many, time is a commodity to be bought and sold, wasted or used productively. Think about how we talk about time: 'time is money,' 'meeting a deadline,' 'spending' time, 'time is of the essence,' 'the ravages of time.' 'I had a good time' usually means 'I wasn't aware of the passage of time since I was very much in the moment.'

Much time is 'spent' fantasizing about how to spend time, planning for the future, scheduling or 'harnessing' time to serve our needs. Or we get lost in reverie of the past, regretting how time has already been spent and wanting to go back and relive certain events, conversations and decisions, thinking we could do better if only given another chance.

The delightful movie, *Peggy Sue Got Married*, is based on this theme of going back in time to high school to re-make past decisions – but this time with the knowledge and maturity of an adult. This movie was effective partially because it captured one of our favorite fantasies of being able to undo the past. Peggy Sue finds herself back in her high school years and lets herself do all the things she was too shy, naive, or scared to do when she was actually that age. She is able to make realizations about herself in reliving it a second time that could only come with the perspective of an adult. It is an incredible realization for many when they notice how much time is spent mentally in the past or future.

One consequence of this is that large chunks of our lives go by without our awareness of where our attention is focused. We miss much of the quality and sharpness of our lives which can only come through our senses when we are focused in the present, not on yesterday or two hours from now, nor lost in fantasy without knowing we are lost.

We spend a lot of time 'spaced out,' forgetting where we have been, what we have said, and very unsure of how to control our own orientation in time. So we go through periods of 'boredom' or anxiety when time seems too slow or too fast. Allowing yourself to become bored is simply the inability to perceive the subtle changes taking place in each moment so that you are feeling inadequately stimulated to stay interested.

WORKING WITH TIME

Here are some healthy ways of viewing time and some unhealthy ways, as well as some ways of working with your sense of time. It is best if you don't just read these and move on but pause long enough to really consider them and try the suggested exercises.

(1) *Time is not something you need to battle or struggle with*. No matter how 'busy' you think you are, try to remember that the pressured feeling of 'not having enough time' is an indication of scheduling more than you are comfortably able to handle and/or not being able to focus your attention sufficiently to use what time you have to achieve your goals. Use this harried, scattered feeling as a tip-off that you need to *schedule less and focus attention more*.

(2) *Become aware of how you speak about time*. Do you find yourself 'killing' time when there is insufficient stimulation to keep you excited? Do you find yourself often giving as an excuse, 'I just don't have the time'? Begin to take a closer look at what this means to you – not having 'enough' time.

Do you talk about time as if it were a precious commodity to be parceled out carefully, or is there more than enough time for you to do personal and business projects. Is 'not having the time' a polite way of saying 'I really don't want to spend the time'?

(3) *Pay attention to your experience of time*. Does time seem to go very quickly for you? Or does it seem to crawl along – barely passing?

Notice how you are feeling when you experience time as passing swiftly as compared to passing slowly or standing still.

Notice how often you find yourself mentally compartmentalizing time – for an appointment or a project – and how you feel when you break up the flow of time into discrete portions.

Pay attention to how much time you spend rehearsing for future projects. How far into the future do you tend to project time? A few hours, days, weeks, months, or years? Do you think about five years from now? How about fifteen years from now?

Are you impulsive, always 'going for it' without regard to consequences, as you feel the urgency of time? Or does taking a risk seem scary, with the future as something to secure yourself against because of its vast uncertainty?

Begin to sense your own primary orientation in time – whether you are predominantly present-centered, replay the past a lot or are mostly concerned with what is 'just around the corner.' Guilt-ridden people and depressive personalities, for example, spend a lot of time going backward, trying to undo perceived past mistakes. Investors, stockbrokers and many business people spend much time in the future, with the next project, the next vacation, the next new car, etc.

Memories and planning for the future are part of the richness of our mental life. I am not suggesting they have no value or place in the breadth of our experience. But they should not overshadow our present perception of aliveness, our sense of what it is like to be immediately involved in the living of our lives **right now**.

Since things are constantly changing, the only real security we have is the present, the ongoing 'here and nowness' of our life. When we lose the present, we lose the fulcrum or balance point between past and future and put ourselves on shaky psychological ground.

(4)   Being able to do six things at once is not a virtue or a sign of high intelligence! Give up the delusion that reading while you eat, as you listen to music and converse with a friend makes you a highly skilled person who is 'saving time.'

What it *does* make you is scattered! Most people who try to do more than one thing at a time are unable to give sufficient attention to each thing at once. Notice, for example, how you feel the next time someone you are trying to talk to is doing something else while they attempt to hear you. Try doing one thing with complete awareness at a time.

(5) Give up the notion that you are being 'more productive' or 'more efficient' by scheduling more appointments than you can possibly handle. The harried lifestyle begins for many when they delude themselves into believing that, like airlines, overbooking is 'necessary and economically wise.' Airlines pay a literal price for overbooking and so will you!

(6) Begin to pay attention to the feeling of time flowing – the unboundedness of time which cannot be discreetly broken down into clock units. You will notice that when you really come into the present, time does not seem to exist! Clock-time is a concept – but a vital concept in co-ordinating our daily world.

But in reality, time perception is a very personal psychological experience, as we all have discovered. We know that 'time passes quickly when you're having fun' but crawls along when we feel bored or are forced to pay attention to something in which we have no real interest.

THE RELATION OF THOUGHT TO TIME

The relation of thought to time is that *thought occurs in time*; our experience of time is usually *in relation to* our own thoughts. If we are present-centered we will be in touch more of the time with bodily sensation rather than thought. But when we get lost in the reverie of past experiences, conversations, or regrets, we are more 'caught' in the web of time.

More of our present action will be influenced by these past experiences when we are unable to pull ourselves out of these experiences (no matter how pleasant or unpleasant they may have been), and come back to the here and now. The same is true if we get lost in the future, even though people who prefer the future are many times more hopeful, optimistic and energetic.

If we are able to stay with the present as the balance-point of our lives, we have the 'full weight' of our attention to use to take care of ourselves in the world, as compared to being caught in the 'webs of time' created by losing ourselves in the past or future.

Keep in mind, we are *not* saying the memories of the past are not valuable. Nor are we saying that flights into planning or anticipating the future are not important. Quite the contrary, planning and anticipating helps us save time by rehearsing for the future as well as providing juicy anticipatory excitement in our lives.

We *are* saying that the relation of time to thought seems to be that *thought 'moves' time while the present keeps time right here and now*. We don't experience the 'arrow of time' stretching into the future in the same anxious, foreboding way when we can settle into and find comfort in the present. This is why time seems to stop when we become deeply engrossed in some project. Time 'stands still' when our concentration is sharply focused and we feel like we have become one with our project.

For example, when I'm keenly interested in what I'm trying to express in this writing, I lose track of time and can just 'melt into' my thoughts as they quickly get punched into the keyboard and then – presto! – they appear on the computer screen. As it was put in a popular soft-rock tune by Carly Simon a few years ago: 'I'll stay right here 'cause these are the "good old days."'

We seem to fight so hard to escape the experience of time passing. Much of what constitutes 'ecstatic' experience is labeled such partly because the experience is not placed in time. And when you think about those short and extended periods of total absorption you have experienced, you may see that the hallmark of these periods of focused concentration is having *no experience of them moving in time*.

Researchers suggest that this so-called 'flow' experience, of becoming one with what we are focused on, is so pleasurable for us because, for a while at least, we are successfully able to escape our usual sense of constraint imposed by the experience of ourselves in time.

In this chapter we have briefly looked at some of the components of the 'mind in motion' and its productions: thoughts and their relationship to feelings. We have also examined some of the healthy ways of working with time in our lives.

We have looked at how we end up with the dreaded disease of 'hardening of the beliefs' and experiments with beliefs, avoidance and 'mental time zones' were offered. Now let us move on to look at the nature of our most 'prized possession': the self.

3

THE ELUSIVE SELF

To talk about the nature of the self, first we need to define what we mean by the concept of 'self.' But even before this, we need to remember what a 'concept' is: simply an idea conceived in the mind or an abstract idea generalized from specific instances. In relation to the self, this means the *concept* of self is not pointing to a real 'thing' but is useful in helping us understand a constellation of experiences which forge our sense of identity. We do not point to a part of our body and say, 'This is my *self*.'

Nor do we tend to think our 'self' is located physically inside our brain. The 'self' is like a coat rack upon which to hang our identity. We tend to forget that the concept of self is just that – a concept – and not something that has an actual existence of its own.

'Self' is one of those words in psychology that has been used in many different ways, and this has made for some confusion, both within the discipline of psychology and the larger 'pop-psychology' community. And even among those writers using the term in a similar way, there is disagreement as to exactly what makes up the 'self.' In part, this disagreement exists because of the very nature of all concepts. They are, as we said, artificial mental constructs, not real things. And as long as different minds are dealing with these constructs, there is always going to be disagreement about their specific meaning.

The term 'ego' has been another term, like 'self,' that has had different meanings and judgements applied to it. For example, much of Western psychology honors 'the ego' while Eastern spiritual disciplines tend to speak disparagingly about 'ego' and insist that it is the curse that keeps one from reaching higher spiritual realization. What do we mean by it?

By 'self' I mean that sense of solidity of *who we are* from day to day, our sense of personal essence (not soul or spirit) which makes us feel we are the same person over time. Self, then, is another way of saying our sense of 'I-ness' or ego – that which is 'who we think we are when we think about who we are.'

Ego comes into existence when we identify with our own thought. (Think about this for a moment, *as you identify with your own thought*.) It includes the images, fantasies, identifications, memories, sub-personalities, motivations and information related to the separate self.

In tying the concept of 'self' to the concept of 'ego', I am using these terms as they have traditionally been thought of in psycho-analytic theory. We may think of the self, or ego, as the organizing part of oneself that keeps the 'circus' harmonious. Different acts may be taking place under different circus rings, but the self is the ring-leader that keeps the show functioning as a coherent whole.

Our 'I-ness' or sense of self is a composite of all that has happened to us over the course of our lives, including early parental experiences, social values which have been learned, self-perceptions, and those ways we have come to view ourselves based on feedback from our interpersonal world. From all of these elements, a coherent self-structure has been formed which (if we have not been too emotionally damaged along the way) gives us a fairly solid, stable and consistent picture of ourselves from day to day when we first awaken.

Because of this, we can take ourselves for granted to a large degree each day rather than awaken to a complete stranger. We have a picture we can 'count on' when we first try to answer the question: *'Who am I relative to all other separate selves?'*

Disturbances we may have of an emotional nature or distortions we may have in our perceptions of ourself and others many times relate in some way to gaps or holes in this coherent and stable sense of ourself. We will look at some of these disturbances later in this chapter.

Some psychologists and writers on the Eastern consciousness disciplines refer to the 'Self' (with capital S) as that part of us which is our soul, beyond individual personality and having more to do with our spiritual essence. Jungians, for example, tend to speak of the 'Self' in this manner. But for our purposes (so as not to confuse the issue), let us use this term (self) simply to indicate the core feeling we have of who we are as unique individuals.

Now, in this chapter we will talk about 'self' in two very different ways, which, on the surface, may seem contradictory. But we are going to make it as clear as possible why self can be viewed in two seemingly contradictory yet complementary ways. For the sake of simplicity, let us think of these ways as: (1) relative self; and (2) absolute self.

THE NATURE OF RELATIVE SELF

Relative self is the ego-self we are all struggling with on a daily basis. Remember, as we speak about 'ego-self,' we are using what is called a 'hypothetical construct' to make sense of something. Remember, don't take this construct to be a real 'thing.' It is very 'real' in the sense that we experience it.

But when we talk about it, we go away from the experience, and form a mental concept about it. It is what we call 'the ego' (construct) that gets injured when someone 'hurts' our feelings, that feels slighted when we are ignored, and that desires to stand out and distinguish ourselves from the 'herd.' We experience that 'hurt' in our guts but we say, 'My ego was bruised by that rejection.' More correctly, we ought to say, 'That blow to my ego hit me right in the guts.' If we are emotionally closed off, we will experience the blow only to our mental concept, not feeling anything emotionally.

If we want to be even more precise (and at the same time pay less homage to the concept of 'the ego'), we might say, 'What you said hurts *me*, as I notice I don't like to identify with the truth of your words.' This, of course, is not how most people (even 'in-touch' people) talk to each other, partially because it would sound awkward but mostly because we would be exposing ourselves to even further ego-bruising to admit these feelings.

It is this sense of self, or ego, which gets so much of our fantasy time, for example, imagining how others might give us special consideration, believing 'it' deserves special treatment from the world. 'It' has grandiose visions of what powers it possesses to excel

41

above all others and thus gain desired recognition. It is this ego-self which we preciously guard, staunchly defend, and go to such great lengths to fortify.

This same sense of self maintains itself by our constant feeding of it through all our I-statements and I-thoughts. It is this relative self which feels proud of itself, feels envy of what others have that it doesn't and feels competitive with the person who is just a little smarter, kinder, more compassionate, better athlete, or more (fill in the blank with one of your own). It is this ego that turns 'green' with envy at the other guy's new Ferrari, Cessna airplane, lavish lifestyle, gorgeous girlfriend, great vacation, etc.

'Why should he have it and not me? It ain't fair! If he can have it, I deserve it, too!' Or, 'If I can't have it, he doesn't deserve it either!' This same ego imagines others are out having a better time in life than it is and stands always vigilant, ready to use anything in the environment to enhance itself.

Also, it is this ego that tries to talk above others to be heard, interrupts, defends itself, and braves the dangers of the world to make its way by facing new challenges, dreaming of new possibilities, and creating new solutions to problems in daily living in the 'pursuit of happiness' and personal satisfaction.

To make the picture of this self more clear, let us illustrate it more graphically, in type that is befitting its importance. This is the self that is unique, idiosyncratic, individualistic and loves beyond all else its realization that:

It is very important because it is the **Subject**, the **Big Shot**, and the whole rest of the world is only a measly object. What a powerful feeling! Boy, is this ever heady stuff . . . Sometimes it feels like sitting on top of the world. But . . . wait a minute . . . it can't really be this simple, can it? No, it really can't.

The problem here is easy to see. Even though this ego walks around with this overwhelmingly powerful realization, it also walks around with the awareness (at least to some degree, even in those with severe pathology) that all other 'objects' (people) also are subjects in their own little relative–subjective worlds. We are nothing but objects to them. And a lot of the time, parts of us don't like this recognition one little bit.

Why? Because we would rather have a BIG HEAD and not have to deflate it just because of the existence of others. A very over-inflated ego graphically looks (and feels) like this:

How we deal with this meshing together of 'our' subject with 'their' object and how 'they,' correspondingly, deal with being the 'Big Cheese' to our being just a little object is what human interpersonal relations is all about! Do we care, fall in love with, fight with, make deals with, build bridges with and have intercourse with 'objects' in whom we now honor the subjective? Or do we keep others objects and see them only as to how they may increase our own sense of subjectivity, catering to our needs and wants? At what point has this BIG EGO had enough?

Where is the balance here? What is the 'right' proportion in our relations between the subjects? When is it necessary for 'us' to keep 'them' an object and when is it safe to let 'them' become a subject with 'us,' in here close?

Ken Keysey, the psychedelic author and chief 'Merry Prankster' of the 1960s, who gained fame for his novel, *One Flew Over the Cuckoo's Nest*, used to say, 'You're either on the bus or off the bus.' So, you're either 'on the bus,' in here with me as a subject or you're just another object 'out there' who doesn't really matter.

This is what we all face, then, in dealing with our subject–object boundaries of identity. A lot of the time, to put it in overly simplified terms, we're trying to decide who is 'on the bus' or 'off the bus.' So we think, 'Can I trust him?' or 'Is she telling me the truth – *or just treating me like another dumb object again who can be lied to?*'

43

BOUNDARY DISTURBANCES AND THE RELATIVE SELF

Many of the distortions of these subject–object relations which crop up as we develop in our early years end up as problems in our relations with others and, many times, in the consulting rooms of mental health professionals. What happens so that this occurs?

One basic distortion we make is to bias the world too much in our own favor. In other words, the Big Shot never realizes that everyone else is walking around thinking they, too, are Big Shots. We tend not to give others their proper 'subjectness,' needing to keep them objects to be used and manipulated for our own needs.

This is what 'narcissism,' a popular term in the last ten years, is all about. One is unable to make others subjects in their own right. Instead, one deludes oneself that one is the only 'real' subject in the universe. 'I'm a Big Shot Subject and you're just a nothing' is the classic 'I'm OK, you're not OK' position.

When we scratch the surface of the façade, we find a lot of insecurity in this position. But on the surface it looks like inflated self-importance and a lot of tooting one's own horn. 'Look at me, I'm really something!' To be really something, though, the other guy has to be nothing. The narcissist can only see others in relation to what they have to offer him. His motto is: 'So what's in it for me? What do you have to offer that will help keep me the center of the universe?'

A second distortion we make is to 'give away the store' and go too far in the opposite direction – everyone else is seen as a Big Shot but we think of ourselves as a nothing. This is the classic 'You're OK, I'm a nothing' position, which is the favorite stance of masochists and people who like to play the 'helpless victim' role. It is also the stance of those with moderately severe difficulties in ego strength, who have never gotten much ego 'feeding' as they developed. Their sense of self is 'shriveled' – a mere fragment of what it ought to be if they are to take care of themselves in a world where there are bound to be many ego bruisings.

So everyone else looks big and important and they feel stepped on and left out. When severe, these people don't believe they even have a right to be in this world and have great difficulty carving out their own psychological space within which to exist. In a less destructive

44

way, most of us assume this stance when we are not feeling good about ourselves.

One frequent form this takes is to question our value unless we have something 'special' to offer the world. If we aren't accomplished, have some special ability, or simply don't measure up to those around us in education, social status, or physical attractiveness, we judge ourselves as 'unworthy of personhood.'

All neurotic disturbances come about as a result of an inability of an individual's relative self to find and maintain the proper balance between himself and the rest of the world. Let's look more closely at this.

Fritz Perls, one of the founders of Gestalt Therapy, believed that 'the neurotic is the man on whom society impinges too heavily. His neurosis is a defensive maneuver to protect himself against the threat of being crowded out in an overwhelming world (1973, p. 31).' The social and environmental boundaries between an individual and his world are experienced as extending too far over into the individual.

According to original Gestalt therapy theory, there are four main boundary disturbances creating chronic, daily interferences with the processes of growth and continual confusion between the relative self and the other. These disturbances are: introjection, projection, confluence, and retroflection.

A fifth boundary disturbance has been suggested by Erving and Miriam Polster (1973), which they call 'deflection.' Because we will not provide a case example of deflection, as we will with the other boundary disturbances, let us take a moment to define it. Deflection occurs when we, consciously or unconsciously, feel the need to blunt the impact of the other in some manner, to avoid the intensity of our interaction. This is a common phenomenon in psychotherapy, where patients feel the need to lessen the immediate impact of the perceived already-too-powerful therapist.

Deflective maneuvers include excessive language, avoiding eye contact, being abstract rather than specific, politeness rather than directness, and shrugging off the importance of what one has just said. Good contact can be deflected either by the person who initiates the interaction or by the person being addressed. Either way, deflection weakens the excitement that is possible between people, making them feel less alive. Deflection is taking place quite commonly between people in their interactions, most of the time without any awareness. When it is not grossly disturbing to one party (for example, never being able to make eye contact while speaking), it may never be mentioned. And yet, it serves to blunt the ongoing interactions between oneself and the world.

All of these boundary disturbances are defense mechanisms and considered abnormal only when used in a chronic manner, as described in the examples below. Everyone uses all of these mechanisms some of the time in healthy, self-protective ways. It is only when they become part of our ongoing personality style in a chronic and self-defeating manner that they should be viewed as 'pathological.' But, remember, they do not have to be labeled 'pathological' for them to be interrupting a more vibrant contact between ourselves and all those with whom we interact.

When we have some understanding of how these mechanisms work, and are 'in touch' (mentally and emotionally) with ourselves enough to identify them as they take place (or even after they take place), we can learn a great deal about how we protect ourselves in the world as well as how we distort our interactions with others.

INTROJECTION

Like the physiological process of chewing and digesting food, the psychological process of assimilation means that we digest and make our own whatever concepts, facts, standards of behavior, morality, political values, etc., may be taken in. If we take something in but don't make it our own because we have not really understood and assimilated it, we will be uncomfortable and want to throw it up and get it out of our system. To introject something is to 'swallow it whole' without ever really assimilating it and making it our own.

Through the process of discrimination we learn to take from the environment what we need to surive and give back to it what we have to offer. In taking from the environment, it is important that we completely 'chew' and 'digest' whatever is taken. If we do not carefully 'chew' what we take in and assimilate it, we end with a feeling of having a foreign body inside us that has been ingested but not digested. Even though it may be in us it is not really a part of us. It is still part of the environment.

When we introject a concept, for example, we take it in and talk about it as if we are comfortable with it and yet we still feel like it is somehow not really right for us. Concepts and values, which help

46

make up our sense of relative self, need to be destructured ('chewed'), analyzed, taken apart, and then put together again in the form which will be of most value to us.

This is the work of what I have labeled the *discriminating mind*. If they aren't, and are instead simply swallowed whole, these concepts and values make us 'paper people' who throw around our ideas, beliefs and opinons without really knowing what we are talking about, hoping that simply mouthing these ideas will impress others. Clearly, this does not contribute to the overall growth and development of our mind or our personality.

Introjection leads to a 'status quo' personality, because we are putting so much energy into 'holding down the fort.' This means there will not be much room left for us to discover what we really believe, apart from what has been 'fed' to us by our friends, lovers, teachers, or politicians. This defense mechanism also contributes to personality disintegration, as we are forced to reconcile two incompatible concepts, having introjected both of them.

For example, a child may have been told, 'Don't get big-headed just because you hit a home-run,' (it's not good to be feeling too good about yourself), and yet also told he should 'like himself' and strive for accomplishment. So, he hits the home-run and then gets slapped down just as he is trying to feel good about his accomplishment. He is forced to carry two beliefs at the same time which are inconsistent.

We can see how confused this can make a child. And it is exactly what happens in many families when parents and teachers expect (and live) these inconsistent and 'crazy-making' beliefs which are never really able to give a coherent and logical picture to the questioning and spongelike absorbent mind of a child.

In introjection we have moved the boundary between ourselves and others too far inside ourselves, where there is little or no room left for us to exist. The motto of the introjector might be: *'It isn't nice to disturb others with one's own feelings or beliefs – much better to believe and do as I'm told without questioning. Father knows best.'*

James: An Example of Introjection

James was 24 years old, a Seventh Day Adventist, and talented in the area of computers and sophisticated ways of programming them. James had thought of himself as a 'nerd' in high school, but did not let this label stop him from becoming a 'whiz' in writing programs for computers. He focused his attention on one particular form of programming and made himself an expert in it. He was looked at with awe by fellow computer students in college, and gained much needed self-confidence, which later turned into a self-acknowledged obnoxious ego-inflation and rudeness to others, which brought him to see me.

He was invited to consult with companies all over the country. Although still in college, he was considered talented enough that these companies would fly him in for special projects. James would put his 'fast-gun' skills up against anybody's. He could 'gun down' any 'fast-draw' computer expert who had the courage to face him in a showdown. But when it came to values and beliefs, he had much more trouble thinking for himself.

In spite of this recognition for his knowledge and ability to analyze with computers, James was holding many beliefs which had been part of his religious indoctrination, further reinforced by his 'saintly' father, but these had never really been questioned. James simply knew that if the church and his saintly father had told him so, it must be true. He was able but resistant (because of feelings of guilt) to use his quick mind to question the beliefs that he had 'swallowed whole' since childhood.

As James allowed himself to begin to question these beliefs within the security of the psychotherapy consulting room, he struggled with trying to determine whether he was holding certain values because he really believed them or because his father had told him, 'This is the way to live.'

For example, he had long allowed himself to indulge in 'heavy petting' with girls and considered himself a 'moderately good lover' even though he had limited experience with girls and had never had sexual intercourse. He had tried to continue a long-distance relationship with a girlfriend from his home town after he had moved to the West Coast.

Although unaware of it, his way of holding her in the relationship was to say things to her to try and make her feel guilty about her interest in dating other men while they were apart. So he would have telephone conversations with her frequently during the week to 'check up' on her and (because she also had a computer-related job), periodically during the day send her long-distance 'electronic mail' notes from his terminal. It was 'love at first byte,' as computer hackers might joke.

Until we looked at this in psychotherapy, James was not conscious of his heavy-handed tactic. In fact, when I brought this to his attention he was truly amazed he could be doing this for so long without any awareness as to his motivation.

To 'keep her in line,' James had learned to do to his girlfriend (make her feel guilty about sexual interest in others) the very same thing his father was doing to keep *him* in line. It didn't work for too long, however; his girlfriend, without being honest about it, ended up having a relationship with another man (who would give her intercourse) and ultimately, with great shock and emotional pain to James, left him for this other man.

Even after this happened, James held fantasies for some time that she would realize her mistake and come back to him. After all, didn't he excite her with his computer wizardry? That glint in her eye and big smile when he would elegantly solve computer-related problems – he hoped it would be enough to hold her at least until marriage, when he could then 'give himself fully' and indulge in sexual intercourse. But, of course, it wasn't. And he missed seeing that glint when she recognized his elegant solutions. But he had no easy or elegant solution to get her back.

In psychotherapy, James began to see that he was afraid of disappointing his father, whom part of him truly viewed as a saintly man and from whom he desperately wanted (but never received) total approval. James had always been able to view taking the next step (indulging in intercourse) as a 'no-man's land' but felt absolutely no guilt in indulging in all of the other 'pleasures of the flesh.' His father had made it clear: 'Don't get taken in by temptation. If you do, you're not as strong as me.'

Upon closer examination, James began to understand that he had psychologically equated his genetic father with the Holy Father (the Pope), and that actually, his father's moral and political views were as rigid, conservative and parochial as the Pope's. This was a big step for James: to be able to begin to acknowledge and disagree with his father's positions without feeling he was betraying his father or the Holy Father, or even the Lord Himself.

James began to 'spit out' those beliefs that no longer seemed right to him, like discriminating against homosexuals, and acquired a set of beliefs more in line with *his* true feelings, not his father's. In this way, he was taking a growth step toward becoming his own man, not just a carbon copy of his father and was able to get a more balanced picture of his father.

PROJECTION

The reverse of introjection is projection. As introjection is the tendency to make the self responsible for what originates in the environment, so projection is the tendency to make *the environment responsible for what originates in the self*. In its extreme form, projection leads to paranoia. The paranoid person is unable to bear the responsibility for his own wishes, feelings and desires, and so attaches them to objects or people in the environment and sees them aimed back at him. Although he thinks he is being persecuted, actually he would like to persecute others.

Projection exists in much less extreme forms than this. The sexually inhibited woman who complains because everyone is making passes at her or the cold, haughty man who accuses others of being unfriendly to him are examples of neurotic projection.

Projection is, it is safe to say, the most frequently used defense mechanism in our daily interaction with the world. It is occurring much of the time when we believe others are responsible for what happens to us. One of the signs of a more mentally healthy person is that she is less involved in this boundary disturbance and therefore distorting less of her relations with the world.

The chronic projector uses his primary defense not only in relation to his relations to the outside world but also against himself. In addition to disowning his own impulses, he also disowns those parts of himself in which the impulses arise. He gives them an objective existence outside of himself so he can blame them for his problems without having to own them as part of himself. Instead of being an active participant in his own life, he becomes a passive object, the proverbial 'victim of circumstances.'

In projection we shift the boundary between ourselves and the rest of the world too much in our favor – in a way that makes it possible to disown those parts of personalities which we find ugly or offensive. We want to believe that if we can deny some ugly part of us and then push it apart from us, we won't have to deal with it any longer and we won't suffer any consequences. But it just isn't true. What we try to push away will always come back – in some form – to haunt us, even if we aren't aware of it.

For example, one of the primary ways I notice the mechanism of projection taking place in psychotherapy is when patients come in to a session and immediately imagine that I am feeling angry or irritated toward them. Perhaps they did not receive a warm enough reception from me or I might be momentarily focused on adjusting the thermostat or closing the window blinds. They will rarely ask themselves how they are feeling about me, instead choosing to see me as feeling something toward them.

Because they are uncomfortable with feeling anger toward me (and even more uncomfortable trying to express it), it is easier for them to disown their anger altogether and then believe it is *me* who is feeling the anger. They take my momentary distraction as a sign that I am not interested in them and this slight makes them angry. Most often, all it takes to bring out their feelings is my asking them if they are angry at me for not being 100 per cent present for them when they come through the door. But, too often, they start with wanting to know why I am angry at them, already assuming that this is what I am feeling.

Also, when they are used to getting such intense focused attention for such a prolonged period of time (usually forty-five minutes) they get 'spoiled' and can't stand it when I avert my eyes or do anything that takes my attention off them, even for very short periods of time. They have come to expect the most focused kind of attention they get in their relations with anyone, including loved ones. If I look at my watch toward the end of the hour to make sure we don't run over, they think I've lost interest. All of this is just more grist for the therapeutic mill.

This is why the competent therapist is always on the look-out for projections in the patient's verbalizations, and always asking the patient to 'try on' as true for himself those statements, especially critical remarks, made about others. It seems that we would always prefer to see the world 'doing it to us' than own our desire to 'do it to the world.'

Linda: An Example of Projection

Linda was 38 and worked as a high school teacher. Although about fifteen pounds overweight, she had a certain inviting sensuality that she was able to 'turn on' when she wished. She had been divorced for three years after an eight-year marriage.

She frequently complained to me that male teachers at her school would invite her for coffee after school, make suggestive remarks to her, and that she couldn't understand why these men were 'after her body.' When I would ask her what her part in eliciting this reaction from men might be, she insisted, 'I don't do anything. I go out hoping they will treat me with respect but within a half-hour, these guys somehow bring the conversation around to sex.'

Linda had been taught by her mother that it wasn't OK to admit to any outright sexual interest in a man. To do so would make her 'sleazy' and a 'tramp.' Ultimately, according to her mother, 'tramps get dumped.' She enjoyed a normal sexual life with her husband for the first three years of their marriage.

But after the birth of their first child, she then began to deny his requests for sexual intimacy and claimed to lose much of her own desire. She was more interested in their growing child. Her withdrawal from sex and loss of interest in giving affection, along with some other relationship problems, eventually led to separation and divorce, some time before she came to see me.

Rather suddenly after her divorce, for a period of about six months, she became, as she put it, a 'sex maniac' and began casually 'sleeping around' with a number of mostly younger men to prove to herself she was still sexually desirable. This promiscuity, although re-affirming her sexuality, and physically enjoyable, made her feel guilty and lose respect for herself.

Because she could not tolerate her feelings of guilt for her 'cheap' behavior, she once again began to deny that she even had any sexual needs and projected her own desire on to the men who would show some interest in her. She preferred to see them after her rather than admit to her own real needs for sexual intimacy. To do so would be to risk losing control of herself and ending up just the kind of 'tramp' her mother had warned her about. After all, hadn't she already lost control after her divorce and slept around with anyone who showed an interest?

It was only after she could separate her real sexual needs (and accept them as legitimate) from the judgements made by her mother about women who open themselves to their 'animal needs,' that she was able to re-own her interest in teasing men and trying to get them to 'come on' to her.

Then, the men who showed interest started to look attractive to her and no longer like the 'beasts' she had chosen to see them as. She was now more able to tell the difference between what feelings were hers, which belonged to her mother, and which belonged to her men friends. It was now more possible to let go of pointing the condemning finger at them.

CONFLUENCE

Confluence means 'flowing with,' as two streams flowing together would make a single larger stream. When we feel confluent with our environment we experience no boundary between it and ourselves. The sense of being in the present and totally focused on what we are doing brings us into confluence. Positive confluence occurs when we have an ecstatic experience and become 'one with the universe' or 'melt' emotionally and physically during sex with a loved one (otherwise known as 'core meltdown').

But when this sense of total identification with something becomes chronic, one is unable to tell the difference between oneself and the world. It is no longer clear where one's sense of self leaves off and the other begins. In its most severe form, this leads to a complete breakdown of ego boundaries and may be seen in certain types of severe mental disturbance, like schizophrenia, and other forms of psychosis. But, like the other boundary disturbances, its more 'garden variety' form is not nearly so dramatic or debilitating, even though it may create some real problems in knowing who's doing what to whom.

One common example of confluence in its negative (but not too debilitating) form would be the need for one's partner to hold certain beliefs exactly as oneself, with no tolerance for difference. For example, demanding that one's wife vote the same way, root for the same team, or have the same taste in furniture, art, etc.

Another example of confluence is the need of some to placate a partner when angry to get them to shut up. They cannot tolerate the differences between them so they immediately apologize so that things can return to 'harmony.' Not so surprisingly, in this culture, that means much of the time the woman placating her husband to keep the peace. However, the dominant, critical wife–passive, whimpy husband is also a popular form in which this one gets acted out.

The motto of the person in pathological confluence might be: *'Peace and quiet at any cost, even if it means forfeiting my separate identity. Flow with it and create no waves or disruptions. Cool out, man. Whatever you want is fine with me. Better to be seen than heard.'*

Another common example of negative confluence (and one that helps keep psychotherapists in business) is the need by some parents to have their children become extensions of themselves. Their children should think just as they do, act like they do, and even look as much as possible as they do. The example given above under the mechanism of introjection pertains here.

Remember, James was unable to sort out his own thinking from his father's, and thus was a reasonable facsimile of his father in thought and behavior. Because he had introjected his father's beliefs, he had become confluent with him, so it was impossible to tell which thoughts and beliefs were his father's and which were his own.

Confluence is the hallmark of passive people, who have long ago learned that 'the best way to get by with others is to get along with them.' Unfortunately, the price paid by these people to get along includes never developing their own sense of individual self that can tolerate (and even thrive on) establishing clear boundaries between themselves and the world.

Rita: An Example of Confluence

Rita was one of the most obedient people I had ever met. She came to psychotherapy initially because she was unhappy with her relationship with her boyfriend, with whom she had been living (and financially supporting) for over a year. She presented herself as being as innocent as the fresh driven snow, one of those people who seemed to be born yesterday, just overflowing with naivety.

Rita was 30 and never married when she first sought me out and was so helpless her boyfriend needed to make the initial appointment for her. In spite of seeming so helpless, she was able to work for a high-powered electronics company, where her job included doing direct sales to executives. She was very bright, spoke quickly and with some self-assurance, and had high hopes of someday owning her own business.

She was very sensitive to any perceived slight she might hear in my voice and bent over backwards to comply with all the routine policies regarding appointments, payment of fee, etc., that I request of patients. She would never disagree with any interpretation I might make, smiled even when it wasn't appropriate, and had great difficulty saying anything the least bit critical about anyone in her life. She hung on for 'dear life' to her boyfriend, who used her for financial support but had little real interest in her and certainly wasn't interested in a long-term commitment.

Her history was of choosing men who were somewhat younger than herself whom she could then take care of and help through their own searching to find themselves. She would earn the money, pay the bills and emotionally prop them up. They, in return, would help neutralize her fears of never having male companionship and make her feel needed as a nurturing mother-figure whom they depended upon for guidance.

Rita just couldn't say 'no.' She had been terrified of her physically and verbally abusive mother, who could only see Rita as an extension of herself. Rita's father was passive, never able to protect her from her mother's outrageously sadistic rampages, in which she would destroy Rita's personal possessions without a second thought, pull Rita's long hair until she cried out in pain, or simply call her enough insulting names to make her want to run away or wish she hadn't been born. She could never comprehend how any mother could be so cruel to her own child.

Both parents were alcoholics and would frequently entertain friends and neighbors in their home by throwing booze parties. It was Rita's job to help serve the drinks and entertain the guests with her charm and wit. As her mother would get progressively more drunk, she would begin to flirt with some of the male guests. Rita, only a ten-year-old child, was forced to watch her mother's antics. She knew she could say or do nothing which might displease her mother or she would be risking a beating. She was a virtual prisoner in her own home, never being allowed to decorate her own room the way she wanted or to live like a normal child.

55

Rita could not go into certain rooms because of her mother's neurotic compulsiveness regarding cleanliness and was forced to repeatedly scrub floors when her mother was angry with her. She could not play with friends after school like normal children, nor could she come home with any dirt on her out-dated and overly formal dresses which her mother forced her to wear. Put simply, Rita was not permitted to be a child. She was expected to be an up-tight, perfect little girl acting like an adult who could make mommy look good.

But what Rita couldn't stand the most was her mother's insistence that she personally be the only one to touch Rita's hair or have anything to do with her personal hygiene. So Rita was forced to submit to wearing exactly what her mother wished, style her hair exactly as her mother wanted, and speak only the words her mother found acceptable.

Consequently, as Rita got into her teenage years, she felt like a puppet whose strings were completely controlled by mother. Her only escape was to make up stories in her head and then write them down. And even these attempts to find some refuge of separateness from her mother were sharply attacked when her mother would burn any stories she might find, after searching through Rita's room when she was away at school.

Her most vivid and painful memories were of her mother physically holding her down on the floor so she could pluck Rita's eyebrows. For Rita to survive in the world she learned one must do what you're told without complaining. To voice one's own opinion could lead to self-destruction. It took us a number of years of intensive treatment for her to learn that she need not allow her mother to control her for the rest of her life. Rita, like Allen in the next example, would rather do harm to herself than risk dishing out to the world what it deserves.

RETROFLECTION

To retroflect means to 'turn back sharply against.' The person who over-uses this defense mechanism has learned how to draw a boundary between himself and others. Unfortunately the boundary line he draws ends up going down the middle of himself. As Perls (1973, pp. 40–1) succinctly put it,

The introjector does as others would like him to do, the pro-jector does unto others what he accuses them of doing to him, the man in pathological confluence doesn't know who is doing what to whom, and the retroflector does to himself what he would like to do to others.

Instead of taking action in the world to bring about changes that will satisfy his needs, the chronic retroflector directs his energy back toward himself rather than toward the world. One way retroflection shows up is in speech patterns. The retroflector tends to use the word 'myself' a lot, as in, 'I must keep control of myself,' or 'I am angry at myself.' It is as if he believes he and 'himself' are two different people.

He has learned at an early point in experimenting with his own self-expression that it was forbidden to express, for example, anger directly at a parent who is frustrating him by denying him some want. Maybe he tries to express his frustration at mother. The parent responds with, 'Don't you **ever** speak to me that way! – I am your mother!!' And so the next time he is angry, he allows his anger to be recognized but feels unsafe directing out toward mother. So this anger is 'turned back against the self' in an unhealthy way. These words then reverberate in his head forever:

'Don't you EVER speak to me that way again, you understand me? How DARE you sass your mother like that?'

That's all it takes – hearing the above command a few times from a raging mother or father as you are being back-handed across the face. We are small enough to be terrified by the strength of the threat implicit in these words. And the slap in the face tells us this is serious (and hurtful) business. We begin to translate questioning a parent as 'sassing.' We know we could be risking not getting mother to take care of us when we really need her.

So it is really not so surprising that as one etches these words into the psyche forever, the result is a turning back against oneself all the 'evil' things that mother never again wants to hear coming from one's 'foul' mouth . . . A mouth that needs to be 'washed out with soap.' A good example of the terror instilled by this kind of behavior is seen in Rita, in the preceding example under confluence.

We are not saying that every impulse to blurt out something to others should be expressed or that we don't use the normal degree of tactfulness in expressing critical opinions. But recognizing the destructiveness of expressing certain impulses is not the same as turning these impulses against oneself. And this is exactly what the retroflector has become an expert in doing.

Allen: An Example of Retroflection

Allen was a 42-year-old systems engineer who came to me with severe marital strain and problems relating to both subordinates and superiors at work. His company had suggested he seek psychotherapy because he got frustrated easily at work, mostly blaming himself for mistakes he might make.

Allen had suffered from a stomach ulcer when younger, and periodically was still forced to take medication to lessen its effects when he would put himself under too much strain and re-experience symptoms. He also had skin problems that were clearly stress-related. In addition, he had been a stutterer as a child and continued to have difficulty clearly verbalizing when confronted or under pressure to speak in front of others.

Allen did to himself what he would like to do to the world. Rather than risk speaking up to superiors he would boil inside and aggravate his ulcer. Rather than let superiors know of his good ideas for policy changes in the company, Allen would hold in his ideas and silently stew about the lack of appreciation he received for his work.

Like Rita, he had decided early in life that risking uncovering his head from the sand was just not worth the price of possibly getting it chopped off. Instead, he forced himself to suffer through various psychosomatic ailments that might not have developed or at least have been so severe had he learned to 'do unto others what you do to yourself.'

And, of course, Allen (like all 'good' retroflectors) had all kinds of 'good reasons' for not speaking up and even after two years of psychotherapy, in which he learned to manage his frustration, he still found it very challenging to say to his superiors what needed to be said regarding his desire for promotion in the company, his desire not to work overtime, and his treatment in his department.

Now that we have looked at the boundary disturbances of the relative self and some examples of how these disturbances are influenced by early developmental experiences, let us look at what we labeled the 'absolute self' and see how it relates to the relative self. *If the relative self keeps our feet on the ground, the absolute self allows us to soar in the heavens.*

THE NATURE OF ABSOLUTE SELF

Absolute self is the self that is not separate. It is what we are before we split ourselves into subject and object, observer and observed. It is the 'other side' of the relative self, and represents both something we wish to unite with and yet fear the actual experience of. So instead of letting subject and object come together and giving up the observing ego, we hold on to the feeling of being always a relative self – and a very important one at that. We are afraid to let go and give in.

Although it is not the way we look at the process of consciousness and self in the West, the Zen Buddhists have a picture of the dance of consciousness that is very helpful in our trying to understand the nature of self. They see there existing an absolute realm of pure consciousness wherein we experience no sense of separateness. There is no boundary between ourselves and the world. A state of spiritual or mystical confluence occurs which is extremely pleasant and from which part of us does not wish to leave.

And yet our relative self is fearful of staying in this state, fearful, of course, that it will lose itself and be unable to re-experience its own nature.

So we are caught in this predicament – part of us wanting to lose our separateness and join with the larger whole and 'soar in the heavens,' free of the burden of worry associated with the relative self and its continual needs for self-protection – and part of us holding on for dear psychological life as a unique separate self. For to give up separateness is to give up uniqueness, and that's a big price to pay to find oneness. At least, that's how the ego looks at it from its relative-self perspective.

From the absolute-self side of the picture, to take the next step, we are having to let ego 'die' a relative-self death in order to stay in oneness. And because we are afraid of merging with The One and The Many we always seem to want to come back, even when it is time to physically die. We struggle with physical death in the same manner we struggle with ego death.

59

How can the ego ever be sure what Oneness will be like on a permanent basis? How can we be sure we would want *anything* to last forever, even oneness? You can see how this ego-self is threatened with annihilation. We could think of it this way: nuclear war means to the physical body (death) what Absolute self means to the ego.

Are we really ready to give up a relative self which we have worked so hard to develop over a lifetime just to become one with Pure Consciousness? And, most of us, because we rarely or never experience a sense of connectedness with everything, or 'oneness with the universe,' don't believe it is actually possible to have these kinds of experiences. We tend to write them off as the talk of mystics, spiritual fanatics, or 'New Age' cult groups. You know the people who are responsible for this stereotype I'm talking about, where you get that vacant, spaced out look when you look in their eyes. The message they give is: 'The lights are on but nobody's home.'

In the midst of Absolute self, we do not recognize ourself. For example, in the moment of embracing your lover you do not think about your relative self as you merge with your loved one. It is only after separating and coming back into relative self that you may think, 'You are so beautiful, I just love to embrace you.' Actually, we have this experience repeatedly but without awareness.

Without dissolving the separate self, we cannot experience the absolute self and if we only stay with the relative 'I am' experience of the relative self, we are in for conflict. We tend not to value and respect all things in life. When we understand that all other people and living things as well as (some believe) inanimate objects have an absolute self, or what one Zen Master calls a 'center of gravity,' we then see our place in the world and are able to respect all life.

When we embrace our lover or put attention fully into any action, there is no need to assert the relative self. Because this kind of notion is foreign to the thinking of most Westerners, it is difficult for us to understand this idea of Absolute self. We don't recognize the moments of Absolute self because the relative self, that would be watching as an observing ego, is dissolved in merging with the other and therefore not around to make this realization.

We have simply never been trained in the activity of Absolute self. We think that if we aren't aware of it, it can't be happening. And yet we know it is possible to have the observing ego doing its job watching and enjoying as we feel one with nature, swimming underwater with our eyes closed, getting lost in music as we play our favorite instrument, or merging with our partner in sexual embrace. We can also bring on this state through meditation and other focusing tools.

This activity of moving from relative self to Absolute self and back to relative self again in a never-ending cycle is how the Buddhists conceptualize the nature of consciousness. When we don't recognize the absolute aspect, we tend to become lost in the search to 'find ourselves' externally in the world. We don't understand that we do not need to search outside of ourselves to find out who we are or how we are related to the larger world. So, the gold of self-discovery comes when we

Look Within
what do you find?

When we are able to experience the absolute in our lives, the frantic search outside of ourselves is no longer necessary. To experience our absolute nature is nothing special, as it is the very nature of our being, according to the Buddhists. This is why the 'awakened' mind is considered awakened: *It realizes not only the nature of relative self but absolute self as well.* Two sides of the same valuable coin. You can bank on it.

One way further to make sense of this idea of absolute and relative selves being two sides of the same coin is to think of a helpful analogy. And that is the process of making motion pictures. We all understand that when we watch a motion picture, what we are really seeing is the illusion of movement created by speeding up thousands of individual frames to make them seem like one ongoing picture.

The motion picture appears to be one continuous picture because we are unable to notice the stringing together of individual frames, as they are moving too quickly for the eye to notice. This is called the 'flicker–fusion threshold.' At a certain speed the eye can no longer see flickering frames – it only sees motion. And, we could say, this is the same process involved in deciphering the absolute self.

Because we are constantly moving from relative to absolute self and back again, we are unable to notice melting back into absolute self. It is occurring too fast for most of us to be able to slow down the 'flicker–fusion threshold' enough to notice. So instead we tend to experience 'blankness' or a feeling of being 'spaced out' when the relative self is no longer being asserted.

Think about your experience of certain activities, like intensively listening to music. When we get lost in the vibrations of sound, we no longer are asserting the relative self because it just isn't necessary. We are merging with the absolute self in a very natural way. Just as we are when we are very tired and ready to 'turn in' to sleep. The relative self isn't necessary to protect us so we are able to just drift off.

Our point here is that this oscillation back and forth between these selves is happening continuously and must be recognized as a healthy, normal process which helps us feel whole as human beings. When it is not recognized or understood, we tend to become attached to things in the outside world as the way to find peace, security and happiness, and yet we are never really able to be satisfied. Like Pacman gobbling up energy dots, relative self can 'gobble up' the whole material world and still it will be 'hungry' for transcending itself and melting into the absolute.

We began this chapter saying that we would present two ways to look at the self. We said these ways (relative and absolute) were contradictory and yet complementary. They are complementary because they are two sides of the same coin of human consciousness. We looked at the boundary disturbances which lead to the chronic and pathological use of certain defense mechanisms. And then we briefly examined the nature of the absolute self and its part in the dance of consciousness which is taking place just **now**, as you read this.

=== 4 ===

THE DISCRIMINATING MIND

In Chapter 1 we said that as we learn to think more clearly, we begin to develop the *discriminating mind*, the mind that is able to make distinctions and see subtle differences between ideas, relationships and forms. We said that the discriminating mind doesn't confuse 'apples with oranges.' It is the maturing mind that knows what it values and what gets priority, and yet doesn't get so overly identified with its beliefs that it can't alter them or even, when necessary, let go of them.

It is, as we said in Chapter 2, the mind that wants to stay nimbly on its toes, so as not to turn 'cherished beliefs into stone.' The *discriminating mind* is both a metaphor for a process of knowing our own minds and a real, practical state of mental development which we can call on for everyday guidance.

Because it is on 'speaking terms' with itself, the discriminating mind is able to choose from a wide variety of inner personality parts that have been developed by listening to a respective inner voice which represents each of them.

In other words, the more we are able to hear and understand our inner voices, the more we are able to accept and integrate the part of us that each speaks for. The discriminating mind acts as organizer, welcoming all of the different parts that make up our personality. It is as if this organizer shouts out to the various parts, 'Stand up and be heard! Have your say so that we may all work together to form a fully functioning whole!' We hear that grasping voice inside, for example, that says, 'Ah yes, if only you could live in Switzerland for three months of the year – then you'd be even happier than you are now!'

We see that this voice 'speaks for' the part of us that wants the world to be *just a little more* perfect than we already think it is.

How do we get to be on 'speaking terms' with ourselves? – again, by first hearing, and then working with, all these different voices we hear inside, and the parts of us they represent. Instead of fighting an ongoing battle, with some parts of us always at war with other parts, we can learn to make friends with these parts, even the ones that make us sick of ourself and feel disgusted.

With patients in psychotherapy, one of the primary tasks on the road toward the development of the discriminating mind is the ability to identify, sort out, accept responsibility for, and then make friends with *all* the 'hideous monsters' inside. We begin to face all of the parts that we have for so long tried to keep outside the self-boundary. Sometimes the internal dialogue might sound like this:

'You mean I have to accept the part of me that has lustful thoughts?' *Yes, that one.* 'What about the one that fantasizes running away from my responsibilities and becoming a vagabond?' *Yep, that one too.* 'How about the voice that sometimes wishes the worst for those who cause me pain, and doesn't really care very much what happens to others?' *Yes, you've got to own that one.*

'But please, you can do anything to me – throw me in the briar patch, even – but don't make me hear that voice that cries out in terror at the horrors of life!' *Well, it's up to you – you can let it in now, or struggle with it for awhile and then be forced to face it later.* 'Oh . . . in that case I'll deal with it later – I've got all the pain I can handle for now, thank you.'

So, we end up putting off until the vague future what we need to deal with today. And the price we pay is a sense of alienation from ourselves and a fear of exploring our own minds.

With the sharpening of this aspect of our minds, we are able to develop what we may call 'discriminating wisdom.' We can think of discriminating wisdom as the sword that cuts through to the truth, a truth about ourselves based on personal knowledge that goes beyond the usual rationalizations and stories we tell ourselves about how things are.

And with discriminating wisdom, we are able to make wise,

healthy and self-loving choices which make our lives more content, satisfying, and as free of pain and fear as possible. We learn to honor and respect our relative ego-self and become friends with ourselves at deeper and deeper levels. We begin to understand what is meant by the dictum that 'you can't really love anyone else until you've learned to love yourself.'

Discriminating wisdom is the ability to decipher what is real in our lives and what is 'make-believe.' When we have developed this quality, we have a powerful tool to utilize our highest mental powers in combination with our intuitive and emotional knowledge. In combination, these qualities act as 'searchlights' to help us find our way when there is not always a lighted path ahead. We then have the necessary courage to believe in ourselves to take the next steps in our personal journey through life.

With discriminating wisdom, we aren't so afraid that the world is going to 'knock us out for the count.' It may knock us to our knees in utter shock, surprise and disbelief at times, but after 'coming to' (becoming conscious once again, as we wake up from the shock) we will once again stand on our two feet and be ready for 'whatever life has to dish out.'

Our discriminating wisdom can act as a guide to inform us as to when to say 'yes,' when to say 'no' and show restraint, and help us stay in touch with those values in our lives that are going to lead us to the greatest degree of personal happiness and freedom from unnecessary suffering.

As well, our discriminating wisdom can help us know when to take care of ourselves and when to take care of others. We are able to tap our own compassion for, and respond appropriately to, the suffering of others when we have squarely faced and, at least to some degree, overcome our own suffering. Discriminating wisdom gives us the courage to face the world and the existential choices that make up our daily world.

When we accept some of the realities of life and stop fighting them, the journey becomes easier, even if we don't always like what may be happening. For example, what if we were to allow ourselves to really accept the reality that this physical body – no matter how hard we try to nourish, preserve, alter, or exercise it – is slowly but constantly decaying and will ultimately die? Then we might not attach our sense of relative self so strongly to this body.

This doesn't mean we don't take care of this body. And it certainly doesn't mean that we abuse this body in gross, masochistic ways. The better shape this body is in, the better vehicle it will be to take us through our journey. We can learn so much about our relative self by paying attention to the desires, sensations and actions of this wonderful body.

But, the truth is the truth. This body is only here for such a short time and we're going to suffer so much if we hang on too tightly to it. Even beauty queens must face the last dance.

When we really accept the reality of this natural process of birth, decay and death we can with some courage, let this body go through its ultimate journey. Physical pain can make life at times so excruciatingly trying that we understand why some people might choose to die rather than go on facing it. And for others, the emotional and psychological pain can bring them to the same point.

Far too often, life seems to have a way to push us right to our limits, so that we are forced to find creative adaptations to our predicaments and thereby gain added emotional and mental self-support. We see that we can find solutions to most of what we look at as our problems. And we see as well that when we can't find a 'solution' to our predicament, most of the time we can more fully accept our predicament, even if we don't like it. The discriminating mind knows that there are so many shades of possibility in the way we might perceive the world. And yet it is not afraid to make a definite choice; it is willing and able to *discriminate*.

How should we deal with the unpleasant but undeniable reality of suffering all around us? Should we run away from these 'unpleasant' realities or somehow find a way to work with them? If we don't find a way to accept them as HOW IT IS and realize that we don't have to like it but not let it knock us out, this very short trip we take through life can seem at times like hell.

Or, when we are able to accept what we don't like but are unable to change and not ask for things to be any more perfect than they are right now, life can be experienced as floating on a bubble, where we simply bounce ourselves (and get bounced around) from here to there, able to land where we land, and find wonder, strength and meaning in all that happens.

The discriminating mind helps us pick and choose those experiences that we think will best nourish and challenge us. It helps us refrain from doing those same stupid things over and over again, as if we are simply unable to stop our unconscious robotic behavior. Discriminating wisdom is the kind of knowledge that helps us know when *enough is enough*. In this way, we are more likely to be clear on our own relative-self boundaries, knowing what we will tolerate and what we won't. We know when to stand firm and when to yield, when to protest and when to play.

The discriminating mind is the mind that can turn back on itself, looking as clearly as it is able to see the truth about how it operates. It realizes, when it looks at itself, that thoughts come and go. Nothing needs to stay if we don't fight it and get lost in it. We let thoughts do what they love to do best – come and go, one after another, like sheep jumping over the fence, in the various forms they may present to us.

When the discriminating mind is underdeveloped or absent altogether, discriminating wisdom is nowhere to be found. We feel lost, unable to trust our own judgement about what is right for us. We then tend to introject, or 'swallow whole,' bits and chunks of information, values, and beliefs learned from authority figures and act as if they were our own.

We also tend to make decisions 'by the seat of our pants,' allowing whatever impulse of the moment happens to come up to sway us one way or another. And even if we are not swayed by the impulse of the moment, we still find it difficult to know when we are thinking clearly and when our mixed feelings are contaminating our desire to be as rational as we are able. We don't know how much to trust our emotions and intuitions. 'They may steer me wrong.'

Perhaps we don't really understand a certain concept that we might toss around, for example, 'self-actualization.' When we talk about it, we may sound unsure of ourselves or sound like we are simply regurgitating what we have memorized. It is not so difficult to tell when we are uncomfortable with the expression of introjected beliefs. Inside, we know something isn't quite right.

Close listening (and questioning) of ourselves and questioning by others reveals a lack of real understanding of what we are talking about. Of course, we never like to admit this, and will even become defensive at being too closely questioned regarding those of our beliefs that we aren't too sure about. No one likes the feeling of not knowing what they are talking about but almost everyone has experienced this uncomfortable sensation at one time or another.

So we do our best to 'get by' by faking it. It is not so surprising that so many people walk around with the fear of being 'found out,' feeling like impostors who are not really sure of themselves and the roles they are playing. This is such a popular topic with which we can identify that a whole pop-psychology book has been written about it and has been well received by the public. Great numbers of people go out, read about the 'impostor phenomenon' and say to themselves, 'Yes, that's me. That's just how I feel!'

And then maybe they come in for psychotherapy (if they are sufficiently motivated) or growth workshops to learn how to feel more authentic and less phony. Or maybe they just learn how to better cover up these feelings of inadequacy and be better impostors, inside feeling like they are clever enough to 'dupe' lovers, bosses, friends and colleagues and even taking a secret delight in not being discovered. But inside they know it's all a charade.

And why might we end up feeling like impostors, fearful of being discovered by the people in our lives? Basically, because we don't know who we really are. We don't trust our skills, talents and knowledge and don't believe we deserve to be thought of as competent. As since we know inside we are really lost, we imagine, at some point, others will see this in us, just as we do.

And while this so-called 'impostor phenomenon' might be of most concern to us in our work-place, where our being found out could cost us our means of livelihood, certainly this isn't something we can turn on and off. If we don't feel worthy of our standing in our jobs, why should we feel any differently when it comes to our love relationships? Why should we feel any more real in our role as a parent or as a friend?

How could we possibly know who we are without at least some knowledge of our own minds and how they work? This is why we keep coming back to the need for us to take time to learn about our own minds. Without this understanding of our minds, the discriminating mind discriminates poorly or not at all, and the wisdom which could be available to help guide us is just not available for us to call on.

And so, once again, we are forced to rely on the knowledge and judgement of others, who we believe will help us find our way. Nothing wrong with this when the other has a skill, knowledge, and training that we don't have, like building a room addition, fixing broken pipes, our car, or our television, or diagnosing some disease, or pulling a bad tooth. But not so great when it means we give away our own responsibility for knowing our own minds!

Sometimes, it is simply mental laziness that leads to the introjection of certain beliefs, opinions, or values about our world. We don't want to take the time or effort required to read, inform ourself about an issue, critically look at various positions, and then come to an opinion after this kind of critical analysis. And, of course, this is especially difficult to do when the subject matter has something to do with ourselves.

And, if it were as simple as just attributing our lack of discrimination to 'laziness,' then all we would need to do is learn how to discipline ourselves to use our minds in a more analytical and penetrating manner – in itself, certainly not the easiest task in the world. But, it is not so simple – because the real problem is that the power of our impulses (discussed in Chapter 1), can be so overwhelming that the rational mind is unable to 'step back' and get the mental space it needs to critically look at an issue without our impulses taking control. The result – we get in our own way.

Let us use an example to make the point that is common and that frequently comes to my attention, as it is often brought in by those seeking psychotherapy. As will become evident, this example is one representing a great many in our society, most of whom will struggle on their own or seek advice of well-meaning friends but not present themselves to a mental health professional.

Randy: An Example of Poor Discrimination

Randy comes in complaining that although he knows he 'shouldn't be doing it,' he cannot stop seeing a woman he is involved with in an extra-marital affair. Randy is 27 and has been married two years. He is bright, verbal, and has a college education, and works as a sales representative, where he is able to make his own work hours. Randy is attractive, quick to smile and, on the surface, presents himself in a pleasant, inviting and lively manner. He is co-operative, with little of the defensive posturing that is commonly displayed in the early stages of establishing a psychotherapy relationship.

I notice immediately that he has a glaring incongruency as he talks about his predicament of being 'torn between two lovers,' or, more accurately, torn between a non-loving wife and a loving girlfriend. And that incongruency is that he has a big smile plastered across his face as he is talking about the pain of having to lie to his wife and be pressured by his girlfriend, whom he has come to care about after many months of exciting outings and sex play. He is not aware of this perpetual need to smile until I point it out.

Because this is a behavior I have seen countless times before in others (and frequently in people with attractive smiles), I can, with a high degree of probability, assume it means he has learned that it is 'not OK' to talk about something important without having to 'sugar-coat' it with a smile to make it more palatable for me, the listener. I also realize that this smile is one of his 'tools of the trade' to make his way through the world. Usually behind this kind of habitual smiling is a lesson learned early in life: SMILE EVEN WHEN IT HURTS AND MAYBE IT WON'T BE SO BAD (AND EVEN IF IT IS, OTHERS WILL BE ABLE TO TOLERATE YOU EASIER IF YOU SMILE).

Randy had been involved with his girlfriend for a number of months and had recently moved out of the home he shares with his wife, who is an artist and musician. He has not revealed to her that he is having an 'affair,' fearful that if he did, she would divorce him. And yet, as he put it, he hasn't 'covered his tracks' very well, leaving the phone bill remains of lengthy conversations he has had with his lover.

And although confronted by his wife regarding the calls, he is able to lie his way out of the jam, and she apparently has 'taken the bait' by believing him. He secretly wishes his wife had cared enough to get angry and care what he had been up to. But he now feels he can't really be honest with her.

And to make things even more complicated, his 'loving' girlfriend has a boyfriend on the side, 'just in case,' whom she calls into duty whenever there is some trouble between Randy and herself. 'Who is doing what to whom?' was the first question I had to answer. Then, maybe I could help him sort this thing out.

Randy felt 'squeezed in,' unable to decide whether he wanted to work out sexual incompatibilities existing before marriage with his passive wife, with whom he thought he made a 'good team.' But he would then be forced to give up the excitement of his somewhat older 'take-charge' girlfriend, who made their time together exciting by planning just the kind of activities his wife couldn't quite motivate herself to initiate.

"I feel **squeeezzed** in ... as if I'm living in a box"

Randy, to put it simply, didn't know his own mind. He didn't know what he wanted and was fearful of ending up with neither his wife or his girlfriend if he couldn't make up his mind. In our first session, he thought he wanted to find a way to return to his wife but wasn't really sure why.

One of his complaints, not so surprisingly, was feeling that he had lost his ability to make up his own mind about political or social issues, instead listening to and then 'swallowing' the opinions of others around him, whose views he respected. When he would try to think for himself and take a chance to counter other people's arguments on a given issue, he many times felt overwhelmed by the force of their arguments, and ended up simply 'buying' their way of viewing things.

His not knowing his own mind came out in another way. His wife, although initially encouraging him to seek psychotherapy as a means to get him to make up his mind and hopefully come back to her, didn't really trust that he *could* think for himself.

So if he made a decision, for example, after sorting out his feelings in a session, to spend more time alone, and not contact either his wife or girlfriend, his wife saw this as his being 'influenced' by me, his psychotherapist. This told me that she perceived him as someone whom she didn't really believe was capable of making up his own mind without being swayed by someone else. In other words, because *she* made it difficult for him to think for himself, she believed anyone he talked to would most likely do the same.

One short side comment about this: The curious thing about this charge of 'influencing' a patient is that I sometimes wonder what people expect is going to happen when a friend or marital partner submits herself for help. Although I don't make people's minds up for them, *of course* I am going to 'influence' them by anything that comes out of my mouth (unless they aren't listening or choose to take my words with a grain of salt).

Randy became more aware, after about ten hours of therapy, that he did not want to give up his marriage just for the excitement he felt with his girlfriend. And even though he cared for his girlfriend, he did not believe their relationship was worth leaving his marriage for. It took a long time for his wife to deal with the pain of the truth of his affair. But Randy and his wife are continuing to struggle with the gaping hole of mistrust that was created in his deceptive affair with his girlfriend.

Some people, like Randy, spend a good deal of their waking life feeling various degrees of confusion. Ongoing confusion that never 'clears up' is a good sign of our simply not knowing how to think clearly in the face of more powerful emotions and more subtle feelings which pull us one way and then the other, like a small sail-boat caught in the emotionally choppy waves on the ocean of life. To trace this confusion, we must go back into the past.

INTO THE PAST: A PERSPECTIVE ON YOUTH

It is normal to be confused while we are children and even through our teenage years and early adulthood. Let's face it: being a child, even in the best of circumstances, can be frustrating. The mind takes time to develop fully and the ability to do rational problem-solving and high-level abstract conceptual thinking is something gained as we mature. In the next section we will summarize this developmental process. But first, some comments on how it subjectively feels for many as they go through this process.

As an adolescent turning into a teenager, as our body changes and we face the wrath of our peers, things can seem so tough that even the frustrations of childhood, in comparison, may seem like 'child's play.' For example, take one simple but telling statistic: *40 per cent of all adolescent girls will become pregnant before the age of 18.* The United States has one of the highest rates of teenage pregnancy in the world. And research shows that most teenage pregnancies are not wanted, so the pregnancy is almost always an emergency and provokes a psycho-social crisis.

For most of us, it isn't so simple as caterpillars turning into beautiful butterflies. Growing up isn't easy! And although loving and supportive parents, pets, fun activities and school friends are nice and can make the journey easier, the truth is that for too much of the time, life for a teenager can be a continual series of frustrations, disappointments and humiliations.

Ask any 15-year-old. As teenagers, we just can't comprehend what this big mysterious world is all about. We aren't sufficiently able to *discriminate*, to know what we really need for ourselves (versus what we want or *think* we need), and even when we are, there are parents, teachers and other authorities to answer to, who are going to frustrate our wishes at every turn of the road.

For far too many, what is appropriate as teenagers (confusion), unfortunately does not cease to exist as we become young adults and move into adulthood. We battle over the course of a lifetime to learn to think clearly for ourselves, and develop the discriminating mind, the mind of knowledge and experience that will help us find our way in this uncertain and scary world.

And because of this, the analogy of sitting in the caboose as the train chugs forward, where we are only able to make sense of our decisions or see the rhyme and reason of our life (presented in the Introduction), seems very close to the truth of how we actually experience our lives, especially for teenagers trying to grow up and stand on their own feet. But, again, who wants to deal with the fear and even terror of not being in control?

It has long been maintained by philosophers that 'youth is wasted on the young, who don't know what to do with it.' What this means, of course, is that by the time we have developed the ability to think clearly, make reasonably intelligent decisions in life, and have finally learned some of the 'ins and outs' of life and how to (hopefully) live it wisely, we might feel too old to really make the most of it, because our bodies aren't any longer able to do some of the things we wish they would and because we believe there isn't enough lifetime left to make the most of our knowledge.

A short way to say this: by the time we 'get it together' in life, we have already wasted so much of it learning to get there. Why couldn't we, we lament, have both the knowledge, understanding and wisdom of our middle and later years *and* the strength, beauty and freshness of youth? Nice fantasy, but it's not possible and because it isn't, we spend too much time suffering, cursing our predicament and the basic 'unfairness' of life.

You might think this a 'pessimistic' view of growing up, but I think it is closer to reality than a perception that views childhood, and especially adolescence and the teenage years, as nothing but wonderful 'care-free' years to have a good time with few of the 'real-life' trials and tribulations of adulthood. In this nuclear age we live in, as we stand ready to plunge into the 1990s, there are simply too many teenage drug overdoses, pregnancies and suicide attempts to hold this old-fashioned, Pollyannish view.

Things are simply moving too fast these days, and in a world where information can be transmitted instantaneously to all corners of the globe by computers, tele-networking and 'fax' machines, we simply don't have the luxury to have a leisurely period of bafflement. If you reach age 10 and haven't yet learned how to use a personal computer, you are going to be behind your peers.

One of my favorite stories about this 'high-tech, low touch' awareness by children and teenagers is one I read in the newspaper not so long ago. A local high school girl, taking a required biology class, refused to participate in the ritualistic and obligatory experiment that all students taking this class are subjected to: the dissection of a frog.

She didn't want to have anything to do with such a 'barbaric' experiment which, in good conscience, she felt was wrong. And what was her thinking regarding learning the anatomy of a frog? She not only believed it was wrong to cut up dead frogs but further maintained that she could get a much better lesson in anatomy by working with computerized drawings of the subject matter without ever soiling her hands! This kind of thinking was not of this world (nor were personal computers!) when I was in high school. And it illustrates nicely the permeation of 'high tech' and computer literacy and its effect on today's teenage mind.

Even 'good kids,' who are able to sidestep the obstacles of drugs and some of the foolhardy experimentation with speeding cars, alcohol and exploratory sex are unable to sidestep the extreme pressure to excel in school, athletics, etc., in order to 'make it' to the big leagues of a 'name' college. They are unable to escape the confusions of relating to the opposite sex and the trials and tribulations of trying to establish and solidify a strong ego-self that can weather the painful ego-bruising that is part of growing up, with a body that is changing monthly.

All of this is not to say that childhood and the teenage years do not have their own particular magic, especially childhood, when we are relatively innocent as to what is really happening in the world. And certainly, for some, the exploratory, 'devil-may-care' times of being a teenager have their own special poignancy that are unmatched in later years.

When you're a teenager, everything in the world is so important! Every decision, every outing, every new date or activity with one's peers is almost bigger than life. Everything matters! Nothing is too small to potentially be the 'end of the world' if it somehow doesn't come out just as it should. And with everything riding as one's self-confidence is put on the line, there is little time to relax and simply enjoy the passing show.

Why? Because the adults (parents, relatives, teachers) in one's life are always expecting the best performance from us, no matter what we are engaged in. From one generation to the next, the rationale is always the same: 'You need to learn early how to compete in this world – otherwise, you will buckle under the pressure when you go out into the cold, cruel world and fend for yourself.'

As adults, as we have said, *the most difficult task in the world is to learn how to control our own minds*. And much of the misery we experience is directly related to our inability to think clearly about ourselves and the world we live in. And if it is so precarious for us as adults, it is clearly even more so for us as teenagers and young adults. No wonder so many want to change their state of consciousness through various chemicals to escape the pain of their normally painful and confused mind. Now let us look at how this mind develops.

HOW DOES THE THINKING MIND DEVELOP?

Very briefly and as simply as possible, let us summarize how the mind and sense of self develop. Then it will make more sense when we talk about the discriminating mind and the use of discriminating wisdom and why it is so difficult to call on this wisdom. How does this ego-mind come from nothing?

To begin with, the infant at birth does not possess a sense of ego-self. There is no real sense of separation between the body and the environment. Although the infant is aware of events taking place in his world, there is no sense of these events as separate from himself.

To put it simply, the infant's sense of self and the world are one. This is the confluence or 'oneness' with the world that is prior to the development of a separate self and not to be confused with the mystical oneness that transcends the personal ego, once it has been developed. To put it in the terms of theoretical psychologist Ken Wilber (1980), the oneness of the baby is *pre-personal*, that is, before a sense of ego-self has been developed, while the oneness achieved by the mystic or spiritual seeker is *transpersonal*, or beyond the full developed ego-self. You can't go 'beyond' an ego that has not yet been developed!

Now, the above picture of the infant's state following birth has been our conception for some time. The infant was seen as basically uninterested in making contact actively with the world, instead bathing in the bliss of fusion with the outside world. This 'oceanic bliss' of the infant is a bliss of ignorance, occurring, as we said, before the development of self-consciousness, in which there is no sense of time. In between, where we spend most of our lives, is the realm of the personal, which is the realm of the developing relative ego-self. This is the realm we looked at in the last chapter.

Slowly the infant begins to sense the difference between his body and the world and to develop reflex actions that still have nothing to do with a sense of self. This happens at about 4 to 6 months. This does not mean the baby can't interact exploringly with his environment. Recent infant research suggests that we are born into this world eagerly seeking out information in the world 'out there.' This emerging picture contradicts the earlier conception of the baby unable to do this kind of exploration. The new picture gives the baby more 'credit' for immediately trying to make some sense out of his world.

It is believed that the infant begins to be able to hallucinate wish fulfillment: whatever he wants will magically be given. There is a very basic sense of hunger and need to survive but still no sense of time.

Sensations and perceptions begin to develop and by 15 to 18 months, the infant is able to distinguish self from not-self. Primitive emotions also are presumed to develop, such as fear, greed, rage and pleasure. The most significant image, according to psychoanalysts, is that of the breast. The infant fears the loss of his mother's breast as, without it, survival is threatened. The baby begins to differentiate between pleasurable and unpleasurable sensations and begins to look for bodily pleasure and avoid that which will bring discomfort. All attention is focused on bodily sensations.

Now, instead of the 'bliss of ignorance' which was reality at birth, the infant begins to divide the world very simply into 'good' sensations and 'bad' sensations. There is still no ability to conceive of past or future. The self is still a body-self, as the infant realizes his body is different from the larger world that is not his body.

As a child begins to speak, what has been termed 'verbal-logic' begins to develop. In learning what linguists call the 'deep structure' of the language of his culture, he also learns to mentally construct and then actually perceive a certain reality when he looks out at the world. He becomes a member of the consensus reality (the 'way it is') of his society and is forced to accept the limits and blinders of this cultural reality as well. Slowly, the child moves away from what psychologists call 'magical thinking' toward a more logical, verbal and linear thinking. The events of life are put into words and communicated to others.

The child has gone beyond the awareness of immediate sensory input and can now think of a past and future, no longer mentally imprisoned in the present. But with this new gain in consciousness, the relative self is more aware of its place in time, and therefore more able to understand its separateness and mortality. He has, in a sense, 'woken up' out of the sleep of subconsciousness and become a relative self, with all the privileges and responsibilities it entails.

Through word and thought the child internalizes the early parental prohibitions and demands and develops the 'inner mother,' or early conscience of right and wrong. The child is now able to transcend, through language, the immediate present and, as we said, now able to think of and plan for tomorrow. He can control his present bodily urges and therefore, at least to some degree, can transcend them.

By around the age of 7, the child is able to do what the psychologist Piaget termed 'concrete operational thinking.' This means that the child is able to apply concepts, or 'operate' on the concrete world and his body. By the time of adolescence, the child is able to differentiate his self from his thought processes. He can operate on his thought process, just as he learned to operate (and therefore transcend) his body. He can now think about his own thinking process. The relative self is learning to transcend the verbal ego-mind. Remember that the verbal ego-mind is the mind that contains the ongoing internal 'chatter,' which we have referred to as the 'monkey-mind.'

The *discriminating mind* is the fully developed use of the verbal ego-mind of the relative self at its highest level. But it is not *just* the verbal ego-mind – it is also the integration of the verbal ego-mind with emotion and intuition. The discriminating mind, while of the same 'stuff' (thoughts) as the verbal ego-mind, is what is left when we have stripped away much of the chattering monkey. It is from the ages of around 12 to 21 that we shape and attempt to perfect this discriminating mind, usually through the development of logical analysis and rational thought through education. This takes place as we learn to live with the various parts of our personality that emerge, as we play different roles in our growing up.

But one of the main themes of this book is that for most of us, this discriminating mind is never really developed to its highest capacity. Because we are unable to master the confusion we feel, we believe that all our rational powers are just not enough to overcome the sense of randomness and irrationality we feel.

We want so much for the world to work logically but it doesn't. We can apply our own rationality but this does not make the world itself rational. And it is when these different parts become confused, tangled and unclear that we are unable to make the kind of discriminations that we have said lead to what we have called 'discriminating wisdom' which we can trust to help us.

This is where the personality problems are felt. Whatever doesn't get taken care of internally as we develop the verbal ego-mind is waiting to make itself felt in the form of pathology, as indicated in the last chapter, through the descriptions of boundary disturbances.

And it is exactly the need to balance and integrate the rational intellect with emotion and a sense of intuition that makes the discriminating mind so difficult to fully develop.

It is only when we are able to transcend these various parts (through the identifying, understanding and acceptance of them) that we are able to 'operate' on them rather than be baffled by them. This, it seems, is one of the distinguishing factors between having some control over our mind versus feeling it is totally in control of us. The way to control it is to be able to transcend it.

And that is exactly what is possible when we have come to grips with our various internal voices, and outward roles that we play in the world of social relations. We sign a 'truce agreement' with ourselves. So, instead of being in perpetual battle, we can go beyond the various parts and end up with a fairly stable sense of relative ego-self. Then we are more ready for allowing Absolute self to be comprehended.

The discriminating mind is the mind that can exercise restraint upon its desires. The thoughts that come up, for example, to acquire a very fast and fancy sports car can be taken as passing pleasant distractions that don't then necessarily or compulsively lead to any action. The thought just comes and goes as a pleasant fantasy, nothing more. We don't need to feel envious of the guy we know who has one – we can even feel 'sympathetic joy' that he is able to enjoy his extravagant toy. Nor do we need to begin scheming to find a way to get one for ourselves.

What we have is enough. We don't feel less than him just because he has the fancy toy and we do not. We remember that toys are just toys to help us enjoy passing the time. They may or may not bring us some satisfaction. We don't need to disparage the other guy who may have more. We can let go of the bitterness and resentment that we feel when we feel 'cheated' that he has more than we do.

How does the feeling of having enough relate to the discriminating mind? In this way: we begin to be able to tell what is worth spending time thinking about and what isn't. That's what the discriminating mind does for us – it helps us learn to discriminate between what to pay attention to and what is just scattered, repetitive, non-present, negativistic associated thought loops which don't lead us anywhere of much value.

=== 5 ===

DISCRIMINATING PERSONALITY

We can think of 'personality' as an enduring and persisting set of attitudes, traits, motivations, beliefs and response patterns that characterize one person from another. Sometimes we think of our personality as who we 'really' are. For example, 'John is a person who is in favor of a woman's right to have an abortion (attitude), compassionate (trait), motivated to succeed in his profession (motivation), believes in the Bill of Rights (belief), and responds with irritation when aggravated by incompetence (response pattern).'

For the most part, our thinking about personality is synonymous with our thinking about our relative self. 'John has an intense personality' usually means about the same as 'John is intense.' In this chapter we will look at just a few personality characteristics and their relation to the development of the discriminating mind.

HONESTY

Let's start with a tough one. Although in this society we like to 'talk up' being honest (as in 'honesty is the best policy'), if we are going to be honest about it, the reality is that our culture also teaches us to look at a person who is too honest as a 'sucker.' For example, the guy who doesn't cheat in some ways on his income taxes (regardless of the new tax cuts), is looked at like he is a 'dummy' for losing out when *everybody else in the same hemisphere* is doing something differently!

At least, this is how it is presented to me by countless acquaintances, colleagues, patients and the media. The guy who is too honest, we tell ourselves, is the guy who is going to be thought of as 'tactless' when he can't hold in his tongue at the right time. Further, we will be seen as 'naive' if we are totally honest, in our foolhardy assumption that others in the world can handle our honesty. Instead of appreciating our honesty (as we think they should), they end up being insulted, needlessly ego-bruised, and disliking us forever.

There is no shortage of examples in everyday politics and government, business, the professions and the academic world to verify our very mixed feelings about honesty, ethics and a sense of fair play in our dealings with others. The blatant lying about their backgrounds by political candidates for President, insider-trading scandals on Wall Street, fabrication of statistical data in academic research, and various other assaults to truth and honesty belie our popular valuing of these qualities.

For too many, unfortunately, behavior is only limited by what they think they can get away with. This is apparently especially true for the world of business. Any behavior in the pursuit of power, money, sex, or fame is considered acceptable if the possibility is high enough that one will somehow get ahead of one's dishonest acts.

A good example is the willingness of Olympic athletes to use steroids to get every strength advantage possible in hopes of outperforming the competition. A Canadian sprinter (you know who I am referring to), considered the 'fastest man alive,' in front of millions of TV viewers around the world, betters his own world record in the 100 meter dash, and is then humiliated by being caught with traces of steroids in his urine. He loses his new world mark, his Olympic gold medal, and disgraces his country. In hopes of becoming very rich and proving he is the 'best,' he uses steroids, gets caught, and ends up blowing his entire running career. Another sad story in the big city. But nothing that isn't occurring every day in one endeavor or another. This one was just more dramatic and pathetic than most.

Being honest is one of those personality characteristics that brings up strong feelings of ambivalence for many of us. We, as they say, 'like the concept' but many times have trouble with the reality of doing it. So, we may 'speak the truth' about Brenda's new dress to Jane, but *perish the thought* that we would ever tell Brenda the truth when she says, 'Now, give me your *honest* opinion'!

We don't believe Brenda can handle the truth, no matter what she says about wanting our 'honest opinion.' We convince ourselves that we are not only saving ourselves, but also saving poor Brenda from the insult of our critical judgement.

Better we should gossip behind Brenda's back! That way, we don't hurt Brenda directly but we do get all the enjoyment of 'confessing' our true opinion to a trusted third party. If this third party, Jane, follows through with her part in this often-played-out scenario, she will find a way to get our real opinion back to Brenda, who will then feel even worse, knowing we didn't tell her the truth and that we made a fool of her behind her back. Too often, like this, it backfires, and we lose when we can't control our own tongue!

Perhaps the most significant therapist-modeling behavior about which I have received feedback from psychotherapy patients over the years, is in the area of honesty. Most patients have never had a relationship in which honesty was actively encouraged and reinforced, as it is in the therapy consulting room. I invite patients to speak honestly and truthfully, and to let their behavior be congruent with their words. Even though I may react to their honesty in some manner they may not like, this does not mean I don't appreciate their open and honest feedback.

I try to model honesty in my dealing with them in a number of ways, including standing behind my words, being direct and clear about contract matters related to time and fee, and my honest reactions to their words and behaviors in the therapy hour. I believe I would be less than therapeutic if I were unable to be completely honest with patients. And even though I say I ought to be 'completely honest,' the truth is that I many times refrain from saying things that might clearly injure someone until I feel confident they are strong enough to handle hearing me. Or I may find a gentle way of giving them the feedback that I believe is important for them at the time.

Those who cannot handle critical feedback of any kind tend not to stay in treatment very long with me, even though I am never cruel, seldom loud or angry, and most of the time able to gauge how firmly something needs to be put to impact the other.

Some people are just not ready for directness or hearing the truth, no matter how important it may be that they face themselves or else continue to suffer psychological pain. For those who require strong doses of heavily supportive therapy where analyzing

83

oneself critically is too much to handle, I have a number of gentle, warm and highly supportive colleagues to whom I can refer, if appropriate.

In the termination phase of therapy, where time is spent discussing how patients experienced my methods of working with them, comments regarding my modeling of honesty in the therapy relationship are the single most often expressed appreciation.

Often, *at the time it is happening*, patients don't like my irritation or anger that might have been openly expressed to them. But in looking back, they are appreciative that I would be concerned about them enough to feel and express anger to them. Many comment that they only wished their parents had shown the same concern that would have evoked real emotion.

The ability to be honest with others is going to relate directly to our willingness to be honest with ourselves.

If we are not willing to be honest with ourselves or are too out of touch to really know what the truth is when we speak and act, it isn't going to be possible to be honest with others. We don't need to be brutal or cruel with our honesty to others, just as we don't need to be cruel in being honest with ourselves.

As we get more and more comfortable with telling ourselves the 'real story' about how we feel and think, slowly it becomes easier for us to risk being more honest with our friends, lovers and outside world. Many people tell me they don't have such a hard time being honest with strangers with whom they come into daily contact as they do with those closest to them, even though they feel much more intimate with loved ones.

Why is this? If we think about this for a minute, we see that one reason for this feeling of greater comfort in being honest with strangers is that we don't worry so much about the consequences of our actions in the same way as we do with those closer to us. So we might let ourselves get mad at the way an employee treats us in the market but not let ourselves express our anger at our mate who continues to cut us off when we are speaking.

When I notice that patients are more able to tell me honestly how they feel, especially when they are hurt or angry about some perceived slight of them on my part, I know they are getting stronger. The more congruent their communication of displeasure, the more I know they are developing their own integrity. They are standing more solidly on their own two emotional feet and able to risk whatever reaction they may imagine will come back from me.

Experiment: Honesty
Think of one area of your life where you have not been entirely honest or truthful with someone. Ask yourself what you imagine would happen if you were to tell them the truth. See if you can imagine at least two other possible outcomes of your being honest, at least one of which you believe to be positive. See if you can contact how it feels when you focus on your knowledge that you have not been honest. If your dishonesty relates to not telling the truth, see if you are aware of other times recently when you have not told the complete truth. What was your reasoning in not telling the truth?

Now see if it is possible to uncover one thought or feeling that you have not been honest or truthful about to *yourself*. Perhaps it is not OK to admit the truth to yourself regarding your ability in a certain area of interest, perhaps a hobby or avocation. Can it be all right for now to just admit to yourself exactly what you believe the truth to be, *whether or not* you like it?

For one week, notice the tendency to alter the truth in your daily interactions with others. For one week (even if you are fearful), experiment in telling the complete truth whenever it is possible. If you choose not to be truthful, again notice what your rationale is in choosing to lie. Notice how you feel when you do tell the truth, especially when it might be easier to tell a 'white lie.' If you choose not to follow through with the experiment, notice why you don't want to do it.

CONFRONTING FEAR

For many men in our culture, the unconscious acquired philosophy of choice has been 'rugged individualism,' or the 'cowboy mentality.' The 'cowboy mentality' is the mentality of those who originally settled the Wild West. Since no one knew how long they might live due to the 'shoot-'em-up' law and order of the time, men couldn't very well admit to fear, as to do so could mean losing the psychological advantage over an enemy that could mean the difference between life and death.

'Men like to be men.' This means they want to take care of their own

problems and not feel dependent on anyone to help them, no matter what. Ronald Reagan is the cultural archetype of this cowboy mentality and because of this, it is not so surprising that he was elected President of this country. In his movies and his thinking, he represents the rugged individualism that forms the backbone of our 'manly' thinking.

This cultural programming, passed down from one generation of 'brave-warrior' fathers to another, makes it very difficult for many men in our culture to reach out for help to a mental health professional. Often, unless overwhelmed by depression, anxiety, loss of self-control, or the threat of losing one's partner, men will simply not come in on their own for psychotherapy.

This is, however, slowly changing as the general stigma attached to seeking psychotherapy has lessened. To admit the need for professional help is to admit that one does not have all the answers and that one is unable to sufficiently help oneself. This is just not an easy thing for many adult men to do.

In the same way as many men are not able to reach for professional help without being threatened, they also are not willing to allow themselves to openly admit the experience of fear. Many who finally do come to see me are unable to express any fear they have regarding their situation.

So, a couple may be experiencing severe marital stress, where there have already been extramarital affairs, separations and chronic poor communication. And still the male, who has been threatened by his wife that if he does not come in for marital therapy, she will leave, is unable to express any fear regarding his wife's threat. In fact, sometimes, especially if his wife isn't in the room, he may cavalierly and smugly tell me the story of his marriage with a smirk on his face.

It is not permissible for these men to show me they are really afraid of their wife's threat. They need to continue to pretend they are *in control*, that no one is going to scare them with threats of divorce. Until they allow their own fear of losing the relationship to be experienced, usually little real change takes place in the relationship. When they accept their fear, they are many times ready to make the compromises necessary to allow the relationship to become unblocked.

Many men (and some women) learn how to block the awareness of fear as they grow up. Realizing that fear is unpleasant to experience, and believing their own father's admonition to 'not be afraid and fight back,' they begin to tighten certain muscles in the body, stop their breathing, and block the physical sensations of fear.

At the same time, they tell themselves they are not afraid, that they can stand up to and conquer *anything*. The consequence of this learning to block the awareness of fear is that one ends up becoming numb instead.

When others are emotionally reacting – for example, feeling excited about walking through a beautiful forest – Mr Fear-Blocker feels little or nothing. While he has successfully learned how to keep out fear, he has also incidentally (and usually unintentionally) learned to block out all kinds of other emotions, like empathy, excitement, joy and surprise. The same psychological dynamic that allows us to make ourselves blind to the awareness of certain negative emotions also works to block out some of those emotions we *do* want to experience.

Women, for the most part, are not as burdened by this 'cowboy mentality' as men. In over thirteen years of experience with over a thousand patients in psychotherapy, one generalization I can safely make is this: women are somewhat less defensive in forming a therapeutic bond, much more trusting of experiencing and expressing their emotions, and more ready to change their thinking than most of the men I have treated. The 'cowboy mentality' wins again . . .

Because women come in more in touch with their fear, are more ready to admit they are not able to take the next step by themselves, and therefore are more ready to learn new ways of thinking about themselves, the process of psychotherapy sometimes seems to flow easier. In contrast, the more a male needs to feel he knows everything and needs to be 'right,' the less productive a psychotherapy relationship with me tends to be. Because I am a rather strong male figure and present myself as sure of myself and my words, many of these men immediately feel the need to show me they won't be 'pushed around,' just because they have come in for help.

This, of course, is my own experience and does not necessarily mean other male psychotherapists would have the same experience. But anecdotal reports and clinical literature seem to agree that male therapists experience female patients as being less defensive, less competitive, and less interested in power games than male patients. To the contrary, women are more used to controlling through being subtly seductive and by playing weak and helpless, which they have learned many times will help them get their way.

What about outside of psychotherapy? How does fear motivate us toward or push us away from certain choices in our daily life? Much of the time when we tell ourselves that we are not interested in something, we may be passing over what could be a landmine of fear.

For example, an acquaintance of mine, Charles, tells me he really isn't interested in learning how to snow ski. When I ask him about his feelings about the snow and skiing, he says he used to love the snow where he grew up. But when he was young, he watched an older brother take a severe fall while skiing. Charles had become paralyzed with fear in watching his brother's fall but was unable at the time to express his fear.

Because of his brother's fall, Charles had decided then and there he would never learn to ski, to make sure this kind of accident couldn't happen to him. Yet even with this very reasonable 'excuse' for his fear, Charles would not outrightly admit to me he was fearful of the snow and everything connected to it.

Experiment: Fear
Think of something that brings up fear. Even if you don't actually feel fear now, as you think about it, you will at least know that it is something that can make you afraid. For example, we don't need to feel afraid, right now, when we mention death, to know that at least once in a while, when we think about death, see an accident, hear that someone has died, got sick, etc., we FEEL FEAR.

What is the nature of your fear? Is there a particular place in your body related to the sensation of fear? What is this sensation? What makes it unpleasant, if that is how it feels? How does your experience of fear relate to the present?

Are you actually afraid of what is happening at the time you experience fear? Or are you fearful of something that is not real now, but that you imagine will take place sometime later? Let me give a simple personal example to clarify this.

I recently had a tooth pulled out. It was the first one in twenty years, since I had had all my wisdom teeth pulled at once just before going away to begin college. I felt mildly anxious when I arrived at the dentist's office. It was hard for me to 'say good-bye' to my tooth, even though it was now causing me nothing but pain. I told myself I had good reasons to be anxious. Here they are . . .

I had only three hours warning that my tooth should be pulled today, this being the opinion of the periodontist I consulted. Therefore, I did not have the usual psychological time I would have planned to accommodate myself to losing a long-appreciated tooth, although I did know that it would have to be pulled in the near future. The dentist said, 'What are you waiting for?' I said, 'I was waiting for you, a specialist, to ask me what I was waiting for.' So we immediately scheduled the extraction for that afternoon with an oral surgeon.

I didn't like looking at all the people coming out of the office in some form of pain. I didn't want to just sit there and get more fearful watching others. Not being able to leave the waiting room and thus escape the pained looks of others made me more anxious. I rarely get anxious about anything except making sure I catch long-distance flights. Wasn't I the 'Meditation Maven'? Why not just go into a nice little trance state? Lower the old heart rate in preparation, maybe? Didn't I know all the psychological gimmicks?

No, I thought, stay here and face the music (or, more accurately, the dentist's extraction pliers). I'll use this opportunity to see how having teeth in a mouth, on a head that sits on a body, means physical suffering. 'Ah yes,' the voice inside chimed, 'the old Buddhist position of not identifying with the physical body. Good idea!'

All ages were in there suffering together – one 5-year-old clutching a teddy bear, anxious about three teeth being pulled out, and adults and older people in various states of suffering. Either suffering the apprehension of what pain they are about to experience, or, like me, with the immediate pain from the tooth in their mouth and wanting to find relief but not wanting the dread and anticipated pain of a tooth yanked out.

There is something, to be sure, quite primitive in the pulling out of one's tooth, no matter how sophisticated dentists' methods become in creating a less painful state of consciousness for the patient. I was curious about having my first experience with laughing gas, and was able to clearly see how it had earned its name. But still, you know very well that some primitive thing is happening inside your propped-open and numbed mouth.

I still had trouble accepting I was going to lose one of my beloved teeth before the age of 40 because of a gum problem. I wondered, 'How could I, with all my self-knowledge, be suffering from something that could have been caused at least partially by stress?' If this was true, what were all those thousands of hours of meditation good for? All that meditation, and my reward is a (possibly) stress-related gum problem now costing me a tooth? Could this be possible? I didn't want to entertain that it could.

I preferred the explanation that having braces when I was young created the pocket around the gum that was now going to cost me my tooth. After all, stress-related gum problems would be a systemic problem, meaning all of my mouth and teeth ought to be affected. But, only one tooth was affected. Even the two dentists agreed that it was hard to understand.

I found myself thinking of only the worse results: pain, swelling, sensitivity for years in the area where the tooth would be pulled, and further problems with my gums, the cause of which no one could tell me, even though I had dutifully asked them to keep the tooth for me when they pulled it out, just as the referring gum specialist had instructed. Even after looking at the rotting tooth, he wouldn't make any definitive statements.

But the reality was that the whole thing was actually not very painful – the tooth was pulled in seconds and the nitrous oxide and local anesthetic made for little actual painful sensation. The recovery was pain-free, with no swelling at all. Had I known ahead of time it would be experienced as RELIEF, I could have saved myself some unpleasant days by having the tooth pulled out some time ago!

'How do you spell relief?' Tooth extraction, that's how!

The moral of the story? *Even things that we have good reason to be fearful of many times are not fearful in themselves. What is scary is the story we tell ourselves about the thing or event.*

I would not have believed it possible to have my tooth pulled and not feel any sensitivity the next day, have no bleeding, no swelling and experience nothing but relief. And yet, that's what happened.

So, I had my reasons for feeling anxious and even fearful. But these feelings were not too terribly unpleasant because they are uncommon feelings for me. Rarely do I get too anxious about anything short of immediate physical jeopardy. And in my (discriminating) mind, this qualified as 'immediate physical jeopardy.'

On the other side of the coin, we have those people who are constantly warding off fear in one form or another. They are basically afraid of living and all the choices living presents. They are afraid of the weather, afraid of competing in any form against others, afraid to be intimate, afraid to show too much of themselves, afraid to lose the approval of anyone they may meet, etc.

Some of us get to a point of being overly fearful of what poisons may be in the food we eat, the water we drink, the air we breathe, and what may be inflicting various systems of our body. We notice all signs of getting older, and worry a lot about the natural consequences of ageing. We are not talking about a normal healthy concern for the integrity of the body – we are referring to a chronic, complaining, preoccupation with the physical body. Fear of the ongoing changes of the body may be accompanied by fear of any significant changes in one's life.

For some people, the business of life seems absolutely overwhelming. They give us a sense of being out of control and barely able to keep up with the melodramas which they create and which are created in the whirlwind around them. And yet, when I ask some of them about these dramas they create, they tell me they would think life 'dull' without some excitement.

They may not like the painful emotions which inevitably surface as they play out their soap operas but neither are they willing to give up on being the focus of attention around which the suffering of others is inevitably played out. They rightfully decide to be the 'star of their own show' but unfortunately only know how to play parts that create pain for themselves and others.

In therapy, one goal with these people is to help them learn more positive, healthy and satisfying scripts where they continue to be the 'star' but no longer unconsciously play out such destructive roles.

Experiment: Creating our own drama
Think for a moment about one area of your life in which you are aware of over-dramatizing to others. Maybe you make something sound worse than it really is so they will give sympathy. Or maybe you just believe something is so important that you can't stop talking about it to others.

Whatever it might be, just take a moment to let yourself admit fully that you do, indeed, complain more, exaggerate, inflate, or otherwise embellish certain stories to others about events in your life to gain a certain response. Maybe you just want the other to be impressed. So you inflate the story a little bit. The idea is to make it OK to admit the truth about how we write up the scripts for exactly how dramatic we want to make our lives seem to others.

One way to realize how we tend to dramatize our lives is to think about our mental rehearsing behavior. If something nice happens to us – say we spend the weekend at a particularly beautiful vacation setting – we can notice that as we are driving back home, we are already thinking about how to best share our experience with those around us. 'Should I focus on how beautiful it was, or how wonderful the experience was?' We begin to notice how the words we use to describe our experience to others actually helps shape our own memories of what happened. 'How dramatic should I make it this time?' is a question we face in relating our stories to others.

If we can catch these moments, when we are rehearsing how we want to present our experience to others, we can learn a lot about our tendency to embellish our experience to create a certain impression.

Every bit as important as how we relate our experiences to others is whether or not we are able to allow our own experiences to nourish us and be satisfying. Or whether we need others to tell us how wonderful our experience was once we share it with them. If we don't get just the right response from them, this somehow diminishes our actual experience. Although this doesn't really make much sense when we think about it, it seems to be a rather common occurrence. It's as if we need others to reaffirm that what we think is true is actually true, even if they are in no position to know!

It may be that we want others to think we have all kinds of fascinating and deep experiences – then they will see us as a deep and fascinating person. Or, if we are looking for sympathy, we might make all our experiences seem overly unfortunate, miserable and depressing.

The important point here is to emphasize that *we are always coloring our experiences one way or the other, then rehearsing how we want to present them to others*. And, this may not even be in our conscious awareness. But if we can be aware of this rehearsing, we can begin to see that it is very much up to us as to how melodramatic we wish to be.

In spite of the truth of the above, the fact that we embellish the stories of our lives is not necessarily so bad. Why? Because it is better to at least be caring enough about our own life that we wish to make it as exciting to ourselves and others as possible. Even if we tend to exaggerate at times and become melodramatic, this at least indicates a healthy enough ego. We want to be taken seriously. It is healthier than squandering the 'authorship' of our own lives, where we choose to live through others rather than create a meaningful and suspenseful life for ourselves. As usual, what we need is the balance of the discriminating mind – a pinch of drama without getting carried away.

This stance, even though able to cause some distortion in our perception, is not as bad as caring so little about our own lives that we try to live vicariously through others, such as movie and TV stars. It is indeed pathetic that some believe that the real excitement in life is reserved for the 'rich and famous' and that the only way they can get some of that excitement to 'rub off' on them is to become fascinated with them, rather than do whatever is possible to create excitement and interest in their own lives.

So, the person who might blow up the everyday experiences of his own life is at least a step ahead of the person who is too low in self-esteem and ego-strength to be able to go through this process. Instead, they remain satisfied to identify with others and indirectly get a little 'piece of the action.'

If we can become interested enough in our own life, we can lose some of the glittery star-struck fascination with which we view others and instead feel compassion for the suffering of those who are 'poor and obscure.' Actually, although their material life style may not compare, the minds of the 'poor and obscure' are many times just as interesting as the 'rich and famous.'

Carrying the heavy burden of an incredibly inflated ego that can never get enough of itself can be part of the baggage that goes with being either rich, famous, or especially talented. Of course, it doesn't have to be this way and sometimes isn't. But it is hard to find two groups of people more obsessed with their three favorite things in life – 'Me, Myself and I' – than those in show business and those who have accumulated great wealth.

We can't really blame anyone, however, for wanting to 'cash in' on the attention given those in our society who have great financial wealth. They are just enjoying the spoils of having played the game as it is supposed to be played in the Western world, according to its materialistic values: 'HE WITH THE MOST TOYS, MONEY, STUFF, WINS!' Can we really blame anyone for simply enjoying having 'won' the game they were taught to play? **Their motto is**:

> # He who thinks money can't buy HAPPINESS DOESN'T KNOW WHERE TO
> # SHOP!!

The discriminating mind knows the difference between greed and 'right livelihood,' in which we find something that we can do well and enjoy and make a living with, something that will not harm or exploit anyone else. Greed is, in the long run, a losing proposition. Only in the short run of some years, will those who are greedy and need more and more feel good for a while, if they are able to keep Just One More Thing coming.

There is so much to distract ourselves with to avoid feeling our pain! We become experts at learning how to distract ourselves from deep dissatisfaction, suffering and emptiness. But, in the longer run, greed is never satisfied. The greedy person can never get enough, no matter how many times he tells himself, 'If only I had Just One More . . . (car, airplane, office building, girlfriend, etc.), THEN I COULD REALLY BE HAPPY!' And yet, even without ever attaining real satisfaction from being greedy, the fascination of accumulation is one of the main pursuits in life for a great number of people.

Everyone wants to be comfortable, have a decent roof over their head and have enough to eat. But, of course, we are nowhere near satisfied with simply taking care of our basic physical needs. Our psychological needs then demand that we be respected by others, feel safe and secure, and feel companionship, love and a sense of belongingness.

Further, we want to be doing work that we find meaningful and rewarding. These are all psychological needs, meaning that we can survive physically without these things, but not very well. Mentally and emotionally, we are in pretty bad shape when these needs are not attended to.

And after we have attended to our emotional and psychological needs, for many, spiritual needs to connect to something beyond oneself then become part of the picture. For those 'malcontents' who have everything that money can buy, finding one's place in the universe becomes important if one is to have a deeper meaning in one's life. While we are on material goods, let's bring in one of the more insidious parasites that lives on the back of the desire to accumulate wealth and material goods.

ENVY: THE DISGUISED EMOTION

We can think of envy as 'the painful or resentful awareness of an advantage enjoyed by another joined with a desire to possess the same advantage.' In other words, we want what the other has and we can't stand seeing them have it when we don't! Why is envy an important feeling? Because it is being experienced much of the time without our even being fully aware of what we are feeling.

For example, many times when we are aware of not liking somebody or feeling annoyed by them, when we look more closely at what is going on, we see that our annoyance is because we see them having something – a quality or possession – that we would like for ourselves.

Maybe we see John's assertiveness and would like more of that quality ourselves. Rather than see that this is what is happening, which means granting John a quality that in comparison we feel lacking, this is too painful a recognition. So we prefer to put him down and maybe even tell ourselves he is too pushy, in this way, not even having to admit we want to be more assertive, let alone that John has something we don't. Envy is many times unrecognized as a motivating force behind many of our responses to those whom we find it easy to disparage.

To keep envy distinct from jealousy, we can think of jealousy as being 'apprehensive of the loss of another's exclusive devotion.' One who is jealous is 'disposed to suspect rivalry or unfaithfulness.' We feel jealous of John getting Mary's attention because we like Mary and want her attention. As long as John is getting what we want, we can't have anything but a competitive, hostile feeling for John. Even if he is our friend, as long as we want what he is getting, we are going to be jealous of him. OK, that's jealousy.

Envy is more for things and possessions that you have and that I want. One patient of mine put it like this: 'If you have a fancy new white Mercedes 560 SEC with beige leather interior, I might have a hard time feeling "sympathetic joy" for you. Instead, I may wonder why you have one of these beauties and I don't. I may think to myself, he only has one of these because he sells real estate to big shots all day. He cares about showing off. At least I sit around helping suffering people all day. If I did what he did, I could have one of those, too.' And that, folks, is the sound of envy!

One of the obvious ways envy shows up in daily psychotherapy work is when patients have difficulty dealing with their desires to have certain things they see in the life of their therapist. So, for example, if patients see artwork hanging in the waiting room, nice leather chairs and furniture that they know is expensive, many have ambivalent feelings. On the one hand, they use these things to tell themselves this means the therapist must be good because he is successful enough to afford nice furnishings.

On the other hand, they themselves desire what the therapist has but are unable to express this desire in the form of outright envy. Instead, they may make remarks that try to devalue the furniture. This is the old 'sour grapes' attitude. Sometimes, patients catch themselves with this sour grapes attitude sometime later and are able to admit their envy more directly. Other times, they continue to make remarks indirectly and unconsciously to let me know that they feel some resentment that their fee is going to my nice furnishings and comfortable lifestyle.

Another even more blatant form of envy in the psychotherapy relationship may be witnessed when the therapist takes a vacation. Many patients are naturally curious to know where I might be going when they know I will be taking time off (which I don't do often enough!). Their responses to my telling them, immediately let me know how they are feeling about my leaving (possibly abandoning) them to have a 'good time.' Some will make oblique references to the place I am going as not being all that great a place. Others will launch into a story of how it was when they went there.

Some, by their absolute inability to show the slightest interest in me, make it clear they don't want me going to a place they can't afford to go. And some genuinely seem able to 'allow' me the time off without resentment and hope for a pleasant trip. Of course their various responses upon my return are also telling as to their feelings about our separation.

In the 'real world' outside the therapy consulting room, we see how envy pops up all over the place in human interactions. It seems almost 'natural' for many to put someone else down for something they possess rather than admit their envy for what the other has. Why is this? What seems to be happening a lot of the time is this: *to admit that we feel envy makes us feel less than the other*.

We are, in other words, unable to let the other have more than us without taking it as somehow diminishing our ego-strength. So we are left with putting the other down and never then having to feel less than the other. We see we want what the other has; we tell ourselves we can admit we want what he has but we must also put him down and then we can handle our desiring what he possesses.

All of this rests on the basic assumption that what the other possesses makes the other a more valuable, worthy human being. And because we so often believe this assumption, we are unwilling to let the other have his higher value by having more possessions than us. We need to, as they say, 'carve him down to size' so we will not feel inadequate compared to him.

Experiment: Speech

Listen closely to your speech for two days. Pay attention to all statements made regarding other people who are not immediately being spoken to. In other words, notice all gossiping about others who are not present and part of your conversation. Consider anything said about anyone not being directly spoken to as 'gossip' and pay as close attention as possible to the content of your gossip.

Are you being complimentary to others, perhaps saying things you are not comfortable telling them directly? Is the content of your gossiping critical of others? Are you judging some characteristic or behavior of theirs? If so, is this a characteristic or behavior that you can identify as one which is yours, as well? Notice whether your gossip has anything to do with what others possess.

This 'possession' of theirs may be their situation in life – for example, they are happily married, or happily single and you would like to be in their Reeboks. Or maybe they have had a special opportunity to achieve something that you, too, wish were possible for you. Or maybe they just have that new fancy Jaguar that you are panting for.

It doesn't matter what the content may be. The important thing is to notice how much time is spent gossiping about people who are not in front of you and how much gossip-time is motivated by envy of the one who is being gossiped about.

Simple Examples of Envy in Everyday Speech

(1)   'Did you see the size of Jane's diamond? If that thing were any bigger and brighter she'd need sunglasses to keep herself from going blind! How can she wear something so obnoxiously large?'

(2)   'Look at Kristin shake those hips! Can you believe the gall of that girl to parade around like that, looking like such a floozy?'

(3)   'How much did your sweater (car, house, fur, computer, etc.) cost? Are you sure you got the best price for it? I think I could have gotten it for you for less – why didn't you call me first?'

(4)   'Look at the gold chains around that guy's neck! Can you believe this guy – looking so confident smiling at those girls? You know these guys just think they're the hottest stuff in the world!'

(5)   'Who do you think you are, sitting there on your throne – some big shot or something? Who are you to tell me anything about alcoholism? You don't even drink – how can you help me if you weren't ever a juicer?'

(6)   'Your office isn't so great. If you didn't rip people off by charging so much, you'd never have these fancy leather chairs to begin with!'

(7)   'What's so great about going to the Alps in Switzerland? I can have just as much a lot closer in the Canadian Rockies.'

(8)   'Look at Candi stick out those tits. I'll bet she stuffs her bra with Kleenex to look like that. Her tits are too big, anyway, don't you think? Anything bigger than a handful is too much, I always say.'

(9)   'He doesn't know how to manage all that money, I can tell you

that. If I had the chance to manage that kind of money – man, could I really do a lot with it. You think he's any happier than me? No way, man!'

(10)   'She doesn't look too pudgy in that designer dress does she?'

A final but very common example of envy is found in the psychodynamics of the family system. In many families, especially those in which siblings have grown up competing with each other in various ways (as most do in one form or another), envy shows its face through an interesting phenomena I have had reported to me by many patients over the years.

It seems that in order to maintain a stable family system and psychological equilibrium, whenever one family member accomplishes something special, there is only so much support he or she can receive from other family members. It is as if other family members can't tolerate any one member feeling too good about himself for too long.

Initially, they can identify with the person who has won some award or been specially recognized for some project. During this phase, they can celebrate the accomplishment of the family member and feel good that someone close to them has been recognized. This helps them feel better about themselves as well. 'She has the same name as me – we are 'blood' – therefore, I am sort of special, too.'

But if this recognition should last too long or be a source of good feeling in the one who has achieved for too long, then the family seems to need to bring back the family system balance by either directly 'bringing the achiever down' through comments suggesting that one is really not so wonderful since, after all, 'we knew you before you were such a big shot.' This happens in more gross or subtle forms depending on the dynamics of the family. God forbid the one who has stood out should stand out for too long!

But I think the purpose of this behavior is to express indirectly the envy we feel when someone related to us accomplishes something we haven't. Even in relatively healthy families, family members can only stand a certain amount of good feeling by any one member before seemingly needing to 'bring the person to his senses' by reminding him that he used to be such a klutz and couldn't dance the Watoosie twenty years ago. Of course, sometimes, it is much more cruel and vindictive than this. Because of the built-in dynamic of competition between siblings for parents' attention, especially in families with children close in age, the accomplishment of one becomes the pressure to 'measure up' for the others.

No matter how great one may be feeling about oneself, there is 'no place like home' to have oneself instantly reduced to feeling like a nothing. Besides not letting anyone feel too good for too long, another dynamic that take place is the need for grown children to be infantilized by parents. This means that parents seem to need to act like parents, and this means making grown children feel like infants.

I imagine Henry Kissinger, over a decade ago in the mid-1970s, returning home from a stressful shuttle diplomacy effort halfway around the world with some of the most politically powerful men in the world, involving issues of the most sensitive national interest. He walks into his home, very tired and suffering from jet lag, to find his mother has decided to make an unscheduled visit. She is in his bedroom, folding his underwear and putting things where *she* thinks they ought to go. She greets him by looking up and says, 'Oh, meeting with the Poo-bah sultans again in the mid-East, are you? Well, tell me, Mr Big Shot, you couldn't find time to pick up the phone in that fancy-schmancy jet of yours and call your mother? Look at this – [shows him underwear] trying to solve the world's problems but you can't match your socks and you're still wearing underwear with holes in them!'

DISCRIMINATING PERSONALITY: SUMMARY

The discriminating mind is the mind that is able to identify with and indulge in various personality parts, balancing strength with vulnerability, power with gentleness and sharp intellect with emotional sensitivity. It knows when to cry and when to hold back from emotional indulgence.

It can tell the difference between sloppy sentimentality and real emotional longing. It understands the difference between honesty and self-deception through rationalization and distortion. It understands the difference between feeling fear out of manufactured catastrophic expectations and feeling fear as a healthy sign of actual threat. It know when it is in danger and when it is simply fearful of trying something new because it challenges one's ego and conjures up pictures of failure.

We must be willing to accept that we are very much limited by what we don't know about ourselves and be willing to learn by the feedback from others. And yet we must also be able to dismiss feedback when it comes from a place of envy, vindictiveness, cruelty, or manipulation. It isn't, of course, always so easy to tell when to listen and when to realize the other's words have little to offer us. As we practice sharpening the discriminating mind, we learn to better trust ourselves and our actions. We spend less time feeling guilty or feeling sorry for ourselves and more time enjoying being alive.

In this sense, the discriminating mind is more than our rational mind being developed to high degree and more than a developmental step in our maturation. It is more than the integration of intellect with emotion and intuition. It is a *state of consciousness* that stays with us at all times and can be used to help no matter what situation confronts us and no matter how rough our lives may seem to be. 'When should I trust emotion?' 'When should I trust intuition?' The discriminating mind knows which path to take.

With this mind we are not so liable to surprise ourselves with behavior over which we have no sense of control. While the world remains a mystery and the actions of others are beyond our control, we steadfastly maintain a high degree of conscious control over our own actions and our attitude toward them.

= 6 =

THAT WAS THEN
AND THIS IS NOW

We said earlier in Chapter 2 that if things are truly changing from moment to moment, we need to learn to let go of the past, without getting overly attached to any pleasant or unpleasant states of consciousness that make up the memories of the past. We need to let go of the distant past as it pertains to blocking us from a more vibrant present. And we need to let go of the immediate past – the last few months, few days, and even few hours – to the degree these memory traces, too, keep us from being more present.

We said that while we like to assume it is *obvious* that things are changing, the reality is that we live much of the time as if things are *not* really changing at all, especially our cherished attitudes and beliefs. We are not talking about 'forgetting' our pleasant memories. We are talking about letting go of those habitual, obsessive tape-loops which keep us from making the present the place where we 'hang our hat,' where we focus our attention.

Of course, it is one thing for the physical world to be continually changing and for us to be aware of the passing of time but it is quite another for the contents of our minds to be changing. And yet this is exactly what is occurring at all times: the contents of our minds are changing!

Sure, we continue to hold the same old beliefs, worship the same values, carry the same fixed responses and same perspectives in the form of attitudes. But the reality is that the moment-to-moment activity of the mind is characterized by the continual passing of thought. It is only when these passing thoughts are crystalized into frozen attitudes (leading to rigid behavior) that we end up looking at someone and thinking, 'He will never change – he is too stuck in his ways.'

It may be that the passing of time and the changing nature of the contents of our minds have something in common. When we have a strong sense of ourselves in time we also tend to have a stable sense of our own minds. When we experiment with what we called 'mental time zones,' we begin to notice how our orientation in time has something to do with our sense of security in the world. If the present means nothing to us but immediate choices and is fraught with the anxiety of which way to choose, we are not going to be very able to 'settle' into the present and enjoy it.

We said that the relation of time to thought is that thought occurs *in* time and that our experience of time is usually in relation to our own thoughts. When we are present-centered and in touch with our immediate senses, we don't experience time passing as we do when 'lost' in thought. Because we either project forward or back into the past, the stories we get lost in all 're-mind' us of the passing of time.

We further said that if we are able to stay with the present as the balance-point of our lives, we will have the full weight of our attention to use to take care of ourselves in the world. Otherwise, we get caught in the 'webs of time' created by losing ourselves in the past or future. In this chapter, we will look at how the past and future affect our ability to stay in the present.

'OLD' ANGER AND RESENTMENT

One of the primary ways we keep ourselves from enjoying the vitality of the present is by getting lost in past resentments. We can think of resentments as past hurts in which we feel an 'indignant displeasure' at some perceived wrong, insult, or injury. The old saying of 'adding insult to injury' fits here. When we 'add insult to injury' and then don't say, 'Ouch! You hurt me!' we end up with resentment.

This resentment is usually accompanied by anger which is experienced inside but not expressed. Because we hold on to our anger (and still feel angry inside when we think about the incident) but are unwilling to express it directly, this anger becomes 'old' anger that continues to dig at us and affect our relations with others. We may become tense, anxious, irritable and chronically feeling as if we have the proverbial 'chip on the shoulder.'

We may complain a lot about all kinds of things and feel little or no real excitement in our lives. We also tend to see the world in a negative, overly critical way and don't feel much sense of hope. Sometimes this stance leads to clinical depression, which is more than just the normal up and down mood swings we all go through from time to time. But depression is only one possible outcome of holding on to our anger and resentment.

Another outcome is a pent-up frustration leading to explosion. We hold on as long as possible and then at some point, a small straw breaks the camel's back and we explode. Perhaps we may be the silent type who piles up one resentment upon another all the while, saying nothing until we just can't handle the burden any longer. And then it happens: the 'big bang.'

A variation of this type is the person who always looks like he is going to explode but instead has temper 'releases' that prevent the big explosion. As long as he is given periodic opportunities to 'let off steam,' he is able many times to stop short of real explosion.

Unfortunately, the price he pays is to be continually on edge, over-responding to perceived slights and unable to be comfortable with other people. How can you be comfortable if you have to continually be watching to make sure the other person is not getting some edge? The ego must be watching full time to make sure the other doesn't come out one-up.

But the explosion may actually be an implosion, if we have learned that it is not permissible to express any negative feelings out toward the world. Instead, we implode, turning back against ourselves what deserves to go out toward the world. This is the defense mechanism of retroflection, which we discussed in Chapter 3.

Experiment: Resentment and old anger
Take a couple of deep breaths, being sure to exhale fully. Let yourself relax in your chair, feeling the full weight of your body in the chair. After you read the following instructions, *put down this book and close your eyes* to make following them easier.

Let your mind wander to a past, unfinished incident in which you ended up feeling some resentment. In your mind's eye, see the details of the incident as clearly as possible. If you can, let yourself feel your resentment right now, as you recall this incident.

Take a moment to get in touch with what you would like to have said but didn't. Now imagine the person or persons your resentment is aimed toward were present with you. Do your best to imagine them sitting next to you, receptive to your words. *What do you want to say to them?*

Go ahead and tell them directly and clearly that they in some way injured you. And be sure to include the following statement: '**I resent you and have not been willing to tell you until now.**' Tell them anything else that will help you feel finished with your resentment related to this incident. Notice how you feel after expressing yourself in this way. Take a moment to stay with this feeling. Make sure that you have said everything that you believe necessary to finish your 'business' of expressing resentment.

If you believe you have, now say 'good-bye' to this person you have been talking to and tell them you are now ready to let go of your attachment to resenting them. If you are unable to feel this is true when you say it, this will let you know that you haven't yet expressed everything necessary to let go.

When you return from the exercise, pause for a minute or two **before going on to the next exercise**. Notice and stay with any thoughts or feelings that may come up in reflecting on your experience. **NOW, put down this book and close your eyes. Then begin the exercise.**

Think of two more incidents in which you are aware of lingering resentment toward someone. See if you can think of two separate incidents with two separate people. If you were to confront these people directly and express your resentment toward them, just think of what you might say. After pushing the 'save' button for your memory to record your responses, file these responses away in your computer-brain for future reference under the heading 'Rehearsal of Unexpressed Resentments.'

Even if we are unwilling (or unable) to express directly to those involved our resentment to them, we may still at least allow ourselves to be in touch with whatever persons and incidents continue to come up and remind us that we are feeling resentment. If we are aware of this resentment, we will be less likely to relate to this person as if we have no unfinished business. So, even if we choose not to share our resentment we can notice how it affects our inter-action.

ANGER: OLD AND NEW

Anger is another tough one for most of us. Perhaps you know how good it can feel to allow yourself to express anger firmly and directly, without having to lose control. But so many of us have not had this experience, as we have been taught from the earliest years about holding back the awareness, and certainly the expression, of anger. For most of us, learning how to express anger directly without having to fear being abandoned by the person we are expressing our anger toward is a positive, healthy emotional step.

For a smaller number of us, our imbalance is in the other direction: we need to learn to hold back and control ourselves, as we are all too easily able to burst out with our anger with little provocation. For these people, learning to contain is the answer. But for most of us, we have learned to contain and restrict all too well and learning to express is the desired direction for growth.

We need to call on the *discriminating mind* to help us see that the ability to express anger directly and with a sense of self-restraint is *not* the same as walking around as a chronically angry person.

This chronically angry character, who has the proverbial 'chip on the shoulder,' is *not* the result of expressing anger all of the time but the consequence of someone who is attached at a deep level to the battering he or she has taken from the world. People like this are unable to see the world without perceiving continual threat to themselves. This world is never a safe place for them and their 'old' anger is one tool to help them survive. Without it, they imagine they will simply not make it.

These people are emotionally troubled and not the kind of people we are talking about who are overly inhibited, fearful of expressing any strong negative emotion, and many times prone to develop physical problems caused by emotional stress from all that gets held in. They suck in their gut instead of getting angry and do this repeatedly over years until they develop an ulcer. Or they get high blood pressure from being so tolerant and understanding of all those in their life.

Dealing with anger creates so many different avoidance responses

107

in people because most of us have grown up with the belief that anger and civilized relations between people just don't go together. We learn that people will avoid us, be fearful of us, and generally not want to deal with someone who 'hurts' others by expressing emotions so directly and openly rather than in more socially acceptable passive–aggressive ways.

We, unfortunately, have learned that letting people know something is 'wrong' and that we are angry at them is best done by passively withdrawing from them. So we don't return a phone call, a letter, or answer an invitation. And this passive response is our way of showing our anger without really ever having to say anything. And so these people live by the following motto:

> # BEING PASSIVE–
> # AGGRESSIVE IS
> # NEVER HAVING TO
> # SAY YOU'RE ANGRY!

Pamela: An Example of 'Old' Anger

Pamela came to see me when she was 25. She had been referred through a professional referral network with which I am associated. She presented herself as a woman who had nothing but 'bad things' happen in her life and claimed that the pain of her past made her feel like nothing any longer really mattered. She had little interest in her work as a legal secretary (but apparently did a reasonably good job) and unabashedly claimed that if she could find a well-off lawyer to marry, she would no longer continue working.

Pamela was blonde, attractive and able to be assertive when required. She was able to tell me when she didn't agree with an interpretation I might make, which showed me a certain degree of ability to confront. But she felt motivated by almost nothing and could not muster up the interest to form any meaningful relationships outside those demanded by work.

Although frequently asked out by men, she denied most requests, despite claiming that finding a suitable mate was something that mattered to her. The belief that it 'mattered' did not seem to do much in the way of motivating her. She could not understand why. But she knew she felt depressed a lot of the time and that there was no joy or playfulness in her life. She claimed that the only love she got in this world came from her three-year-old dog. Males she would not trust – but her dog was a female, so it was OK. So she said.

When I asked about her relationship with her parents, her eyes bugged out, her body tightened, and she began raising her voice. She told me her father was a 'no good greasy sleaze-ball' who had left her mother when Pamela was 15 (ten years ago). Ever since then she could not stand to spent time with her father, and did her best to avoid visits with him. Her father had gotten sexually involved with a younger woman who, coincidentally, had been a previous dance teacher of Pamela's.

She strongly supported her mother's 'throwing him out on his ear,' and later supported her mother's initiating divorce. And yet, because she was terrified of her father due to beatings she got while growing up, she never was willing to risk telling him how she felt about his involvement with her dance teacher.

How did she feel, you ask? She hated the son-of-a-bitch! For so long she wanted to explode in rage and tell her father how she really felt. And for so long, she was forced to sit on her anger and find more safe passive–aggressive ways to get back at her father. She would forget appointments she made with her father and be late anytime she couldn't get out of seeing him.

She would do her best to make snide remarks and subtly put him down when they were with his new girlfriend, the dance teacher. The dance teacher (to hear it from Pamela), seemed unable to understand how Pamela might object to her being an 'accessory' to the crime of abandoning her mother.

Pamela's father had trouble understanding how she could be so overwhelmingly against him and supportive of her mother. After all (from his point of view), didn't Pamela's mother 'drive him away' by not sleeping in the same bed as him for the last six years? Pamela did not care about her father's side. From her value system, there was nothing in the world worthy of her father having an affair and wanting to leave her after her devotion to him for a good twenty-two years.

Working With Pamela's Anger

As we began to work with her suppression of anger, Pamela had a chance to finally and in a safe manner express the full force of the rage toward her father. First, by having her speak to me as if I were her father, telling me about all of the times she had wanted to kill me for doing this to her mother. Spewing out more and more venom at me (as her father), pointing fingers at me and cursing me with every name she had ever heard to try and make me feel pain, the same pain she and her mother felt for so long.

Next, I had Pamela beat a couch with a tennis racket while she made short, explosive exclamations aimed toward her father. Things like, 'I hate you!' as she hit down with the racket. Also, 'How dare you!' and 'I don't respect you!'

In allowing Pamela a chance to take as long as she needed to finally 'dump' her load of old anger, I was reinforcing her right to feel anger and to express it. By coaching her in technique and feeding her exclamations to use, I was helping her express herself as deeply as she could allow herself.

Although Pamela chose not to go and express herself all over again to her father (as some patients do), our work with her anger helped her lose her deadness to the world and woke her up all over again to her strong emotions and her aliveness. She became more accepting of her anger and other stronger emotions and began to find things looking meaningful to her again.

With further work in the area of the mistrust she had learned for men, she was slowly able to give up some of her hostility for the male species and began to give men another chance. She lost a great deal of the fear she had felt of her father, and while not wanting to go and actually confront him, did begin to let herself make tentative contact and try to build some bridges toward getting closer. This process took us three years together, so I don't want to pretend that all of this happened in a short time.

DEFENSES DEFENDING THEMSELVES

When we are talking about allowing ourselves to experience and express old anger, it is never a simple or short-term process. And don't let anyone tell you it is! If they try to say you can do it in a weekend workshop, or in three sessions with hypnosis, or by using some other technique – just smile politely as you turn in the opposite direction and RUN – DON'T WALK – as fast as you're able. Again, the key thing to remember is this: although your thoughts are constantly changing, your basic personality is not going anywhere so quickly. It has taken you a lifetime to equip yourself with your present defenses.

These defenses are not going away just because you might like them to. In order for us to let go of any defense we have invested much time in, we need to feel safe enough to give it up. And we're not going to feel safe enough to give it up unless we realize we don't need it anymore, or we have something better to put in its place. Because of this, we need to be especially careful of any program, workshop, class, guru, or teacher that promises instant change.

Although we can be 'turned on' and have profound emotional and even spiritual experiences designed by a knowledgeable teacher, these turn-ons don't mean we have altered our basic personality structure. After we 'come down' from the intense 'peak' experience (as we always do), we pretty much feel trapped by the same ways of thinking and same ways of behaving.

The point is: we need to remember that although we may wish for instant personality transformation, our wishes should *stay* in the realm of wishes. When we realize that we don't really change this way, we can give up this wish and not put so much pressure on ourselves to make some amazing transformation overnight.

Although we can't expect to change the deeper parts of ourself so quickly, what can we change, then, by giving up the resentments that come up on a regular basis? How long does it make sense to hold on to the 'bad feelings' that come up as we relate to people in our everyday interpersonal world?

We can think of these 'bad feelings' as making for 'new' anger that usually stays in the form of 'new' resentment because, again, we determine it is not safe to let others know when they are hurting us in some way. After all, who wants the other to think we're weak? Who

111

wants to have them think we can't take it? We think, 'If Mike Tyson could take a right to the chin without flinching, then so can I!'

Experiment: 'New' resentments

Think for a minute about the last week of your life. Have there been any incidents with people where you noticed yourself feeling hurt by something they said, either directly and consciously or indirectly and unconsciously – something that hurt you in some way? Maybe you just didn't respond when you heard it, not wanting to make anything of it. But you noticed the little sting when it was said and you didn't forget it.

Identify anything that you think wasn't said to someone that has something to do with your feeling hurt by their words or actions. Maybe they just didn't think of you when asking others their preference and you felt slighted. Feeling slighted is a good way to know that there is a breeding ground hot for 'new' resentment if it is allowed to gestate for long.

So, once again, let yourself now imagine what you would like to say about these words or actions by others that have hurt you. Do you want to hear 'I'm sorry'? Do you want other people to know that you are sensitive to their words? Do you feel exposed in imagining the others knowing your 'weakness' in being hurt by their words?

Notice any obsessive thoughts that have been coming up in the last few days. What are they about? Who didn't you say what to? What are you holding on to? An image that was dented? A belief that was attacked? A mistake that you made? Maybe an embarrassment or humiliation in front of others?

If your obsessive thoughts are helping you in any way in the present, see what you're holding on to and see if you'd be willing to let go of whatever it is that warrants so much thought-time.

Begin to notice how playing back the last few days, few hours, or even few minutes keeps you from feeling alive and vibrant in the immediate present. See if the thoughts that keep coming up are about something immediately threatening to you in some way (like not having enough money to pay a bill) or whether many of these thoughts relate to what you *imagine might* happen. Begin to notice how often you find yourself on 'instant replay.'

What do you think you are wanting for yourself in playing back a conversation or incident again and again? If you really could do it over again, do you think it would make much difference? If so, why? What do you think doing it 'just right' would mean to the other person? In other words, how do you think they may see you differently if you had come off the way you wanted to?

OK, I realize the last four paragraphs are filled to the brim with questions. **See which ones you quickly jumped over without even considering.** Why did you want to jump over these questions? Without judging yourself, get in touch with whatever fear might be attached to your avoidance. Try to remember that each exercise presented in this book can have some effect on your thinking if you will take it seriously. To 'take it seriously' means to experiment in good faith without strong preconceived notions about what is supposed to happen.

WHY DO WE AVOID THE PRESENT?

It doesn't take a lot of insight to see how adamantly we wish to avoid the present. Yes, we are told to 'live for today' by credit card companies who want to see us get in over our heads, and 'charge it to the max.' And yes, we are told by enthusiastic supporters to 'GO FOR IT!' and to take risks in our lives and thereby make them potentially more meaningful.

But when it really comes down to it, we are much of the time terrified of the immediate present. We become experts at learning how to take ourselves out of the present by perfecting all sorts of mental gymnastics into the past and future. We love to 'space out' to avoid the anxiety that we experience when we come into the present.

We can see it continually as we watch ourselves and others around us. There is something anxiety-provoking about the present, especially when relating to another. Even when we begin to be able to settle into the present by ourselves and really enjoy what happens from moment to moment with hardly a trace of anxiety, being with someone else and allowing ourselves to stay focused in the present is something that is an art and not something most of us learn very easily.

We light a cigarette to handle the anxiety, or begin tapping our feet, playing with our hands, scratching, swaying, jerking, coughing, averting our gaze, and so many other little mannerisms to deal with the fright of confronting another person in the here and now.

Why do we experience all this anxiety? You may have noticed it comes through in more subtle forms with those we know and with whom we feel some degree of familiarity. Simply because **we are more sensitive when we come into the present** to the multitude of choices we have at any given moment for what we might think, say, or do. Faced with so many choices (but usually not aware this is even facing us), it is not so easy for us to gracefully make decisions, big and small, in a flowing, consistent and sensible manner.

Spending time in the present is usually 'awkward' for most of us and we simply want to avoid this awkward feeling. It is awkward because we can't handle the pauses, the poignancy, or the possibilities. We pick up our own fragile nature being reflected in the 'all-too-humanness of the other. And if we can escape the present, we can escape our discomfort at seeing and feeling these things about ourselves and others. To 'keep things light,' as they say, is to keep things at a level at which we don't have to open to these anxious feelings.

What else about the present makes us want to avoid it? When we come into the present we are reminded of *possibility*. We don't like to have to come back, over and over again, to remembering that, once in the present, we can choose (and therefore are responsible) for our own actions for the next moments, minutes and hours of our life.

'What do we want to do with ourselves now?' Always we are forced to return to this provocative question. And, by leaving the present and going to Fantasyland (wishful thinking about how 'fair' things ought to be), Adventureland (the past), or Tomorrowland (the future), we can escape this predicament, even if for only a while. Sounds too good for many to pass up! When the outside world stops giving us enough stimulation, we can always 'space out' to our favorite mental wonderland.

Avoiding the present is one culturally conditioned way of avoiding the poignancy and the immediacy of our lives. We think that if we can lose the 'here-and-now' quality of our aliveness, in other words, deaden ourselves, we won't have to feel the world impinging so heavily.

How else can I say this? We want to avoid the sense of life demanding a response from us, forcing us to respond to being alive in some way. We know the story – a need coming up and clamoring for attention until it is satisfied, followed by another and yet another.

Continually, it seems, we are repositioning our bodies to make ourselves more comfortable, to rid ourselves of some kind of physical discomfort. Or we are dealing with the 'monkey-mind', with its never-ending flow of thoughts. Or we are in emotional pain, feeling sorry for ourselves or for others. Not so surprising, then, that we are looking for a 'way out' and various forms of drugs serve this purpose, along with simply leaving the present.

We want to escape our sense of the repetitive nature of life, in which we are never getting too far away from something coming up to pose a threat or demand a response. We want to escape the pain and suffering that is always just below the surface. And when we come into the present, we feel in each other that suffering.

All we have to do is look into the eyes of the other. We can see his suffering, which gets us back in touch with our own. If we can avoid the present, we can then more easily avoid coming back to the suffering inherent in basic nature of human life.

When we leave the present we, in effect, say to ourselves, 'OK, that's enough – I've had it – time to go to Tomorrowland for a while.' We don't always do this so consciously or intentionally, of course, but this is really what we're doing. I don't think anyone would disagree with this rather obvious assumption, would they? All we have to do to verify that this is true is to pay attention to our own mental fluctuations. Anyone can then see how we avoid staying too long right here in the present.

LIVING *IN* THE PRESENT – NOT *FOR* THE PRESENT

We need to understand that we are *not* talking about living *for* the present, as in 'Eat, drink and be merry, for tomorrow ye may die.' To live *for* the present means that we can't see past today, this hour, this minute. We then don't value our mind's fine ability to plan and project into the future, fantasize various possibilities for the future, or anticipate events in the future with excitement and hope. Planning, anticipating, hoping, imagining are all part of our sense of the continuity of our sense of relative self over time.

So, we are *never* saying 'live for the present.' After all, what kinds of people are living for the present? The answer is: people who are in pretty bad shape; like heroin addicts who can only think about scrounging up enough money to buy their next fix, and so self-destructive they don't care about clean needles or AIDS-infected blood; and people so poor they can only deal with their needs from moment to moment, with little or no security of having a tomorrow; and criminals, who can't think past their immediate impulsive need to steal something, escape from someone, or just stay one step ahead of the law.

Desperate people live *for* the present. More highly conscious people live *in* the present. The difference between *for* and *in* is all the difference in the world – because each is living in a very different psychological world. One can see no future because he can barely survive in the present. All his energy goes toward satisfying basic security-level needs.

The other is secure in knowing that basic security-level needs for food, shelter and a human environment in which to live are surpassed and higher level psychological needs such as respect, love, affection, recognition, work that is personally satisfying, and a sense of meaning in one's life also, have been pretty well satisfied.

To be able to come into the present and make it the center of one's life can only occur after we are sufficiently able to jump, at least for a while, outside of the whirlwind of continual stimulation offered by the world. Otherwise, our minds will never be still enough to tolerate staying in the present. If our minds are too active, we just can't handle staying in the present, it just creates too much anxiety and confusion.

The desperate person, who is forced by circumstances (sometimes of his own making) to recklessly and disgracefully experience the anxiety of living *for* the present, should never be confused with the 'normal' sense of uneasiness that is experienced by many trying to live *in* the present. It is not the desperation of having *no* future that burdens these people but the realization of having *too many possible futures* that weighs them down. They can't tolerate having to make so many choices. How did we make this distinction? By calling on the discriminating mind to help, as usual.

One short life but so many important choices! So much room for regret of decisions made. 'Oh, I wish I could do it over again!', say so many people in psychotherapy. But most of them, whether they know it or not, would not use whatever knowledge they have since learned to make the earlier decisions any differently. In other words, even when we do have information after the fact to help us the next time, when the 'next time' comes, we many times make the same old decision, even when we know the negative consequences.

To understand why this is true we must be willing to accept that so many of our decisions are being made at least partly unconsciously. Because of this, when an unconscious motive is operating, we will make the same decision again and again, no matter what the consequences. Let's give a fairly simple example.

Suppose I tell myself that I want to notice as soon as possible each and every time I mentally leave the present. I may do this experiment just as a mental exercise to sharpen my attention. I am aiming to be aware of even the slightest diversion or mental fluctuation. I am not interested in judging myself negatively, just to notice as soon as possible and then bring my mind back to the present. So that's the task, simple to formulate, not so simple to do.

What happens when I try it persistently? Sometimes I may discover I am pretty sharp and able to stay for very long periods in the present without going into the past or future nor blanking out for short periods.

But other times, because unconsciously something else may be more important for me to attend to, I will be unable to stay present-centered for very long. I may be thinking about an ongoing project that I am involved in, like the writing of this book, or something that happened with a patient in psychotherapy. I will be unable to stay too long in the present because the world seems to call me in some form to mentally attend to it. Or something may be mildly uncomfortable in the present, so I may 'space out' to a mental place where things are more manageable and where fantasy is in control.

The world of my body may demand that I come out of my head, or the world of 'objects,' including other people, may call for a response. Concepts have no place in the present because concepts are mental constructions and anything that is mentally constructed pulls us into our heads and out of touch with the sensations of the immediate present. There is nothing 'wrong' with this, but we need to realize that the world of mental conceptions is exactly that: a mental world that is not the immediate world of our senses. So, our task is to learn to balance the rational intellect with the power of immediate sensations in the present. We do not need to sacrifice one to partake of the other.

117

SETTLING INTO THE PRESENT

We said that one reason why we avoid the present is that it is anxiety-provoking. What is interesting about this is that when we can really learn to settle into the present, as if we were settling down into our favorite lounge chair, all anxiety vanishes and we are able to feel a strength and peacefulness that eludes us when we jump into the past or future. This is the power of a special focusing method, like meditation.

Initially, we may have all kinds of problems dealing with the physical pain of sitting absolutely still and the mental anguish of having to watch the 'garbage' contents of our mind spill out for our observation. When we are able to get past the discomforts, the quietness and sense of mental–physical harmony that we can experience is well worth the initial discomfort we may experience.

Meditation helps us learn to get comfortable in the present, without the need of mental gymnastics to help us escape. Any contemplative discipline, for example, the movement meditation of T'ai Chi Chuan, can help us focus attention in the present. We will devote a chapter to meditation and inner awakening later in this book.

If we don't learn to get comfortable in the present, much of our life can seem to be various acts of avoidance of the anxiety of the fleeting present moment. We don't want to see it because then we will be reminded time is passing and we are not going to live forever. Who wants to face this on a daily basis, let alone be reminded from hour to hour, or minute to minute? Who wants to have to deal with this kind of realization?

Settling into the present is like being able to kick your shoes off when you come home and just relax. Beyond the anxiety that initially coats the present we have a soft, inner marshmallow center that is warm and chewy. The present, as we said before, is the power point for all our action. It is the crucial 'launching pad' for bringing all our thinking, planning and creative ideas into light of day.

Can we make them real, in some tangible way? Or will they get lost, like so many other schemes and hopes, in the darkness of the mental labyrinth, never seeing the light of their hatching into the present?

We notice the amount of time we lose in consciously being alive when we are mentally unable to stay for long in the present. This is so because if we leave and go into the past and then return without knowing where we went, it is the same as having 'blanked out' on our own attention. Chunks of our life are spent totally 'gone' and out of touch with the contents of our own minds.

If we are going to take the trip to Adventureland (the past) or Tomorrowland (the future), let us at least be able to do two things:

(1) Let us be able to recognize where we have been and what previous mental association led us there; and
(2) let us be able to communicate to others where we have gone should they see that blank look on our face and inquire as to which world we are mentally residing in.

We need to have 'mental zip codes' so we can remember the terrain of our thoughts. So, we notice, 'Ah, yes, going back to the 1959 Dodger game when I was 10 where my father caught the Norm Larker foul ball – the night the world was perfect and I was in seventh heaven.'

We put a mental zip code on this so we will be able to easily go back there again when we want whatever nourishment that memory has to offer. But we realize that no matter how nourishing that (or any other) memory may be, no memory will offer us the freshness, vitality and possibility that we find right here in the present.

=== 7 ===

THE PLAGUE OF PERFECTIONISM

The belief and deeply held conviction that anything less than perfection in our performance is unacceptable can create great torment, self-hate, and lead to the lifelong affliction of perfectionism. It doesn't matter whether the 'performance' is in our job, relationship to a significant other, avocation, sport, physical attractiveness to others, or overall self-evaluation as a person – the result is the same: anything short of perfect is seen as 'failure.'

In order to be a perfectionist, one requirement is that we must see two **and only two** possible outcomes in our performance of any task: complete success or complete failure. There are no places in between. By definition, anything short of 'the best,' whatever we imagine 'the best' to be, is seen as failure and a corresponding judgement of failure as a person is also made.

This means that every time we tell ourselves we have failed, we also tell ourselves we are worthless *because* we have failed. Nobody wants to feel like a failure and yet, so much of the time, it is our faulty thinking that puts us in the prime position for exactly this judgement to take place.

Quite often in psychotherapy practice, I encounter people who do not label or think of themselves as perfectionists. And yet, when I question them closely regarding their attitudes on winning and losing, their willingness to experiment with new activities and be a 'beginner,' and other questions relating to their expectations, they turn out to be perfectionists in sheep's clothing.

The truth is that they don't want to think of themselves as

expecting too much because they are unaware of the grandiosity of their hopes for achievement, recognition and excellence.

It is not that they shouldn't 'aim high' and always want to perform at the highest level of which they are capable. Pushing for excellence is not the same as being a perfectionist. This kind of pushing of oneself can many times be partial motivation for greater effort and discipline. No, the problem is that their hopes and expectations are too often completely out of reach and they are unable to see this. To allow themselves to see this would be to have to admit they are not, in fantasy, every bit as good as they *wish* they were.

Before these people will give up their perfectionistic thinking, they first need to realize that they have totally unrealistic expectations as to what they are capable of achieving.

Not to be willing or able to admit to our own limits is to set ourselves up for perpetual disappointment.

It is extremely helpful (although not absolutely necessary) to have what we call an 'obsessive–compulsive personality' to be a good perfectionist, or at least to have 'tendencies' in this direction. Because the perfectionistic person likes things perfect and is willing to devote a lot of time to organizing his personal world, this person may have many of the same traits and ways of thinking as the obsessive–compulsive person.

Because of this, the compulsive person is a good prospect to develop perfectionism as one of his styles of coping with the world. This is the person who needs to have his personal psychological world rigidly defined so as to feel some sense of control in his life. We are talking about a matter of degree here. Most people want to control their immediate environment to some extent. It is the person who is preoccupied with keeping his world in order whom we are saying is most likely to develop the obsessive–compulsive personality to the point where it causes real problems in day-to-day living.

THE 'OBSESSIVE–COMPULSIVE' STRUGGLE

Just to make sure we are on 'speaking terms,' so these words will mean the same for us all, to 'obsess' is to repeat the same thoughts again and again over something, many times something unpleasant, and not be able to voluntarily stop this thinking. We just can't stop thinking about something, no matter how hard we might try. And of course, we know that it is not so simple as just telling ourselves, 'Stop thinking about girls!'

The mind is far too tricky and subtle to fall for such a simple maneuver! When we do this we usually find that more thoughts come up rather than less regarding whatever we are trying to push away. This is because the effort or energy that we put into pushing something away is going to keep us attached to it.

To be 'compulsive' is to perform certain ritualistic behaviors in a uniform, ongoing manner that help keep one's world in order. Many times, for the person who has developed this kind of pattern to a pathological state, the anxiety of obsessive thinking leads to ritualistic compulsive behaviors that are aimed at lessening the anxiety.

So, for example, the up-tight, inhibited and religious school teacher who can't get rid of the thought that she has 'sinned' by feeling lust when she looked at a fellow teacher, may develop a hand-washing compulsion to symbolically try and wash away her guilt and moral dirtiness.

But we need not have reached pathological proportions such as this before our compulsive behaviors and 'tendencies' tend to limit our psychological world. We'll talk more about more 'normal compulsivity' later in this chapter.

Compulsive people like their outer world in order and once they manage to get their world in order, do their best to keep it that way. In this manner, they are able to manage the anxiety of never knowing for sure what may disrupt their sense of security in the world. We all like to think (especially those of us with compulsive tendencies) that if we can just have some semblance of control in our private little universe then perhaps our sense of being out of control of much of what happens in our lives won't disturb us so much.

The compulsive doesn't want to believe he is sitting in the caboose like the rest of us. And yet at an anxious level of awareness just below consciousness, he knows all too well he is. He fights like hell to resist this knowledge, even though he is always preparing for the world to topple over on his head. He thinks if only he can get 'on top of things,' by keeping his house neat and clean with everything in place, he will then be able to keep the contents of his mind neat and clean, and control the direction of his own life.

And in this desire to control his personal space, it is possible to develop all kinds of constricting, repetitive, and self-destructive habits that, when not performed according to ritual, may create massive anxiety and become literally paralyzing.

Beneath the attempt to control his personal world (and many times, the personal worlds of those close to him, such as his children) is a person who is terrified of facing the anxiety of what we called in the Introduction the 'existential givens' of our life. We said that the 'existential givens' are those aspects of life that we must face just by being alive and are therefore part of the human condition.

They are those aspects of life that remind us that beyond the surface differences in race, color, speech, culture and individual personality, we are, as they say, 'All in the same boat.' These include, as we mentioned, the need to manufacture meaning in our life, the anxiety and responsibility of choosing how we will structure our time, our awareness of our own mortality and the finiteness of life, and how we will attempt to satisfy our needs on biological, material, psychological and spiritual levels.

SAME BOAT OR SAME OCEAN?

No matter how persuasively I may try to explain to certain people I have seen in psychotherapy treatment that 'we are all in the same boat,' some will never seriously consider my words. They are absolutely convinced that those with higher socio-economic status are not at all in the same boat, even if we may all be in the same ocean – and they are not even sure we're all in the same ocean!

They will explain to me how the rich are comfortably cruising in fancy yachts, powerful cruising steamships and speedboats philosophizing on the meaning of life, while the poor are barely able to inch their way in a dilapidated rowboat, struggling just to stay alive from day to day. And who can dispute the enormity of lifestyle difference between the rich and famous and the poor and obscure?

And while it is true that although we are all facing the same predicament in being alive, some of us are able to face it without the financial worries that can become the overreaching burden of everyday consciousness for the majority of us. But this does not mean that the rich and famous don't get old, suffer the loss of people in their lives, have frustrated hopes and dreams, and deal with how to spend this very short and precious life that we are all given to live.

Of course, while some can see this when they think about it, the emotion of envy (and the obvious material comfort and opulence they see others enjoying) makes it too difficult to convince many that life just isn't all that different when you strip away the trappings. Who can blame any of us for at least wanting the chance to have enough trappings to voluntarily strip away?

Let's move away from the related socio-political issues and get back to perfectionism. Being a perfectionist doesn't necessarily mean you have to have an obsessive–compulsive personality or even strong 'tendencies' in this direction. Some people who need to do everything as an 'expert' or else won't do it at all are not obsessed by any thoughts nor are they so rigid as compulsives in their daily habits.

The stereotype of the slobby, absent-minded computer 'nerd' who has his outer world in chaos, books and papers scattered, doesn't care much about his personal dress or hygiene, may be just as easily plagued by perfectionism in his work. Although he doesn't need to have his mind rigidly controlled or his outer world impeccably in order as does our 'good' compulsive, he still may torment himself when his work does not measure up to his own definition of perfection. He can be a 'slob' on the outside but be tormented by the same perfectionistic mental programming. If perfectionism really is a plague and not a virtue, how does it get started?

THE SHAPING OF THE PERFECTIONISTIC MIND

We should remember, as mentioned above, that many who might be quickly and unequivocally diagnosed as suffering from perfectionism by a mental health professional are not really aware of what they do to themselves with their demands for high performance. (Just to be clear – there is no such thing as a 'perfectionistic diagnosis.' One who is afflicted by this plague would most likely be classified as an 'obsessive–compulsive personality disorder.') They may not even think that they expect perfection from themselves. This is, of course, part of the problem, as they would be in better shape if they had some inkling that they have set totally unrealistic demands on themselves and are setting themselves up for sure failure.

Someone will tell me with a perfectly casual air (as if everyone in the world thought the same) that if they don't practice the violin every single day of the week for at least four hours they are 'lazy' and don't deserve to ever attain professional status. When it becomes patently clear that they have *never, not more than three days straight*, been able to play *every single day for four hours*, this piece of information does not seem to sway them from their goal. And this is one difference between the perfectionist and the normal goal-setter, who wants to do the best that he can but is able to think in more realistic, attainable terms.

The perfectionist, even when confronted with compelling evidence, has great trouble realizing that his goals are impossible to attain. The non-perfectionistic goal-setter seems to have a better idea of what is possible and realistic given his past performance and he knows how to use this information. The perfectionist will not use this same information to help himself alter his future goal-setting behavior. He refuses to believe, no matter how often he falls short of his goal, that perhaps his goal has been set beyond reach.

It can take me quite a while (months of therapy) to get some perfectionistic patients to see that they may be expecting way too much if, despite repeated efforts, they have never been successful at reaching their goal. This piece of information has always been available to them, always right in front of their cognitive noses, but it has never been allowed to sink in.

Because, to allow it to *really* sink in would be to have to stop their efforts and admit they have set their target too high. This would mean, of course, having to admit 'failure,' as they would be admitting they were unable to (expertly) set realistic goals. And, of course, more importantly, it means they would have to question everything they have stood for, their whole image as one who is important because they strive for only the best.

Another difficulty in working with the perfectionistic person is that many times, they have come to think of their striving for 'only the best' as a virtue. Now, we're not talking about the people who haven't yet figured out they are in this category that we mentioned above. We're talking about those who know they tend to want and expect themselves to be perfect and carry this around and boast about it as if it were a badge of honor. They like the self-image of one who is a perfectionist. They have confused the idea that aiming over your head means you are striving to be your best.

It is one thing for us to push ourselves to new heights of performance, in the attempt to 'actualize our potential,' whatever it may be. It is another to rarely or ever let ourselves be satisfied with our performance. But this is exactly what the perfectionist does. Because his head is always a bit in the clouds, wishing so badly for perfection, he can't accept his real-world performance, even when it may be at a high level. We will go further into why this happens after an example of the perfectionist mentality.

Arnold: Nothing Less than 'Number One'

Arnold was one of the most interesting patients to find their way to my consulting room. It was not so much his personality, or the troubles he brought in to work with, that made him so interesting. It was his high level of accomplishment in the world, his relative lack of self-insight and psychological naivety given his high intelligence, and his openness to experiment and responsiveness to my interventions that made him interesting and stimulating to work with. I'm sure that I was impressed by his accomplishments, having some idea what it required to excell at Arnold's level in his chosen academic discipline.

There was a little-boy excitement to his realizations as we worked together that made him ripe to learn about himself and enjoyable to work with. He got excited making mental associations that led to self-insight. And because he had the capacity to tie mental associations together and see the relations between things, he made good progress, even though our time together was not long enough to touch some of the deeper issues that Arnold was ready to tackle.

We worked intensively (three times per week) for a few months before a critical business decision forced him to leave the area and prematurely terminate therapy. By the time he left, he was more interested in furthering his personal growth than on working on any issue creating immediate problems. The issue that Arnold brought in is not my reason for using him in this section. I use him because he is a great example of the perfectionistic mind in action. This example really shows the best and worst of the plague to be perfect. We will go into some detail here to make the point.

Arnold was 43 when he came to see me but had accomplished enough, it seemed, to have filled two full lifetimes. He had grown up in a lower-middle-class small town and remembered how hard he

127

worked at a gas station as a teenager to have a few extra dollars. He liked talking about his childhood, and liked the exclusive attention he got from me. He was unable to sit still very long, always a little jittery. Either he would be nervously tapping his foot while he spoke, or he'd be moving around in his chair.

Arnold was a good example of what we consider the classic 'Type A' personality: he did everything fast, had great difficulty totally relaxing and doing absolutely nothing. He had a sense of urgency in his life that, at best, spurred him to produce scholarly textbooks and articles at a Herculean pace and try out a lot of sports activities – and at worst, made it impossible to ever slow down and catch his breath, so that rarely could he allow himself to stop producing or showing off without feeling anxious and unworthy.

As well, his obsession with the power of his own mind and intellectual prowess made it difficult for him not to look at all other people as satellites to his sense of being the Big Star.

And because he was the Big Star, this relegated everyone else in his life – his parents, ex-wife and girlfriend, children, secretary, colleagues, employees in his company and 'all others' into the category of being Little Nothings, who did not deserve much thought as to what they might need from him. All that was important was what others could do for him. And he wanted them to do it FAST, no matter what 'it' might have been.

It was not hard to see how he had developed such an inflated ego – he had done an incredible amount of high-level work and was quite talented in a number of sports and hobbies. Arnold couldn't find anyone to be friends with who could come close to having his range of interests. His friends might share one or maybe two interests in common with him. But he had such a broad range, a lot of the time he just pursued his interests alone. As he put it, 'I work hard and I play hard – nobody can keep up with me.'

What were his particular skills and interests? To me, the most impressive was that he had earned a Ph.D. in his chosen academic discipline in his early twenties and had gone on to write a number of widely adopted textbooks, many of which were updated on a regular basis. He basically made a living on the royalties he earned from the book sales. He boasted to me, once I got him talking about his work, that he had written more books in his specialty area than *anybody else alive.*

'MORE BOOKS THAN ANYBODY ELSE ALIVE'

Of course, a claim of this magnitude did not pass by my ears lightly, and I came to discover that he was telling me the truth about his success, although I don't know about the 'more than anybody else alive' part. To verify (and because I was curious about his writing) that he actually did write books as he claimed, I had him bring in some examples. We are talking about scholarly, tedious, informed and demanding textbooks that he had become an expert at punching out on a variety of subjects related to his field.

Many of the books he was counting were not really separate new books but revised editions of the same old books. But whatever way you look at it, this man clearly had a talent that made him stand out from the academic herd.

But the interesting thing about Arnold was that he wasn't satisfied with being at the 'top of the heap' in just his own area of work. He wanted to be at the top of the heap in *every* area and every activity he took on. Nothing felt right for him unless it was done intensely and for a long time. He had little appreciation for doing a little at a time.

So, I was impressed by his productivity and how he had been able to extract himself from the teach-a-class-and-do-research world of the academic university by having his books sell so well that he could live off the royalties for many years, even if he never wrote another word or revised another text.

How does all this relate to perfectionism? Well, Arnold had to be the best at everything he did. He wanted to be the total Renaissance Man, able to perform all kinds of physical and mental feats at the highest possible level. He wanted to be a Man for All Seasons and did his best to make this a reality. So, he became a good surfer in the summer and an expert skier in the winter.

He could not stand to see someone do anything better than he. So, he would practice skiing until he could handle the downhill as fast and as adeptly as his skiing teacher. He had considered becoming a professional photographer but decided it wasn't demanding enough. He had run in a number of marathons and also participated in and completed at least one 'Strong-Man' triathlon contest. He had worked with weights when he was in high school and college, and enjoyed the respect he got from the 'heavyweights' with whom he worked out.

To top all this, he had the distorted but firmly planted idea that he ought to have sex every single night of his life, or at least once per day. This was not just a pleasant fantasy for Arnold, but something he took very seriously. He felt something was wrong with him and his girlfriend if this daily sexual bout did not take place.

And he was so obsessed with his own need to prove his manhood that he could not possibly appreciate how his girlfriend might feel if she were tired of this compulsive ritual or, for some reason, not feeling like making love. Without daily sex, Arnold believed another opportunity for The Perfect Day had been ruined. And did he just have sex and enjoy it? Oh, no! He had to make sure he was a 'long-distance runner' in bed as well as out on the road. He was into high performance.

By looking at the motivations for some of Arnold's very high expectations of himself and his need to do everything to the extreme, he was slowly able to modify some of his obsessive all-or-nothing thinking as well as alter some of his daily patterns. He began to question his motivation more (or what I call 'thinking like a psychologist'), and slowly became aware of how selfish, self-centered and self-obsessed he had become. He wondered whether he was capable of really loving a woman. He wondered how much he was able to really care for anyone in his life.

He began to see how little regard he had for other people, how little their needs mattered to him, and how he had oppressed those close to him by trying to get them to live up to his perfectionistic standards. He began to see that underneath all of the accomplishments and boasting was a part of him that felt very unsure, insecure and didn't know much about his own mind.

Because he was earning a lot of money and writing a lot of books, and because he was used to having his way, it was not easy for him to cope when his wife left him for another man. He could not believe that anyone could ever want to leave him and his very comfortable lifestyle. If there was any leaving to be done, *he* wanted to be the one doing it, not his partner.

Arnold had the intelligence to understand that his obliviousness to the needs of others was not something he could continue if he wished to be fulfilled. He began to be less demanding and critical of his children, took some time to slow down his usual hectic pace, and seriously wanted to understand the psychological dynamics that were creating the need for this maddening perfectionistic thinking and behavior.

He began to accept the limitations of others instead of ridiculing them and he began to ease up on himself and allow for things not to have to be perfectly in order to be acceptable. Arnold represents both the positive and negative ends of the polarity of our striving to achieve at the highest levels we are capable.

This trying to be the best that we may be is what the psychologist Abraham Maslow meant by striving for 'self-actualization.' He believed that we all want to be the best that we may be in all aspects of our lives and that we will not be satisfied with ourselves if we know that we have not pushed ourselves to do our best. Maslow thought that if we just get by, when we are really capable of more, our self-regard will go down. We can't fool ourselves about our own effort.

But the negative end of the continuum makes for rigidity, difficulties in accepting our real limits and the limits of others, and an itching dissatisfaction that is never relieved because we can never be perfect all of the time in all of our thoughts, words and deeds. Then why doesn't the perfectionist 'throw in the towel' and give up the struggle? Because he is, I believe, really looking for a perfection of a different order. And this 'different order' desire just doesn't go away. It relates to our desire for self-transcendence. But first let's look at the more obvious psychodynamic behind perfectionism.

LOOKING FOR LOVE AND ADMIRATION

On the psychological-need level, the perfectionist believes that if he could only be perfect, finally he would win the approval, respect, admiration and open-hearted love from his parents and significant others in his life that he deserves for his high performance. Like most of us, the perfectionist has learned that good performance is rewarded by acceptance, recognition and, sometimes, love. He also knows that just being himself is not enough to earn approval from loved ones. Never has he really been given the feeling that *just who he is* is enough to be loved.

So, for example, even if he runs into a woman who demands little of him and tells him repeatedly she loves him just for who he is, he is unable to believe her – he knows there must be a catch in there somewhere! He keeps waiting for the proverbial shoe to drop, disbelieving that maybe this time he really is lovable to someone without having to prove his worth by accomplishing some task.

The perfectionist, in a sense, has 'taken the bait' and is unable to get off the hook of trying to please his parents and finally get the hoped-for love. While one sign of healthy emotional development for those who have been emotionally deprived is to realize that one's parents just aren't going to be able to 'deliver the goods' any better now than they could before, the perfectionist just doesn't allow this to sink in.

He is convinced that if only he can do it absolutely perfectly, there will be a FINAL PAY-OFF. Giving up this delusion (after accepting that it is, indeed, a delusion) is what is necessary for the perfectionist to allow for a margin of error and begin to judge himself less harshly.

Scratch the surface and you will find that behind the perfectionist mentality is the desire to be a good little boy or girl.

But that is just the motivation on the psychological level. There is, I believe, an even deeper dynamic at work in perfectionism.

THE DESIRE TO BE ONE WITH GOD

The perfectionist, on a deeper level, wants himself and everyone else in the material world to be perfect. He wants things to be the way they were in the Garden of Eden, where we are all innocent, free of sin, and with all our needs met all of the time. He wants us to live in a perfect world, where sickness, disease, suffering and death are not to be dealt with. He wants everyone to be beautiful and healthy. But, what does he *really* want?

At a deeper level than just becoming a perfectionist because of his toilet training and other psychodynamics of growing up, I believe he wants to join with God. He wants to lose himself in the perfection of creation and never have this perfection disturbed. He wants to be omnipotent and have everything in the world remain in its pristine original radiance, as it would be in heaven. His intuition tells him there is more than just this dirty and disordered world to partake of. And, by God, he is going to do his best to find it!

And that 'more' is to feel as one with the whole world and be released of the chore of having to be separate, living in a world where perfection is never attained. He wants the beautiful rose to never wilt and the beautiful woman to never show age. His relative-level ego knows it wants more than just this imperfect world and wants so badly to join with Absolute self.

Absolute self is like temporarily being one with God.

The only trouble is, to enjoy it you have to snap back into being a separate subject watching some blissful state of consciousness go on. And then some sense of relative self sneaks back into the picture, perhaps thinking, 'Nice state of consciousness we've achieved here. But how long will it last?' So, I am suggesting that beneath (or behind) the desire to be perfect in one's actions and to see others be the same, lies the desire to merge with God and be perfectly One for ever more.

We could say, then, that behind the desire to be perfect in one's speech, thought and action lies the deeper desire to be one with the Absolute self, or that part of us which is PERFECT and God-like. If we conceive of God as a force outside ourselves rather than as inherently part of ourselves, then we would wish to join in perfection with this God-force. For the purposes of offering this interpretation, it doesn't really matter what our conception of God is.

The main point in relation to how some of us become perfectionistic is the desire to find oneness, and therefore everlasting perfection, with this force. But as a substitute to this, we get bogged down with ordering and re-ordering our personal little worlds, and striving for perfection in all that we do.

We can't bite off the whole piece of seeking God-likeness at once – it is more than we can psychologically handle – so we bite off a little corner instead. I should be clear that this interpretation of perfectionism and the obsessive–compulsive personality is my own. It is not something that is commonly shared by other mental health professionals. And while some writers, such as Ken Wilber, talk about the desire we all have to realize our God-likeness, I am not aware of this dynamic being applied specifically to the obsessive–compulsive personality. We'll talk more about self-transcendence later when we get to developing the inner witness. For now, let's go back and look at 'tendencies' toward obsessive–compulsive behavior on the relative ego level.

COMPULSIVITY 'FOR THE REST OF US'

We said at the start of this chapter we would come back and look at how obsessive–compulsive tendencies affect all of us who may not require psychotherapy because we have reached pathological proportions but still notice repetitive thought as well as ritualistic and orderly behavior in our lives.

We all know what it's like not to be able to get a certain thought out of our minds, no matter how hard we might try. We also know the even more uncomfortable feeling when we find our mind going back again and again to some emotionally charged incident that has occurred in our lives, where we find ourselves trying to undo or re-do the incident because we don't like what happened.

A certain amount of obsessing is normal and doesn't need to cause any concern. Likewise, it is no big deal if we tend to want our homes in order, desks orderly and books on a shelf. We may like our bathrooms to look a certain way or the kitchen to be arranged a certain way or

(don't be shy – fill in your favorite compulsive preference in the space).

As long as ordering our thoughts and material world is not something that gets out of hand, there is nothing 'wrong' with it. It simply helps keep our personal world in order so that we have a sense of control and efficiency in our lives. 'Good' habits save time!

But what about when it becomes more than this but less than pathological? We don't need to be 'sick' to suffer certain consequences because of our concern with perfection. Let me give a personal example that seems fitting at this point.

I could have easily written this book six years ago, when I began to relate this material in my own mind. I thought it would be a good idea to combine case examples from my psychotherapy practice to illustrate certain psychological and philosophical ideas that I believed educated people would appreciate. I wanted to include exercises that would further enhance the chance of the reader having an experience of the ideas, beyond just an intellectual understanding. But because I reacted with such distaste to the pop-psychology books which seemed to appeal to the public, I did not want to write something that I thought might be thrown in the same category. I had what I thought were 'good reasons.'

I couldn't stand the idea that I might write just another unnecessary and overly simplified psychology/philosophy book. It would have been much easier for me to write a more scholarly book that would have lots of references and appeal to a relatively small group of professionals.

So, because of what I now label a perfectionistic 'tendency,' I chose not to sit down and write this book. I continue to believe that most self-help books are overly simplified, and promise more than they can possibly deliver. Far too many are, in addition, poorly written and treat the reader like a 12-year-old. I also told myself that because this was the kind of stuff that publishers wanted, they would not appreciate my writing. And because my writing was welcomed in professional journals, I contented myself with the thought that only professionals could appreciate what I had to offer.

But I don't think I needed to let this be so important that I postponed writing for six more years! It was not until I allowed it to be OK to write 'just another popular psychology book' that didn't have to be perfect that I could go ahead and begin the project. I also needed to be willing to face the possible rejection of publishers who might not think my writing worthy of publication.

If this happened, I would be in the uncomfortable position of having been critical of so many pop-psychology books that *at least some editor thought worthy of publication*. Who am I, I thought, to be so critical of all those popular mass-market books when I can't even get published? So this was the predicament I found myself in.

Just one more example of how the Perfectionistic Monster can rise up out of the murk and mire to bite us on the ass . . . Nothing very different from what we go through all the time in postponing tackling a project because we don't want to try if it can't be perfect. Better to keep the book in the realm of Mental Perfection than bring it out into the cold, cruel, rejection-ridden world of publishers, editors and the greater public.

WORSHIPPING THE 'PERFECT BODY'

We would be overlooking a significant area of the perfectionistic plague if we did not at least briefly mention 'the cult-in-search-of-the-perfect-body.' In California, and especially along the Coast, the obsession with looking 'perfect' is engaged in by great numbers of men and women of all ages. This obsession leads many to the compulsion to diet and heavily exercise. All of this has made for numerous TV shows and newspaper articles and is not really new. But the motivation to have the perfect body is more than just to get the opposite sex looking with lust.

Beyond simply knowing and practicing good dietary habits and doing some form of exercise to keep their heart and muscles in shape, these people are psychologically addicted to exercise in pursuit of the good physical feelings it brings and the hope of shaping themselves into the perfect body. Those addicted to various forms of exercise may not always be the hard-core fanatics who spend most of their time shaping their bodies with weights and are not as concerned with aerobic work-outs.

For many women, this 'perfect body' is thin. For many men, it means muscles in the right places. But these people are convinced that their obtaining what they believe to be the perfect shape is going to help them find all the sex and romance they can stand. They base their feelings of self-worth totally on whether they are able to get the 'right shape.'

Tanning salons, weight training, clothes-shopping sprees for the oh-so-latest fashions that will best show off their hard work, obses-sion with counting calories, and so much more . . . It all becomes an obsession 'for the rest of us,' the segment of what I think of as 'normal neurotics,' who may never come to the attention of a mental health professional unless they go to an extreme, such as becoming anorexic, or some other disturbance of extreme body weight or eating habits.

But this does not mean they are not obsessive–compulsive perfec-tionists. It only means that in a culture that worships the shapely, youthful body, these people will not be seen as suffering from any kind of problem. In fact, they will be envied by all those who are not able to obtain the same results. The motto in California of the 'cult of the body' is: 'You Can't Be Too Rich or Too Thin (but Rich and a Little Fat is Better than Thin and Poor).'

The 'cult of the body' may lead to signifant emotional difficulties as one has to deal with age and the loss of muscle tone as one gets older. The obsession will then take the form of abusing plastic surgery, as one refuses to 'grow up and age gracefully' and instead, does everything surgically possible to remain looking young.

Experiment: Perfectionism

Think for a moment about your expectations of yourself. In what areas do you expect yourself to perform at a very high level? If there are no areas you can think of, you may not expect too much from yourself. Or, you may not have developed areas of interest in which you have become highly proficient. But most of us have at least one or two areas in which we have very high expectations of ourselves.

Once you identify one area of high expectations, ask yourself whether you tend to think perfectionistically. Do you find yourself disappointed when you don't reach your desired level?

Do you tend to put down your own performance even when others are complimentary of your skills?

Do you tend to berate yourself and feel like your self-worth has diminished when you don't perform up to par?

Do you become compulsive about your chosen area, so that you feel driven to improve your performance even if it means no longer enjoying what you are doing?

Just for the sake of experimentation, see if you can give yourself credit even if you don't reach your desired level of expertise. See if there are any activities you are aware of avoiding trying just because you can't stand starting off as a beginner.

What have you sacrificed because you wouldn't let yourself take the chance of failing? Keep in mind the difference between continually disciplining yourself through practice to improve your skill and setting expectations that are impossible to meet.

Use your discriminating mind to know when 'good enough is good enough' even if it isn't perfect. Let go of whatever inflated ego feelings go with the need to perform perfectly and allow for your feelings of self-worth to stay in place even if you don't measure up to someone else who may do the same activity better than you.

=== 8 ===

POLARITY AND PARADOX

In Chapter 2 we opened the topic of opposites, or polarities, and made the point that it is difficult to see the opposite side of our own most cherished beliefs. We tried to imagine taking the opposite belief to see if we could notice how we had alienated ourselves from half of the picture.

Now let us examine the concepts of polarity in more detail and introduce the concept of paradox. We don't want to jump past identifying and integrating opposites on the psychological level before we begin to examine the transpersonal, or spiritual level.

Also, we need to grasp the nature and significance of both bipolarities and paradox in our coming to understand ourselves and our world. The concepts of polarity and paradox are part of our everyday world. And yet, they are not widely understood or even identified by most people, unless they have had a background in psychology, philosophy, or logic. We don't commonly learn in college (and certainly not in high school) how to think in terms of bipolarities. Nor do we learn to open our minds to the reality of paradox, as it makes itself felt in our daily lives.

THE BIPOLARITY OF 'OPPOSITES'

One of the more telling insights that appears (on the psychological level) in the process of our individual and collective 'waking up' to ourselves is the understanding of bipolarity. Understanding how the bipolarity of opposites works distinguishes those who are able to identify, discriminate and pay credence to *both* ends of any given bipolarity from those hopelessly caught on one end of something that is fundamentally two-ended.

Because of this 'holding on for dear life' stance to one end, personal suffering is increased and our ability to see ourselves clearly is clouded. We end up thinking there is only 'heads' and we never see 'tails.' This is what we examined in Chapter 2 and called 'hardening of the beliefs.'

It is the fine-tuned discriminating mind which pays homage to polarity. The lazy mind doesn't want to be bothered by looking too closely, especially when it seems hard enough to get in touch with one end and be certain about our feelings, let alone have to entertain the opposite end to discover our investment there, too.

But, whether we like it or not, the picture is more complicated than just learning to 'get in touch' with our feelings on one side of the coin. Let's look at why it is necessary for full psychological growth to see both sides of our own coin.

What do we mean by a 'bipolarity'? When we think of a polarity, a good image to start with is a pair of *apparent* opposites, like the emotions of love and hate. We grow up learning to think of love and hate as having nothing to do with each other, because we think of them as completely the opposite of each other. 'Polar opposites' means the two ends, indeed, are completely and totally opposite. Each represents as far away from the other as it can possibly be.

'Bipolar opposites' means the two ends are intimately connected to each other, even needing each other, for their existence. Unlike a 'true' opposite, the middle point between the two bipolarities is the farthest point from each of the bipoles. When we hear such wise sayings as, 'It takes hardship and suffering to fully appreciate being well-off and happy;' or, 'You can only appreciate wealth after you've been poor,' we are hearing an indication of a knowledge of the concept of bipolarities.

The idea is obviously that our life experiences can be more fully understood and appreciated in the context of the intimately related extremes. The realization of opposites helps us put our experience into some kind of meaningful structure, in addition to getting us closer to the truth about the deep nature of personality.

Look at Figures 8.1 and 8.2 to see this graphically. Notice that with 'true' polar opposites, the middle point **C** is closer to both **A** and **B** than **A** is to **B**. Just as polar opposites should be, **A** (West) and **B** (East) are as far away from each other as possible.

But in Figure 8.2, **A** (love) and **B** (hate) 'collapse' back *toward* each other when one point is stretched to its limit. The mid-point **C** is the furthest point from both **A** and **B**. So, for example, we say to someone, 'Watch out that when you hate someone you don't fall in love with him.'

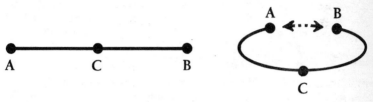

Figure 8.1   'True' Polarities.   Figure 8.2   Bipolarities.

And we take our partner missing us when we're apart as a sign of caring about us – if he or she doesn't miss us, and feels indifferent (the mid-point but furthest point from both love and hate), then we wonder whether he or she really cares. When we think about this for a while, it is not so hard to see why we say that indifference is further away from both love and hate than each is from the other. This is what makes for a bipolarity.

Rather than say that love and hate become the 'same' emotion when stretched toward their limit (which, of course, they don't), instead, it is more accurate to say they 'approach' each other, because *the intensity of each share a common emotional energy.*

And this common emotional energy that is necessary to experience the strong emotions of love and hate can be seen as the 'common denominator' that provides the rhyme and reason behind the concept of bipolarities. This common denominator is the key to the collapsing of **A** towards **B** in Figure 8.2.

'If they are opposites,' we think, 'how can they have anything in common?' This is the fundamental either/or thinking that we are taught is 'logical' and sensible. And when we are repeatedly being told to think that opposites have nothing in common, we soon learn to view this in relation to *all* of the opposites that we confront in our

141

mental and emotional life, and not just those in the physical world in which we live. This confounding of true polar opposites with bipolar opposites, then, is the fatal error in our thinking that limits our ability from going beyond the 'either/or' mentality.

'EITHER/OR' THINKING

Let's take a look at a few simple examples, just to make this clear. Notice which of these polarities seem to be true polar opposites and which qualify as bipolarities. We call the form of thinking that requires *all* poles be seen as true polarities as 'either/or' thinking.

Mini-thought experiment
Can you think of some other polarities or bipolarities of your own to expand the following list? Pay particular attention to those opposites which you can easily identify as part of your own personality make-up. Consider some of the polarities found in the physical world and in nature. What do you come up with?

good–bad	win–lose
happy–sad	inside–outside
stingy–generous	active–passive
strong–weak	love–hate
thought–feeling	loud–quiet
tough–tender	mine–yours
kind–cruel	thoughtful–selfish
excited–bored	easy going–uptight

'either/or' thinking

Notice that some of the pairs given *appear* to be clear-cut polar opposites that could not possibly be open to question. Examples of these would be the following: 'win–lose,' 'inside–outside,' and 'mine–yours.' *Either* you win *or* you lose – you can't objectively do both at the same time! *Either* you are on the inside of something *or* you are on the outside. How can both be possible? *Either* the car is mine *or* it is yours, unless we both happen to own it.

We are taught to treat our personal psychological and emotional life with the same either/or thinking that we apply to the outside world of objects and physical boundaries.

But when we look more closely at even these 'hard' examples, where the boundaries presented appear to make either/or thinking appropriate, it is possible to question the reality of the firm boundaries that appear to be implied in the opposites shown.

For example, we can always question the relativity of winning and losing, the firmness of the boundary dividing inside from outside, and the meaning of something being 'mine' and not 'yours.' Let's take a minute longer here with these examples just to illustrate what we mean.

Let's say Johnny happens to lose to Jimmy in their high school competition for outstanding high-jumper on the track and field team. Jimmy has objectively 'won' the competition, even though he has long thought (with good reason) that Johnny was more skillful in the high-jump than he. Johnny felt the same way – he didn't think he could ever lose (especially to Jimmy) and, in fact, has won most of the high-jump competitions against other schools.

But this time, he loses to Jimmy. He can't understand what went wrong for this to happen. A strong part of his ego-strength comes from his identification as the 'best' high-jumper at Satori High School.

His losing the competition to Jimmy means he learns something valuable about himself – it is possible to lose no matter how good you think you are or how much praise and encouragement you get from others. On the objective level – no question about it – Johnny lost.

But his losing provides a valuable opportunity (which he takes) to learn about being too cocky, conceited and taking something for granted (that he could never lose). On the psychological–emotional level, Johnny has 'won' something that will be helpful in future competitions for the rest of his life. So, the philosopher and psychologist might ask, did he 'win' or 'lose'? Did he, as they say, 'lose the battle but win the war'?

To take one more example of the apparent 'hard' boundaries, we think of being either on the inside or outside of something. Objectively, when there is a real physical boundary, this seems to be true. Either I am inside my house or outside my house.

But what if while I am physically inside my house sitting at my computer and writing these words, mentally I'm thinking about how much I would like to be outside at the beach, taking a walk along the sun-drenched shoreline? Suppose I close my eyes and just drift off in pleasant fantasy?

I may perceive the physical boundary as either all too real, if I am not interested in sitting at the computer and writing, or I may be able to erase much of the actual boundary by using my creative imagination to visualize the seashore, sun, birds, sand, people, and sights, sounds and smells of the seashore that I know so well.

I can be sitting right here at the computer but be indulging in the delicious fantasy of being at the ocean. In effect, I am able to diminish the actual physical reality of being inside by the power of my mental imaging. 'Inside' and 'outside' no longer seem so sharp and defined, nor does the physical boundary seem so hard, real, or limiting.

In this way, I give myself a 'breath of fresh air' and am able to keep writing without feeling like I am depriving myself. Also, I can use my fantasy to follow up with plans to actually go down to the ocean once I complete my session's writing.

The loosening of boundaries of inside and outside also relates to our understanding that the issue is really this: **Where is our attention?** 'Inside' and 'outside' are not as important, in the realm of the mind, as knowing where our attention is being focused at any given moment. Here is a short Zen story that clearly illustrates this.

Muddy Road

Tanzan and Ekido were once travelling together down a muddy road. A heavy rain was still falling.

Coming around a bend, they met a lovely girl in a silk kimono and sash, unable to cross the intersection.

'Come on, girl,' said Tanzan at once. Lifting her in his arms, he carried her over the mud.

Ekido did not speak again until that night when they reached a lodging temple. Then he no longer could restrain himself. 'We monks don't go near females,' he told Tanzan, 'especially not young and lovely ones. It is dangerous. Why did you do that?'

'I left the girl there,' said Tanzan. 'Are you still carrying her?'

This story points out that the physical reality is not as important as the mental reality. When our attention is with the past, it doesn't really matter whether we're 'inside' or 'outside.'

Another example of this idea comes through in the following question: 'Which person is more spiritually pure – the whore who sits in a brothel all day meditating on Christ or the priest who sits in his church all day thinking about his desire for sex?'

Let's look at the alternative to either/or thinking. We can call the alternative 'both/and' thinking. Another aspect of the *discriminating mind* is that it knows when to see things as true polarities (where 'either/or' thinking is appropriate) and when things are actually bipolarities, in which 'both/and' thinking is the necessary mode to get the full picture.

'BOTH/AND' THINKING

Both/and thinking assumes that we do not need to get caught on just one end of what is actually a bipolar, or two-ended personality tendency. Referring back to the list, this means that we would look at the possibility of our being *both* active *and* passive, loving *and* hateful, thoughtful *and* selfish, strong *and* weak, stingy *and* generous, etc. To put it simply, we may be **both** this **and** that rather than **either** this **or** that.

Why is this type of thinking not our usual way of looking at our own personality? How did we get so stuck wanting to identify with only one end of the polarity? The answer is all too obvious. It is hard enough for us to get in touch with ourselves to know what we are thinking and feeling on *one* end of the polarity. How can we possibly learn to identify with both ends when one end seems so difficult?

So, we might prefer to identify ourselves as good, happy, generous, strong, kind, loving, thoughtful and easy going. Who wants to have to admit that along with all these positive aspects we can also be at times bad, sad, stingy, weak, cruel, hateful, selfish and uptight? Do you see the predicament we are in here? And yet nothing less than the integration of both ends of the opposites is necessary for full, vibrant, healthy and self-aware functioning.

To believe that we are only loving and never hateful or only kind and never cruel, or only thoughtful and never selfish is to delude ourselves, plain and simple. It is to not really be aware of what is

145

called, in Jungian terms, the 'shadow' side of our personality. The more self-aware we are at the psychological level, the more we are able to identify with *both* ends of any given personality bipolarity in ourselves.

In the process of psychotherapy, much of my time is spent with patients helping them to get in touch with and then 'own' (assume responsibility for) the shadow, or darker aspects of themselves.

As mentioned earlier in this book, one way patients (and people in general) 'give themselves away' as to their disowning of aspects of their personalities is through their use of language. 'I' versus 'it' language is the most obvious – this is one area you can easily hear in casual conversation with people (if you are listening for it), or just overhearing other people's conversations.

For example, we may hear 'It felt scary to say that to her,' instead of 'I felt scared to say that to her.' Or, 'It doesn't seem to ever go my way' instead of 'I never seem able to make things go my way.' Or, 'It makes me angry when you ignore me,' instead of either 'I'm angry when you ignore me,' or (not quite as good but better than 'it' language), 'You make me angry when you ignore me.'

When we say, 'I'm angry' instead of 'You made me angry', we are closer to accepting full responsibility for exactly what we are experiencing. 'You made me,' still sounds like we are blaming the other person for how they have made us feel. But at least it is more direct than saying 'it.'

Another gross disowning bit of language is the use of 'you' when we mean to say 'I.' We hear football players being interviewed on TV, and they sometimes sound like this:

'Ya, Joe, ya go out there and ya feel da pressure and ya think ya can't shake it and play da way ya needs to but, ya know Joe, somehow ya gotta find it deep within ya to get past it. Ya just gotta shake it off anyway ya can, Joe, ya know?'

Instead of saying 'I go out there . . . and I can't shake it and play the way I need to . . . I find it deep within myself . . . '

Is this asking for too much? Maybe from some football players it is, but not from those who want their words to be congruent with what they are feeling and expressing.

This one is so obvious to the trained ear that it can be used to quickly discriminate those who are in touch with themselves as the center of action in their lives from those who are alienated from their own experience.

How about this assertion for going out on a limb: *never* have I heard someone simply substitute 'you' language for 'I' language without it being an indication of limited self-ownership of thoughts, feelings and behavior. While this may sound like a strong statement, in my experience of listening to patients and non-patients alike, it is true.

On the surface, some of those I question regarding their use of 'you' language when they mean 'I', tell me it is part of speaking and writing in the business world. But, always with people who make this claim, close inquiry shows they simply don't want to own their own statements.

It is much easier to have the company (in the form of 'we') backing up one's opinion. Also, these people are told it is 'too personal' to use 'I' language. Sometimes, the logic of the business world interferes with simple, direct and psychologically sound self-expression.

Listen to the self-expression of those around you and see how true this is. We are *not*, as they say, just getting caught up in semantics (the meaning of words).

The use of our language is fundamental to the way we think about ourselves and the meaning of our experiences.

This has been understood especially by those linguists and developmental psychologists who see the basic structures of our mind being shaped by our culture as we acquire language. Our minds, in other words, are shaped as children by the structure of language and how we adapt it for our daily use.

As adults, the *discriminating mind* helps us choose those ways of expressing ourselves which will be most self-expressive of our ownership of our own experience and most precisely communicate what it is we want to say.

The discriminating mind realizes this is not just a 'matter of semantics' but a matter of being able to 'say what we mean and mean what we say.' We take seriously the words that come out of our mouth and are ready and willing to stand behind them. We go beyond the mentality of simply saying whatever we need to say to 'get through' an uncomfortable situation. We don't make promises that we don't intend to keep. And we don't tell people what they want to hear just so they will like us.

We know when the best response is to simply keep quiet, rather than lie to someone to get out of a sticky situation. We choose one behavior over the other – not because we are trying to be moralistic. We do this because our relative ego-self demands that we respond from a place of congruence and integrity. We don't like ourselves when we lie, deceive, or manipulate other people.

And while formal education definitely has something to do with our verbal ability to pick and choose the best words to express ourselves with congruence and integrity, choosing the best words is also something that can be learned if we are willing to use our ears (to listen) carefully and not be afraid to assume responsibility for what is our own experience.

WHY IS IT SO HARD TO RECONCILE OPPOSITES?

Let me illustrate why it is so hard to reconcile opposites through the use of a case example. Janet comes in and tells me she is 'strong, assertive, and won't let herself be pushed around by men.' She works out with weights, runs daily, and takes pride in looking 'lean and mean.' She is 28 and works as a trial attorney for a public agency. She likes her work but doesn't know how long she wants to remain in a public practice setting.

Janet begins to confront me directly in our early sessions, wanting to make sure I am in no way permitted to 'get away with' anything she may interpret as a lapse of total attention on my part.

She doesn't like it when I shift my attention away from her for even short periods (seconds) of time. For example, when I get up to adjust the thermostat, she angrily accuses me of being bored with her. When I look away from her after prolonged periods of direct eye-contact, she tells me I'm not really interested in her, that I see her as just a slot of time in my schedule. She appears hardened, showing little interest in appearing feminine in speech, dress, or manner.

As we worked together for a while, I learn that Janet has been subjected to beatings by her father, beginning when she was 6 years old. She also grew up in an area where she needed to act tough in order to survive, as any appearance of weakness would be pounced on both verbally and physically by other girls. After suffering some of these 'pouncings,' she decided to put on a 'hard-shell finish' that would not be penetrated.

148

Janet could not understand that it might be possible to allow herself to become more feminine without having to give up her more assertive behaviors. There was not room in her mind for being both feminine *and* masculine, as they are traditionally thought of.

Like many of us, she had worked so hard to develop half of a personality characteristic that she was unable to see the imbalance in her behavior. And, like so many, she had never been privy to the notion that it is possible and even desirable to exhibit both ends of any personality characteristic. She thought, 'If you're tough you're tough and if you're soft you're soft – how can you be both?'

To allow herself to develop any softer, feminine behaviors could spell disaster when she was younger and needed to be tough just to physically and psychologically survive. But 'that was then and this is now,' and now she could not see that she no longer needed to protect herself as heavily and one-sidedly as she once did.

Janet is a good example of the strong lifelong investment we may develop when our early growing up forces us to attach ourselves to only one set of personality characteristics. We become lopsided, unable to flexibly play a number of different roles, depending what the situation may call for.

In terms of accepting the bipolarity of opposites, what do we need? What is the picture of one who would focus on integrating polarities?

We need to be able to be spontaneous and playful with our lovers and children. And we need to be comfortable saying 'no!' to our lovers and children. The *discriminating mind* helps us know when each is right.

We need to know when to emotionally let ourselves 'melt' with our lover and when we need to be able to stand firm at times and be as hard as a rock. We need to be able to be so close to our lover that we no longer know who is who. And, at the same time, we need to be very sure of who is who, that our partner has a mind of his/her own – he/she is not just an extension of us.

We must be able to get angry with those we care about and sometimes, those we don't. And we must be able to say, 'I'm sorry' and emotionally let ourselves 'give in' to our partner.

If we stay with only one side of the bipolarity, we get caught, unable to stay flexible enough with our thinking and behavior so we may be 'just right' for a given situation. Flexibility, then, to meet many situations with the perfect response, is really more mentally

149

healthy and practical than attachment to one end of the pole. We need both ends of the bipolarity, not just the 'right' one that is compatible with our self-image.

But, like we just said above, knowing that lying is the polar opposite to telling the truth doesn't mean we need to indulge in lying in order to be 'whole.' The *discriminating mind* tells us from our past experiments in lying that it just doesn't reduce suffering. Instead, it increases it and makes us feel badly about ourselves. Anyone who experiments with lying and deception for a while tends to make this realization. If they can't or won't, it is often because they are pathological liars who are unable to stop without psychotherapy treatment.

EXAMPLES OF BIPOLARITY IMBALANCE

Bipolarity: Egolessness–Strong Ego

Relative self-egolessness   With a strong sense of ego-self we are willing to let go of some of our concern about the judgements of others. This 'letting go' can be thought of as moving toward egolessness. We don't need to spend so much of our precious time wondering about what others are thinking about us. Because of this, we are willing to be more risky, allowing ourselves to experiment in various situations without having to worry about our self-image being threatened. We can think of this as being able to give up ego for a while, what we might term 'egolessness in the service of flexibility.'

If we don't have to be asserting relative ego all the time with others, we are more likely to be honest with them. We are also less likely to have to try and play games with or manipulate them for our own needs. If ego is not right on the line, we can free ourselves to behave in ways that give us great latitude. Because we are not so attached to needing rewards for our behavior, we may give more freely when we care to without nagging thoughts about others 'paying us back.' Less nagging makes for less resentment.

If relative ego-strength is low, we tend to be passive and unable to assert ourselves when necessary. We tend to shy away from making decisions and rely heavily upon others to gauge the 'right' way to behave and the 'right' way to think. In order to make the state of egolessness a positive one, we need to know that a strong relative self will pop right up to take care of us when required. *This is the same dynamic as with relative ego and absolute ego.* We can't let go into absolute self unless we know relative ego will be there when we need it.

Strong ego-imbalance   The positive aspect of a strong ego have been touched on above. But what price do we pay if we get caught here? When we get caught on this end of the pole, we can use our strong personality as a mask to hide behind.

For example, the physician or psychotherapist who puts up a professional demeanor which doesn't allow for real contact with the patient. We become fearful of showing others who we really are, instead, feeling the need to play a variety of roles. When we get lost in our roles, no longer are we able to bridge the gap between ourselves and the other.

This imbalance on the side of strong ego was what we showed graphically in Chapter 3 as the 'Big Ego.' This imbalance (actually, a compensation for our sense of insecurity) leads to spending a lot of time trying to impress others so they will see us as worthy. Then, we hope we will finally let ourselves feel worthy.

For example, 'When the promotion comes through – then they'll really know how good I am!' We need status, as shown through the accumulation of valuable material possessions. We may treat other people just as we do material possessions. For example, we might view gaining the favor of and developing a relationship with an attractive woman as the 'possession' that others will envy. Then they'll really know how desirable we are!

We tend to 'write off' the opinions of others and put them down for being less than us. We get the 'Big Head' and don't want to take instructions any longer.

I remember a personal example of this, when I was about 15. I was taking drum lessons and began to feel like I could really lose self-consciousness and just hit the drums without a lot of rehearsing. Clearly, these first steps indicating improvement were exciting.

At the end of each lesson, my drum teacher would let me just fool around on the drums, and this is when I would 'let go' and start banging. Afterwards, he would always say, 'That's great, but *don't let it go to your head!*' He didn't want me to stop paying attention to him so I wouldn't be open to learning any more.

151

Actually, he didn't have anything to worry about. Because I was just getting started at learning to be comfortable playing the drums. It wasn't until many years later that this comment would have been more appropriate, although I have to admit that I quit the lessons a few months later. But this was because I realized I didn't really want to learn to read music – I just wanted to learn to play the drums. Learning to read music (even relatively simple drum signatures) seemed demanding, constricting and dull.

Banging the drums was freeing, spontaneous and a good release of tension. I could easily get lost in the motions and the inner rhythm I would hear. I didn't realize it at the time, but what was so captivating about learning to play was this: I had found a method for going beyond relative ego. I could get lost in the sound and go beyond myself. This is one of the wonderful and attractive features about listening (in a passive way), and playing music.

Bipolarity: Yielding–Assertiveness

On the negative end, the person who is overly yielding may not stand up for what he believes, never really caring enough to take a stand. He may become mushy, and unable to pick and choose. He doesn't care about decisions and just follows what everyone else wants. This is the overly passive person who may adopt a yielding stance more out of not having learned assertive skills than *choosing* yielding as a specific behavior response.

This is an important distinction. If we are unable to make a conscious choice to yield, we should think of this position as more of a 'forced passivity.' True yielding must be a choice and this means it must not be our only perceived option.

On the positive end, knowing when and how to yield leads to flexibility, softness and an openness to others and the world around us. We are more willing to accept those things that we don't like or can't change. We give up trying to control the world and everybody in it. We obsess less about whether events are going to turn out just the way we want. This is true because our interest and our sense of what is important is shifted more toward **acceptance of what is** rather than forcing the world to change to meet our needs.

If we are assertive, we don't let others manipulate us so easily or take advantage of us. We are sure of our beliefs and our judgements, and willing to stand behind them when necessary. We have prefer-ences and aren't afraid to state them.

On the negative end of assertion, when we go too far, we become obnoxious to others, pushy and unable to give in to the desires of others. Everything should be **our** way. We try to bully the other to get what we want. We become loud and out of touch with our environ-ment, as we are only able to concentrate on ourselves. We miss the social cues that others give that would help us know that it is time to quiet down, or stop talking and make room for the other.

Bipolarity: Attachment–Non-attachment

When we are able to develop the quality of non-attachment, the positive aspects include a non-clinging, non-possessive attitude. This attitude allows us to see more clearly our predicaments as they arise without getting mentally or emotionally caught in them. What we have referred to as the *discriminating mind* is strengthened by our ability to step back and see the bigger picture.

Non-attachment means not taking ourselves, others, or the world too seriously. We take everything *sincerely* without taking it too seriously. If we are too serious, we tend to become too melodramatic and make a big deal out of everything that happens in our life.

This 'big deal' stance is not very helpful, as it usually means exaggerating the events in our life (as we discussed earlier) and distorting our own perception with the hope of feeling positive about ourselves. We think that if we make a big deal out of everything others will see how important we are and how fascinating, pitiful, exciting, unique, or   (choose one of these, or fill in your favorite if it hasn't been mentioned).

On the negative side, getting caught in the stance of non-attachment can lead to a personal numbing of our feelings and sense of total detachment from ourselves and others. We dissociate, or split off part of ourselves. We watch everything as if it were a movie script playing itself out. We don't care about anything and lose our ability to feel our own pain and the pain of others.

This isn't really what 'non-attachment' means, but much of the time this is how people misunderstand it. They don't understand that being non-attached does not make us uncaring, detached robots. And, unfortunately, there are those who have used a concept like non-attachment to justify turning off from people.

On the attachment side of the bipolarity, our over-commitment to others and a sense of needing them for our survival can lead to an over-dependence on them. It can also mean we are constantly afraid of losing them. We become overly preoccupied of disease and death. We become possessive of our loved ones and end up trying to control them or resentful of them when they don't satisfy our needs for intimacy.

On the positive side, attachment in the form of caring love can mean our willingness to commit to others and become intimately involved with them. We are able to satisfy our needs for love and affection, as well as our need to be passionately committed to some form of work or meaningful project.

It doesn't matter whether the attachment is to completing a book, building a house, fighting for democracy, or whatever. When we let ourselves care in a committed way to a belief, person, or even a material object, in its healthy form, attachment is a psychological and emotional need.

It is possible to both satisfy the need on the psychological/emotional level and also realize that we can't hold too tightly if we do not want to suffer more when something happens to end our relationship. The tighter we are holding on, the more we are going to suffer, whether we're holding on to a belief, a material possession, a loved one, or our very life.

The paradox here is this: how can one both care deeply about one's personal projects, loved ones, beliefs and values and, at the same time, be able to let go of them, or change them when necessary or desirable? Can both of these work together in some way? Is this one like love and hate in that going far enough with one brings us close to the other?

JUST FOR THE SAKE OF DOING IT

For example, I may decide to challenge myself in some way. I decide I want to sit down and learn how to use a computer. Previously, I thought computers were for 'nerds' and people who would rather relate to machines than people. I had to face my own prejudice about computers and those who used them. I had to give up my bias and admit that part of my distaste for computers was that I was afraid I might not be able to learn to use them. Once I realized and then accepted my fear of tackling something very different than I was used to, I could face my fear and decide to overcome it.

I had been dedicated (firmly attached) to writing all my articles longhand and having all the problems associated with this laborious method of writing. I had talked myself into believing this was the *only way* I could smoothly co-ordinate my thoughts with their expression on paper. When I realized the power of word processing, I saw how my limited beliefs had kept me from a simpler, more efficient and practical way of writing. I had to give up my strong beliefs in the face of overwhelming evidence that compared to word processing, all other forms of serious writing were in the Dark Ages. It was time to let 'high-tech' influence my writing style.

I wanted to face my case of computer phobia and prove to myself I could learn something mechanical and technical that had terms like 'hardware,' 'software,' 'utilities,' 'desk accessories,' 'Font/DA mover,' and 'initializing the internal hard drive disk.'

Then something I didn't expect happened – I found myself actually getting interested in Macintosh computers and wanted to quickly learn enough to operate these fascinating machines. So I sat down at a computer for the first time in my life at a local Apple dealer for about three hours just trying to understand how they work. And then I came back a week later for another two hours. And the next week, again I came in to learn for another four hours. Then I decided to buy one, even though I really didn't know much about what I was buying or how to use it.

And now I see personal computers as something that will (as they continue to get easier to operate) someday be as much a part of a typical home as a telephone, television, or video cassette recorder are today. We will rely on them for all kinds of daily tasks to make our lives easier. And they will be simple enough for almost everyone to use without feeling intimidated. Of course, to some degree all of this is already taking place. But it will happen on a much larger scale in the next ten years.

Attachment to Outcome and Expectations

When we talk about our personal projects and our attachment to their outcome (as compared to doing them for their intrinsic value), it is helpful to remember an old Zen saying:

Big Expectations:

Big Disappointments

Little Expectations:
Little Disappointments

No Expectations:
No Disappointments

Our projects need to be meaningful in and of themselves, not just as means to outside ego-gratification, fame, money, or anything else. Of course, we will tend to spend our time with those projects which will satisfy our needs. And these needs include outside recognition from others, finding personal meaning, a sense of belonging, and material security and self-integrity. All of these needs on the psychological level are valid and important to satisfy.

But we need to have the integrity and self-respect to value the projects in our lives, *just for the sake of doing them,* even when they don't satisfy these other needs. The more we can do this without outside confirmation, the more satisfaction we feel with our choices about how to spend our time. Instead of worrying that our neighbor or friends may be doing something wildly exciting when we're not, or that somewhere, someone is enjoying life more than we are, we quieten down and give up the sense of 'losing out.' This, of course, is part of the process of maturing.

156

Final Comments on Bipolarity

From the three examples given in this chapter, we have tried to illustrate how there is a positive and negative side to each pole of a bipolarity. Attachment has its positive and negative consequences, just as does non-attachment. We are always looking for integration and balance of these bipolarities. Just as we want to be able to experience that part of us which is attached, we also need to be able to let go of even the most meaningful projects in our lives. Our task is to remember that we are looking for integration and balance!

PARADOX AND SPIRITUAL EXPERIENCE

We said that a paradox is something that seems to violate the basic laws of logic but, at the same time, appears to be true anyway. Our common logic doesn't take to paradox very well. It tries to choose something that it can handle without 'tilting,' without causing (to use a computer term), a 'head crash.'

Because 'Mr Logical' doesn't think that two contradictory thoughts, behaviors, or emotions can both be true, he quickly tries to resolve the conflict by choosing one side or the other. This of course, reminds us of just what we have been discussing about the nature of owning both sides of a bipolarity.

Whether we like it or not, this world is fraught with paradox, and the sooner we understand this and accept it, the less frustration we are going to have to endure. Things just aren't as simple as we would like them to be. Solutions don't always fit into the square boxes the way we wish they would. And, of course, there are NO EASY ANSWERS, no matter how long and hard we may search for them. Right here we can paraphrase the whole title of this book: *The discriminating mind goes beyond the self-delusion that searches for easy answers. It aims for deepening insight and clarifying outlook.*

One of the areas where paradox is most evident is in the description by people of their spiritual, religious, mystical, or peak experiences. Let us look briefly at spiritual experience as an example of dealing with paradox.

To begin with, spirituality has nothing to do with the external religious programming that we are subjected to as we grow up. It emerges when we connect to our own unconscious and

157

super-conscious (Absolute self). Many now believe that we have an innate need for meaning beyond ourselves that is satisfied through spiritual experience and a sense of oneself being connected to something much larger than one's own brain and body.

Spirituality may be part of the deeper dynamics of the mind. We could say that 'true' spirituality is something that is experiential, universal and mystical. It is not something we read about but something we understand from our own experience. And what are these experiences that pose so many paradoxes for us?

A person having a mystical experience has a sense of overcoming the usual psychological and bodily fragmentation and reaching a state of complete inner unity and healing. There is also a feeling of transcending the ordinary subject–object polarity. There may be a sense of ecstatic union with other people, nature, the cosmos and God.

The positive feelings associated with mystical peak experiences cover a range from peace, tranquility, and serenity, through joy and bliss, to ecstatic rapture, and even sexually colored states described as 'cosmic orgasm.'

The normal limits of three dimensional space and time are transcended during a mystical experience. People experiencing spiritual consciousness often have a sense of timelessness and feel that they are in touch with infinity and eternity.

Descriptions of mystical consciousness are usually full of paradoxes that violate the basic laws of logic. People might talk about the experience as being contentless and yet all-containing. They might refer to a complete loss of ego and simultaneously claim a sense of identity that expanded so enormously as to encompass the entire universe. Some feel overwhelmed and absolutely insignificant and humbled by the experience, and at the same time, have a feeling of accomplishment of cosmic proportions and of being commensurate with God.

Even such fundamental distinctions as that between matter and empty space, or being and not being, can be transcended. It is not uncommon to perceive oneself and the world as existing and not existing at the same time. In line with the Buddhist scriptures, one can see the form of material objects to be essentially empty, and at the same time, understand that emptiness is pregnant with form. So, this is what we mean by the concept of paradox.

For some, an experience of unitive consciousness is associated with gaining access to profound Ultimate Knowledge about the workings of cosmic intelligence in our universe. This 'knowing' can be very strong and seem to overshadow the more mundane, everyday knowledge we carry.

For many, a feature of mystical states is their ineffability. Words just aren't able to describe in a meaningful way the power of the unitive experience. One may perceive a sense of unity with all objects in the world – people, things, animals and all other forms of life. The world may appear as a wonder-full place of radiance and beauty that has a divine intelligence that makes all things 'just right.' There may be a sense of everything being absolutely perfect, all things are in order and everything is planned, just as it should.

One of the telling consequences of a unitive experience is that often people experiencing it tend to be much more accepting of that which they are unable to change in their lives. They tend to see more positive aspects in their own personal life and in the world in general. They continue to view the world as more mystical, changing, positive, hopeful, and have more faith in the goodwill and basic workings of their daily world. They are more enthusiastic about their projects, and more able to enjoy the simple pleasures of daily life. In other words:

They are awake!

Having this kind of spiritual experience makes one more zestful in the living of daily life, less prone to boredom and negativity. And although the positive effects of the experience may slowly 'wear off' over time, there is a yearning to re-experience unity, unless the means by which it was attained (for example, extreme pain, loss, or despair) was so unpleasant that there is no desire to have to go through it again. And even then, the experience of unity is desired, but through a less drastic means.

We have used the mystical spiritual experience as a prime example of the nature of paradox and how it must be incorporated into our usual logic-tight, either/or thinking if we are to have a way to understand the contradictory aspects of our search for meaning and understanding in our lives. Once we incorporate the concept of paradox into our thinking, we no longer are so baffled by what the world presents to our logical minds.

BACK TO OUR PREDICAMENT: EXAMPLES OF PARADOX IN EVERYDAY LIFE

Besides the mystical experience, how else do we experience paradox in our daily life? Remembering what we identified in the Introduction, we could say the most significant paradox is that we strive to find meaning and satisfaction in our rather short time on this earth and yet we are forced to realize during the whole journey of our lives that the journey will end with death. A 12-year-old might say about this, 'How gross!' Ah, yes, how gross but how true!

We watch our bodies grow, and in so doing, cause us pain. We tackle the tasks of the developing mind, learn the skills necessary to survive physically, mentally and emotionally in the world, and all of this leads us to what? To having to grow older, watch ourselves lose some of the skills and sharpness we worked so hard to attain, and ultimately be forced to cope when family, friends and loved ones die around us.

Repeatedly, we are forced to be reminded that while we wish we could live forever, this body just isn't going to stay with us, no matter how much we love our lives. So the paradox is that we slowly build a solid, substantial and meaningful life over many years and yet we are forced to face that at any time, through accident, injury, or just 'bad luck,' this precious life may be taken away from us.

Psychologically, this is the meaning behind the Buddhist admonition not to become too attached to our bodies, our projects, or our relationships to others. If we know that holding on tighter will only cause more suffering when we are forced to let go, it makes sense not to make the existence of any other person, place, thing, or project the 'reason' for our existence.

160

When we understand the paradoxical nature of our lives, it becomes possible to form bonds of attachment and yet be able to let go when circumstances force us to let go. This is what we mean when we say we can love in a non-attached way.

The secret is this: *The more we are ready to let go and realize that we can survive without the other, the more able we are to give ourselves deeper to our loved one.* If I know my world will not end if I get close to you and you leave me, I can then give myself fully to you.

Far too often, I see in the consulting room the results of people who are afraid to get too close to each other out of fear of being abandoned. I watch how powerful this fear of abandonment can be in shaping one's commitments to others and one's daily fear of involvement with others in life. I watch people struggle with their needs for sex, love and affection with each other and yet they desire to maintain a distance from each other so that they don't become enveloped in the other.

How do we deal with the paradox of our very nature? How do we understand the seeming contradiction that we are able to be, on the one hand, so cruel, insensitive, hideous and brutal to each other and yet, on the other hand, so altruistic, loving, compassionate and needy of each other? How does this make logical sense unless we invoke the concept of paradox?

When we are young, we are so vulnerable, so needy, so fresh and pure to the world. And as we grow, we learn 'the ways of the world,' one of which is: 'It is hell out there. Others will hurt you, take advantage of you for their own gain, and you must put on your psychological armor if you are to survive!' How do we get our needs met if we have to question at every turn of the road who can be trusted and who's going to stab us in the psychological and physical back?

How can we expect people to feel safe when they know that at any time, they can be physically assaulted in public? How can we teach people to minimize the use of psychological defenses when their actual experience is that they can't survive without a full armamentarium of defensive mechanisms?

How do we understand the nature of good and evil in our world? Without the concepts of polarity and paradox, many realities of our lives don't make much sense. But when we understand these concepts and, equally importantly, how they actually make themselves felt in our lives, we are more able to comprehend why things can be so illogical and contradictory but exist side by side. We are able to tolerate and even appreciate the 'both/and' mentality instead of fitting everything into logic-tight, 'either/or' boxes.

The paradox that the stronger we are able to build our sense of relative ego-strength, the more we are able to 'give ourselves away' is baffling for many with little psychology background. But the whole idea of Jung's (borrowed from Hinduism and Eastern thinking) that the second half of life is the time for exploring our spirituality and the deeper meaning of our life, is based on this.

I say this because Jung was able to see that without a good, strong relative ego that had learned all the skills to support itself emotionally and physically in the world, one was not ready to pay attention to spiritual needs. If we are overly concerned with work, family, 'making it' and satisfying ego-level needs for recognition, status, belongingness, etc., we are not going to be very interested (or have time for) spiritual concerns. This is why many writers believe that spiritual concerns become a more focused issue for us *after* we have taken care of these other needs. And, for many, this doesn't happen until about mid-life, if it happens at all.

Of course, we are not saying that anyone who has not reached mid-life cannot become interested in spiritual values or make spiritual concerns an important part of their life. When we pay attention to the ultimate life and death issues of our lives, we are, in effect, dealing with existential and spiritual issues.

So, when a 6-year-old asks the meaning of God, or death, he is beginning to address spiritual issues in an elementary fashion. In other words, the answers we give to these questions can only be as sophisticated as the child is capable of comprehending. But the point is this: it is not the same to ask these questions before we have discovered ourselves on the relative-ego level. We need to have a sense of **who we are** as relative egos, establishing ourselves in the world and tackling all the ego-level issues before these questions seem to take us to a deeper level.

If I have lived half my life and learned to take care of myself in the world, form relationships with others, and learn the 'ways of the white man' well enough to find my niche in the social and work worlds, I will have tasted the success of ego-level gratifications, and be more ready to see what else is possible in going beyond the good feelings that relationships, status, material possessions and security have to offer.

This is why the popular 'mid-life' crisis has found its way into our vocabulary and thinking. The mid-life crisis is life's way of reminding us that we won't live forever, and that we had better make damn sure we are spending our short lives doing what will be most gratifying and meaningful for us. No matter whether that be saving the whales, delivering (or having) babies, building tall buildings, playing the violin, selling insurance, making love, running marathons, travelling the world, surfing big waves, holding political office, becoming enlightened or   (fill in your single most meaningful interest).

Now let us leave this and move on to see what the witness is, and how this witness consciousness may be created, nurtured and used to add meaning and a sense of balance and perspective in our lives.

=== 9 ===

CREATING AND NURTURING
THE WITNESS

We have examined, in Chapter 3, both the relative and absolute selves and said that in order to help develop the *discriminating mind*, we need to be able to hear all of the voices inside and be able to see various shadings, or gradations of choice, rather than just all-or-nothing choices. We said that when we get caught in all-or-nothing thinking, one result may be the perfectionistic mentality wherein we lose our self-worth when we judge ourselves short of perfect, as we are most certainly bound to do.

Now, let's look at that part of us that is not caught up in the whirlwind of chattering inner voices; a part that makes it possible for us to connect to something larger than ourselves; a part that helps us transcend the petty relative-ego battles we fight with ourselves and others that only bring us more suffering. And this part, in line with the literature focusing on the Eastern consciousness disciplines, we call the 'witness.'

We can think of the witness as that spacious place inside that is able to dispassionately allow thoughts and feelings to come and go without the need to identify with them but is simply *aware* of their coming and going. It is 'pure' in the sense that it is not there to take sides or help us win arguments. It is there as a natural part of us that feels like part of our essence when we think about our sense of continuity from day to day.

The witness is part of our mind (or general consciousness) but ought not to be identified solely with our physical brain. Although it may feel like the witness is part of our physical brain (because that is where we usually identify the seat of our consciousness), there is reason to believe, according to researchers, that consciousness itself is not something confined to the physical brain. Very briefly, let's see why this is true.

If we think of a general consciousness, or life energy, which transcends individual physical brains but connects us all, the witness can be said to be part of that 'independent' mental connector that binds all human minds. Some would refer to this connection as 'spiritual,' since it is not a material reality that is connecting us. We could also call it a 'mental connector' if we use 'mental' to mean beyond our own individual brain but having to do with a larger 'mind.'

But others (I'm thinking of some orthodox brain researchers) would consider all human consciousness to be a property of the physical brain. They would tell us that any sense of connection we might experience is only a result of our emotional make-up, itself just another aspect of brain centers which control emotion. For them, our consciousness is reduced to the workings of our brain and nervous system.

The relationship between the brain and the larger 'mind' is a complicated one which continues to be the focus of research in a number of different disciplines, including neuro-psychiatry, biology, transpersonal psychology, cognitive psychology, philosophy and neuro-anatomy. But, for our purposes, it is only important to keep in mind (and in brain, too!) that the witness is something that is shared by all of us, even though each of us individually must develop this aspect of consciousness. Some have simply learned how to 'create' and nurture this witness state of awareness more fully than others.

The witness is 'independent' in the sense of not being tied to any particular person. And it is a 'mental connector' in the sense of being something that we all share in common, no matter how developed it may be in any one individual. If this is true, then it is no surprise that people experience such things as mental telepathy, precognition, and other psychic phenomena.

Why? Because if we share an independent connector such as the witness, we may also share other mental and psychic aspects of consciousness that connect us in various ways to each other. So, mental telepathy doesn't really seem all that startling, once we accept that, indeed, there are mental and psychic forces that are beyond our own encapsulated brains which bind us together.

The witness is inherent in the nature of human consciousness itself, and therefore, as our consciousness changes, our relationship to the witness changes with it. We can say 'our' witness since from inside it feels like we are doing the witnessing. But if we talk about it as 'our' witness, we need to remember that this witness consciousness is beyond any individual, personal consciousness.

To put it simply, then: The witness develops as our general state of consciousness develops. And, conversely, our general level of consciousness expands as the witness is more predominant. So, we are saying that these two aspects work together.

If we are continually waking up to new realizations about ourselves and our world (in other words, continuing to grow), we will also be continually sharpening our ability to use the witness to gain some distance and clarity to the ongoing events of our life.

Why do I say this? Because, to grow in consciousness is to grow in the ability to use this expanded consciousness to our own means. We become more in control with the *discriminating mind* and less the victim of strong impulses over which we feel little or no control. And it is the witness which helps us pull back and *discriminate* before we commit ourselves to action. So this basically impersonal aspect of consciousness may be used in a very personal, practical manner.

The more highly developed the witness, the more potent will be our discriminating mind; because we must be able to see without the usual clamor of our strong psychological, emotional and physical needs getting in the way to perceive clearly. The witness is our 'man for the job.'

To the extent that our thoughts (and especially our 'I' thoughts) establish and fortify our sense of relative self, our sense of daily continuity of self will be maintained by thought. But, 'behind' this sense of continuity established by our ongoing thought, we also have a sense of continuity through our experience of the witness.

THE CONTINUITY OF THE WITNESS

From this place, when we think of how we are the same over time, beyond our same old thoughts, feelings, sensations and attitudes we recognize a certain consistent feeling of knowing ourselves. *It is the witness that is this consistent, continuous part that is stable within us over time.* It is the witness that is able to show us that we are more than

167

just what we say, do, or think. And it is the witness that can help extract us from the common suffering that otherwise makes up far too much of our waking awareness.

Remember, at the earlier stages of growth, when we are focusing on relative-ego development, we want to identify with all our thoughts as *ours*, and all our feelings as *ours*. This is what we aimed at in the last chapter in looking at bipolarities.

As well, all the boundary disturbances we examined in Chapter 3 relate to our unwillingness to identify with and take responsibility for our own thoughts and feelings. So, first we learn to be responsible for ourselves rather than stay with the childhood mentality of blaming the world. And we do this by re-owning those negative aspects (see Chapter 8) of ourselves we would rather project on to others and the 'cold, cruel world.'

Once we have developed a relative ego which can carry us through the world relatively unscathed from the ongoing bombardment of assaults to the ego, it is then time to look for what else is possible. And that 'what else' is spiritual development focusing on the Absolute self. Many thinkers in this area now believe that this looking for 'something more' is actually a deeply experienced need that is part of our fundamental nature.

They maintain that once we take care of our basic biological and security needs, and then satisfy our psychological needs (respect from others and for oneself, meaningful work, love relationship, friends, etc.), we are then confronted by the need to find a Higher Meaning that tends to push us in the direction of a spiritual search.

And the search is undertaken because we get to a point of realizing that what the material world has to offer (no matter how high a level of material comfort we may experience) just doesn't satisfy a deeper yearning for connecting to something beyond ourselves. It doesn't satisfy our desire to understand our place in the world and reconcile the reality of our haphazard life in a vast, unfathomable universe.

One of the main contributions of the Eastern consciousness disciplines (the philosophies and methods that have been cultivated for thousands of years), is this: *Growth does not stop with the fully developed relative ego.* And that 'what else' is possible beyond ego development is spiritual development that can offer us meaning beyond the relative-ego concerns that tend to make up the brunt of our waking hours.

In the East, spiritual searching and practices are built into the fabric of the culture. We should remember, however, that most of us prefer to stay at this development of relative-ego stage for our whole lives. In other words, we never get enough 'feeding' of ego to want to move on to spiritual concerns.

Or, if we try to move on to spiritual concerns, our ego keeps getting tangled in using spiritual seeking to further fortify itself. This is the same as saying that our ego, in a sense, 'forbids' us from going beyond it until it is sure it will not be left behind.

So, while we work to own and identify with all the parts of ourselves, including those that we don't like, when we work in strengthening the ego-self, we must go back and *dis-identify* with these thoughts and feelings when we wish to work on strengthening our transcendent self, or witness. And from the witness, it is possible to ultimately achieve glimpses of unity consciousness, in which we no longer experience ourselves as a subject looking at an object of our own consciousness.

This 'unity consciousness' is none other than what, in Chapter 3, we labeled Absolute consciousness. We said that we are melting into this Absolute consciousness repeatedly but that we don't actually experience it because it is happening too quickly. We are unable to let go of our relative level ego to actually experience this Absolute state long enough to actually realize we are in it. This is what we mean by 'glimpsing' unity consciousness, before relative ego pulls us back to 'reality' again.

So, instead, we seek 'mystical' experiences, 'spiritual' experiences, states of transcendence and various psychic experiences as if all of this is originally outside of us. And yet, it isn't. *We really don't have to seek these experiences outside of ourselves.* We will return to this topic in a later chapter. But let's just define the issue for a moment before moving on.

One of the puzzling facts of human behavior is this: even when people satisfy their basic security needs (food, shelter, safety) and their psychological needs for self-esteem, recognition, respect and a sense of one's own uniqueness, they still refuse to seek higher spiritual needs and even refuse to believe that there *are* spiritual needs. Instead they prefer to become 'experts' on the material level, hoping that with enough accumulation they will finally be satisfied they are 'really something.' In other words, they never get quite enough to become satiated. Ego's 'stomach' never gets filled.

If they did get enough, they might realize that there is still a nagging dissatisfaction with the nature of material life that might propel them to something beyond the material accumulation of 'stuff,' to something bigger than themselves. And this would be the experience of their own God-likeness – not someone in a church or temple *telling* them about God and not worshipping a God that is separate from themselves, but the *real, undeniable personal experience of knowing their own perfection*.

Who would need to run around feeling like a chicken with its head cut off, striving to be a perfectionist in the world, if we knew that we really were perfect **just as we are**? We still do the best that we can but our sense of deep self-acceptance would not be on the line. What a relief! Can we do it?

By working with creating a stronger witness and learning how to nurture it, we are able to get one step away from melting into the Absolute without our having to fear not returning to relative-ego self. We are able to gain a clarity in our lives that is able to help us support our discriminating mind when we need to, and when we don't, let go and just watch our inner processes.

So the witness helps teach us that the power of discriminating is *inside* and that basic self-acceptance for who we are is not something that has to be put in the hands of the world outside us, no matter how strong a pull that world may exert, and no matter how badly we yearn for that full and loving acceptance that we may not have received from our parents.

'CREATING' THE OBSERVING WITNESS

How can we 'create' something like the witness that has been with us from the very start? We can't! So, when we talk about 'creating' the witness, we mean it in this sense: *Until we fully wake up to the existence of the witness, it is as if it has never really been created.*

The paradox and irony is that we are having to discover a part of ourselves that has always been *right here with us*, always made us feel 'right at home' with ourselves and yet, at the same time, was not being utilized anywhere near what is possible.

And what is possible? What is possible is to be able to watch all our thoughts, feelings, mood and attitude changes, physical pleasures and pains, and do it with a sense of non-attached observation. What we are forced to create is not the existence of the witness itself but *our conscious awareness of it*. With self reflective practices such as meditation and contemplation, we are able to strengthen our awareness of our witnessing part, and begin to utilize this detached observer to our own benefit.

Of course, part of the trick is to be able to use the discriminating mind to decipher exactly *when* we need to watch with non-attached observation and when we need to identify with our thoughts and feelings and move into action. It is a great skill to be able to move into action and still be able to witness one's movement. We can feel angry and also watch ourselves feeling angry. Both the emotion and the watching of emotion can exist together.

And the watching of emotion, like anger, means that the witness can then tell the *discriminating mind* to alter the emotion, if warranted. Obviously, this is going to give us a sense of increased self-control. In this way, the witness influences the *discriminating mind*, which in turn, shapes action that may be taken.

It is a great skill to learn to be very expressive with a strong emotion, like fear, anger, or joy and, at the same time, be witnessing one's emotional expression. It calls for a splitting of attention that is of a whole different type than the normal scattered awareness that we are trained to think of as 'everyday consciousness.' It is because our everyday consciousness is so scattered that we use the metaphor of being in a 'trance.'

But there is something more here. When we truly wake up to the vibrancy of the present and 'see' (perceive) what we simply could not see before, this idea of trance becomes more than a metaphor. We understand the meaning of: 'we don't see what we don't see.' And then, when we wake up, seeing what we didn't see gives us the sense that we were in a trance. And, of course, we will actually run through this phenomenon over and over again, each time 'waking up' to what seems now obvious but could not be seen before.

'WAKING UP' ONE STEP AT A TIME

Of course, this is what we are talking about when we say to ourselves, 'Why didn't I see that? How could I have been so blind?' And this is the process of our step-by-step awakening. We are continually realizing that our minds, our relations to other people, and the outer material world are presenting us with new information that makes us feel stupid, asleep, in a trance and, even, at times, helpless.

Many of the people I see in psychotherapy are easily overwhelmed by the feeling of how much they don't see. They are in a process of consciously trying to wake up to themselves. And each time they gain a new insight or make a new realization, they begin to sense how much they haven't let themselves see. It gives them both a sense of interest and a sense of the magnitude of the job of self-discovery and growth.

And as we look from one step higher up on the awareness ladder, it can be easy to judge oneself negatively. 'Why can't I wake up at a faster pace?' 'Why can't psychotherapy go faster?' 'Why do I keep repeating the same behaviors again and again? I must be in a trance!' And we make these mini-realizations over and over again, calling them 'insights,' 'creative thoughts,' or 'mental breakthroughs.' They push us forward but also shows us our own present limitations, that we have to be patient with ourselves and remember that growth, for the most part, comes one step at a time, and not as sudden and total 'enlightenment.'

We can only wake up as fast as we are ready to wake up – and no faster! This means that if part of us is not ready, for whatever reason, to make a certain realization, we simply will not be able to make it. And all the self-berating and wishful thinking in the world will not make us awaken any faster. This is what we mean by 'honoring' all the psychological and emotional defenses we have available which protect us from risking 'waking up' if the threat is too great.

When we don't honor our defenses and instead try to push past them prematurely by powerful techniques, gimmicks and tools used to assault and weaken them, many times the result is psychological difficulties. Defenses are there for a purpose! They are not just psychological 'garbage' that interfere with our achieving higher states of consciousness. Too often, by many lay people who aren't psychologically sophisticated (and helping professionals who should know better), this is not understood clearly or taken seriously.

What is the purpose of identifying more with our witness and less with the passing show of thoughts, feelings, mood states and psycho-social dramas that make up our daily lives? The purpose is to be able to see that we are MORE than just the passing show. And if we are so totally caught up in our thoughts, feelings, mood states and actions, we will be unable to make this realization.

Or, to say this another way: until we step back and observe our own mental and physical processes we will be stuck in the mental–emotional content and 'fall asleep' to the larger reality. And what is this larger reality?

The larger reality is that we are wanting to be one with God, however we personally make sense of this concept. If we think of God as that which is closer to us than even our innermost self, we can use the God-concept in this way. We want to merge with a force which is larger than us and which gives us a sense of spiritual meaning in our lives, beyond the healthy psychological and emotional needs which we strive to satisfy.

Or, we can think of wanting to join with some strong spiritual force of current that creates and maintains life and its direction. We can look at it as something we contact inside of ourselves or something we connect with outside of ourselves through inner experience.

Either way, what we are wanting is to find the peace and sense of comfort with ourselves in the world that makes us really feel as though we are 'home,' able to settle gracefully into the present, without having to fight time, always regretful of the past or anticipating the future.

We want to experience a sense of our connectedness to others, and connectedness to the natural world of which we are embedded. And we want most of all to experience a connectedness to something larger than ourselves. We want, to put it simply, nothing less than to actualize our own intuited but not-yet-manifested God-nature. We know it's in there somewhere but just aren't sure how to find it.

We want to feel 'naturally alive' and able to be spontaneous and free in our everyday behavior. And yet, because of our self-consciousness, many times we get in our own way by not being able to refrain from asserting relative ego. **We try to play God instead of melting into God.**

We don't understand that the object is *not* to take relative self and make it a God but to *forget about* relative self once we no longer need to worry about it being annihilated. It will always pop right back up and assert itself when needed. This is what we are not really trusting of and what we are talking about when we say relative self fears

173

being 'annihilated.' But why does it seem so difficult to realize our inherent nature? How 'natural' can it be if so few people actually ever claim to experience it? Good question!

An Example of the Witness in Action

Deena initially felt totally unable to stop herself from getting angry when her boyfriend would look at her in a certain way. She felt he was disapproving of her and letting her know by screwing up his mouth. Each time he would give her this look, she found herself immediately reacting with abusive remarks, and at times, even wanting to come up and physically push him. She knew her reaction was all out of proportion to his look, but just couldn't control herself, nor did she know where it was coming from.

Upon analysis, we discovered that this same screwed up look had long been part of her relationships with other men. It happens that her father had displayed a similar look of disdain when she was young as his way to tell her he was displeased with her. As well, a previous boyfriend had also used the same screwed up look to mean the same disapproval. Once Deena was able to connect the meaning of this gesture to a general message of critical judgement by the men in her life, she was able to see why her reaction was out of proportion to the gesture itself.

But the real work was for her to learn to dis-identify herself from the gesture and learn to use her witness awareness to watch the gesture without her habitual reaction. First, I asked her to depersonalize the gesture by repeating to herself, when seeing this gesture by her boyfriend or anyone else, 'I am noticing a screwed up mouth that has nothing to do with me.' She was to repeat this to herself at least three times every time she saw a mouth movement by anyone even close to the gesture that disturbed her. I wanted her attention to be on simply noticing the mouth movements and not on giving the movement any meaning.

As she continued to carry out this exercise, Deena noticed a growing ability to simply watch her boyfriend screw up his mouth without having to react outwardly by saying anything. I then had her change the message she was to repeat to herself to: 'Mouths move in all kinds of interesting ways and none of them have anything to do with me.' She was now feeling a sense of detached observation and within two months, was no longer aware of any negative reaction associated to seeing a screwed up mouth, including her boyfriend's. As she continued to detach herself from any sense of personal reference to this gesture, I had her cut down the self-statement to, 'moving, moving' each time she noticed something resembling the original gesture. This is a simple but powerful example of how learning and practicing non-attached witnessing can help us un-learn previous habitual reactions. Little by little, we become more in control *from the inside out*, and less ractive to others from the outside in.

Experiment: Further creating the witness

Go to an event where people are doing something that easily and naturally grabs your attention and holds it. It doesn't matter what the event may be, as long as you don't need to worry about being a participant. You want to develop the ability to just see what is in front of you, being aware of looking. (We are trying to work here with first developing a sense of non-attached observation of outer events, before we try to witness inner events. It is easier for most to turn their eyes outward rather than inward.)

When listening to sounds, you want to be aware of using your ears. Or when smelling or touching, we need to be aware of it just as it is happening. In simply noticing what is happening while it is happening, we train ourselves to be more and more able to stay with that impartial ongoing awareness inside us that transcends any personal concern about what happens to us. It just watches the movie.

As an anchor in doing this experiment, while you are looking, silently make the mental note, 'looking, looking.' Be as non-attached to what you are looking at as possible. By 'non-attached' we mean, having no personal interest or investment in what you are looking at. The idea is *not* to become interested, but just to be aware of using the eyes or whatever other sense is being used.

So, when you hear sounds, and your attention is drawn to them and away from primarily looking, notice the moment you make the switch. This kind of watching of our senses can feel microscopic as compared to the usual lack of attention we pay to what sense is being utilized.

Notice any inner reaction which may come up as you simply

observe outward behavior of other people. Don't actively engage in interaction with others – simply be as unselfconscious as possible. We mean this as literally as possible. We want to be able to observe others with a sense of total unself-consciousness, that our own relative ego is not getting in the way. It doesn't need anything and therefore doesn't need to assert itself for any reason.

As you watch this public scene, notice if you tend to reflect any of what is seen and heard back to yourself, wanting to somehow put yourself in the scene, wanting to be 'part of the equation.'

The witness may flourish when the relative self is not having to assert itself but can instead hang back and allow the witness to kick in without being threatened. We are, to put it in the terms of the California lifestyle, looking to create a 'laid-back' relative self. Don't mistake this. We don't mean passive when we say 'laid-back.' We mean laid-back in the sense of being able to give up control, to get out of the way when its presence isn't necessary to hold up the 'coat-hanger' of the self.

Now, this does not mean we don't act in assertive ways and do all the things a good, strong relative-ego self ought to do, like taking stands when important issues come up, feeling pride in accomplishments and enjoying one's uniqueness. We still respond in all kinds of other expected and appropriate ways that relative selves behave.

But, because the healthy relative self is sufficiently 'fed' (feels good about itself), it also can simply pull back and watch the passing show. It can make more space available for the witness to take over and not need to worry about relative-self preservation.

THE WITNESS AND AWARENESS

If we think of the limitations of our common, everyday consciousness as similar to being in a trance (and therefore basically unconscious activity), and 'pure awareness' as consciousness having no object at all, then *witnessing is what happens when we become aware of our usual unconscious behavior*. In this way we can think of witnessing as a method or technique toward this state of 'pure awareness' or, what we termed 'Absolute self.'

When we say our daily behavior is basically 'unconscious' (and therefore, like being in a trance) we mean this in the sense that we

176

experience large numbers of episodes of 'spacing out,' losing our train of thought, drifting off in reverie, 'black holes' of interesting thought that wrench us away from our immediate environment, and other lapses of thought, speech and action that make us feel out of control of not only our minds, but our bodies as well.

We trip, stumble, fall, lose our balance and continually attend to the needs of the body in an ongoing fashion, yet so much of the more subtle picking, scratching, moving, bending, twisting, stretching, etc., is not really fully conscious. The body, in this sense, does indeed have a mind of its own!

Let us use our discriminating mind (and, perhaps, personal experience) to make a further distinction. We can think of *awareness* as distinct from consciousness. Consciousness is a quality of our mind, but *not our whole mind*. We can be both conscious and unconscious but when we transcend our minds there is no unconsciousness and no corresponding consciousness. There is just awareness itself. We are trying here to find a way to describe something that is complete in itself, with no subject viewing an object of any sort.

Awareness means the total mind has become aware. The nature of this 'pure awareness' mind is, as you can see, rather paradoxical. How can we know we are experiencing something called 'pure awareness' or Absolute mind if it takes a subject to know this Absolute mind as object? Does it make sense to talk about 'experiencing' Absolute mind if the very nature of this mind is that there is no object? If it 'takes one to know one,' who is doing the viewing?

In other words, how can we experience awareness or Absolute mind without making it an object? Is a mystical state of 'oneness with the world' the same as Absolute mind? We will return to these questions in a later chapter. But let us at least admit to the logical corner into which we have worked ourselves. We can see there is a paradox here.

Let us think of a 'paradox' as something that appears to be contradictory or defy common sense but nevertheless is perhaps true. Both this *and* that can be true, even though they may, on the surface seem contradictory. This is what we mean by 'paradox.' And it seems to require a willingness to acquire and be comfortable with paradoxical thinking to grasp the larger picture of Absolute self. We have to be able to go beyond the either/or mentality.

Witnessing is a *state*, and consciousness is the means toward witnessing. When we talk about practicing witnessing, remember that we are really talking about practicing working with our own attention. In working with our own attention, increased ability at witnessing is a by-product of this work.

We may nurture the witness by learning to dis-identify with all of those identifications which help fortify our relative ego. In simple words, we need to let go of what we identify with and *identify with the identifier*.

As we develop the relative-ego self, our goal was to identify with what is ours: our thoughts, feelings, moods, attitudes, possessions, body parts and everything else that makes up our sense of relative-self identity.

Now, we are interested in going beyond those identifications. We need to be very clear about this: we do not slip out of our personal identifications as if we were slipping out of a bathrobe. Nor are we disowning everything we have worked so hard to acquire in the firming of relative ego. But we are going beyond these feelings of 'this is me' to a larger identification that transcends our everyday thinking. We keep everything we have *and* we let go of it for a while.

It's like leaving your home when you go away on a vacation. The best vacation is had when you can let go of your home mentally, so you can be totally present on your vacation. It takes away from the immediacy of the experience to keep comparing where you are to home. We don't sacrifice our home when we go away, we don't sell it, or destroy it just because we want to go away on vacation. And when we are totally present-centered in Switzerland, it is like 'home' doesn't really exist, even though we know when we think about it that we do have a home 'back there.'

In the same way, we temporarily let go of our personal identifications to experience something of our nature beyond them. The spacious inner peace and contentment that is possible when we are able to transcend our identification (and therefore, our problems) with who we think we are and what we think we believe in.

And it is the discriminating mind that helps us know when it is safe to let go and relax into Absolute self. It is the discriminating mind that hasn't forgotten (and you can bet won't *ever* forget) that relative self is back there waiting when we are ready to return to it, just like 'home' is back there when it's time to return from Switzerland.

Experiment: Strengthening the witness

Since we need to dis-identify with our usual relative-ego identifications of who we are, the process is an 'undoing' of our building of the normal sense of self. So, one way to experiment with this is to repeat the following statements (Wilber, 1979) to yourself slowly and with total concentration, so as to allow yourself a chance to experience what they really mean.

Say the following out loud and listen to yourself as you do:

(1) I *have* thoughts but I am *more* than my thoughts. I can know and intuit my thoughts, and what can be known is not the true Knower. Thoughts may come and go but they do not affect my inward I. I have thoughts but I am *not* my thoughts.

(2) I have a body but I am *more* than my body.

(3) I can see and feel my body but what can be seen and felt is not the true Seer.

(4) My body may be tired or excited, sick or healthy, heavy or light, hot or cold, but that has nothing to do with my inward I. I have a body, but I am *not* my body.

(5) I have desires but I am more than my desires. I can know my desires and what can be known is not the true Knower.

(6) Desires come and go, floating through my awareness like bubbles in the air, but they do not affect my inward I. I have desires but I am *not* my desires.

(7) I have emotions but I am not my emotions. I can feel and sense my emotions, but what can be felt and sensed is not the true Feeler. Emotions pass through me, but they do not affect my inward I. I have emotions but I am *not* emotions.

When you complete saying the above aloud, begin again and this time say each statement silently. As you do, again try to feel the truth of your words. Stay with each statement until you can sense the meaning of your words. Then move to the next statement. Continue deliberately and with full attention until finished.

This experiment helps us experience how all our senses can be operating but we are not the 'doer' of what is being done. The witness simply notices what is happening just as it is happening, without interference, judging, or identifying with what is occurring.

179

We make the realization that all of these senses can take place without there having to be a relative sense of self that is responsible for the listening, touching, hearing, feeling, or tasting.

This is a rough one for most of us. We have real trouble initially wanting to accept that our senses can be operating perfectly well without our having to think, 'It is I who is thinking, hearing, tasting, looking.'

We don't want to give up 'ownership' of these senses, even when we experience the feeling of just bare looking without the 'I' doing the looking. It is more like, 'Looking is happening,'; or, 'tasting, tasting, chewing, chewing' rather than 'I am tasting, I am chewing.' Initially we think the relative ego's 'I' needs to be in control of the show. But we begin to understand that all of our usual lively processes of life can take place without needing to think 'I am doing it.'

Right now, who is doing this writing? 'Writing is taking place' versus 'I am now writing.' The practice is simply to take the 'I' out of the picture as the one who is making everything happen. Because we want to get a sense of getting out of our own way, to see what it's like to watch our own process unfolding without having to believe 'we' are constantly making it happen.

This is probably the most difficult concept presented in this book, in that we simply aren't used to (and naturally resist) thinking of not being the one to make everything occur. *And this can only be done with any grace and security if we feel safe that relative ego will not get lost in the process.* The sharpening of our ability to stay with the non-attached witness can help us control ourselves from quickly and prematurely jumping to respond to stimulation in the world. We become more able to pause, notice what is happening and not feel so compelled to jump in and have to respond in some way. We go beyond the knee-jerk reaction.

In this way, witnessing is a tool. The object is not to use the witness as a way to dissociate ourselves from our own actions but simply to understand that we do not need to think of all our actions as being 'I' motivated. When we dissociate, we act as if we are split off from our own actions. This is not witnessing! Always, the observing ego is able to realize that although it is witnessing without attachment to the action, it may also choose at any time to 're-own' its thoughts and actions. Witnessing is a state we enter into voluntarily, whereas the negative use of witnessing is splitting off from ourselves and our environment in a way that seems out of our control. This is a very significant difference.

When we are able to fully attend to the environment and then choose how we will respond (the part played by the discriminating mind), we feel more in control when we finally take action. In this way, we are using the witness to help us make real decisions in the real world. So, it is not true that creating and nurturing the witness will lead us to retreat from full participation in the world, or to become 'zombies' who can't respond humanly to other people.

To participate in the world with the full use of the discriminating mind is to participate in the world consciously and with intention. It is to be fully present and involved but where one's involvement is tempered by the perspective of 'who is doing what to whom.' We are able to realize that there is more taking place than just a subject 'doing' to his world and that the 'doer' of our action is not who or what we may think it is.

IS WITNESSING AT ALL LIKE CHANNELING?

We can compare the process of witnessing to the currently popular interest in 'channeling.' Channeling is the ability of a person to focus spiritual energy in the form of the words of a long-dead spirit entity, or more generally, to allow spiritual energy to be focused through one's physical body for some purpose, for example, laying on of hands, or other physical transmissions between two people. In the currently popular form of channeling utilizing long-dead spirit personalities, the channel supposedly opens himself to receive the words of the spirit entity, who presumably has chosen a specific person to 'channel' his message to the living.

There are all kinds of serious questions about the validity of people who claim to be channels, and there is at least some reason (and evidence) to believe that much of what is presented as 'channeled' material is coming from the vivid imagination, intuitive abilities and skillful acting of those doing the channeling. This, in fact, is what has been claimed by some of those working very close to the channels who later become disenchanted. Channeling may be simply the use of the intuitive mind, information that comes from a part of the medium they are normally unaware of or unable to access without the use of the dead spirit's personality.

There are some impressive performances staged by popular channels, and the theatrical performances of channels have captured much recent interest from those hungry for wisdom from the spirit world. While some channels, while in their channeling state, seem to be able to speak in languages that they otherwise claim not to know, there are too many questions that have not been satisfactorily answered from the standpoint of validity for me to take the channeling phenomenon seriously. Too often, these channels simply are not convincing in their affectation of the spirit's manner. And although the messages that they bring us from the 'spirit world' may contain useful information, this does not in any way guarantee us that, in fact, this good information is coming from a dead spirit.

But my bringing up the process of channeling is not for me to share my own opinions or to judge the validity of channeling itself, even though I would suggest that people approach this craze with full use of their discriminating mind. Rather, the purpose is for us to compare witnessing to channeling to help us see more clearly the nature of witnessing. The 'spirit entity' which is being channeled by the human channel purportedly needs to temporarily inhabit a body for its message to be delivered. This is why the body of the channel changes dramatically when the spirit entity is coming through.

In the sense that the channel feels out of control to manage the powerful spiritual force which they claim to experience, the independence of the channeled energy form is similar to the witness being independent of the relative ego. The channel is not in control as to when the energy comes or goes, nor (they claim) to even what form of language or style of expression flows through them. Similarly, the person witnessing is not very able to control how long he will be able to stay with the witness rather than concede to relative ego's wish to be given some good old relative-ego attention (in other words, jump back into identifying with 'I' as the doer).

There is a dynamic tension working here. Ego wants to pull us out of the witnessing state, once again fearful that we won't want to 'come back,' just as ego fears when we lose ourselves (literally) for a moment as we melt into the Absolute self.

In this way, we could say that there is a freedom to the channeled spirit form that is the same with the human mental–spiritual energy that makes up the witness. Remember, while the witness feels very personal (at least relative ego thinks so), it really is common to all of us, making up the larger reality that connects us in ways we are only slowly coming to understand. For those who 'believe' in channeling, the energy force that is being channeled by various humans would be seen as the same common 'channel' or 'wavelength' which carries the witness energy.

As I write, I wonder how clear this sounds to you, and how clear it is possible to make something that is not easy to put into words. But remember, that is one of the tasks of the discriminating mind – to make the necessary distinctions which help us understand the difference between 'apples and oranges.'

When we don't attempt to 'put it into words' and to make the necessary distinctions and discriminations, we end up with mushy thinking, and half-baked decisions based on inadequate information. Or, as one of my former graduate school professors used to say, 'We are jumping to unwarranted conclusions based on unsubstantiated assumptions and inadequate data.'

The obvious difference between the process of channeling and the process of witnessing is that we don't need an outside spirit entity to create and nurture our 'personal' witness. Each of us, individually, *is* the 'channel' for the witness awareness to come through. If it is true, as we have said, that being in the witnessing state of consciousness is 'halfway to paradise' (halfway to unity consciousness), then why should we bother with the 'middle man' of a spirit entity or channel other than ourselves?

The 'wisdom' or information which a spirit entity can teach us, as brought to us through a medium or channel, is information that we are capable of getting for ourselves. This is what many refuse to want to believe. They want it coming through somebody else who is more impressive, dramatic and authoritarian. They want to believe that channels are the special people designated to bring forth the wisdom of the spirit entities. And, of course, the channels themselves are quite willing to have us believe this, too.

This doesn't mean we're all able (even if we desire) to be 'possessed' by the grace of a spirit entity, although there is really no logical or psychological reason why this couldn't be possible, if indeed, this phenomena is able to be convincingly demonstrated under rigorous examination. I mean, in the realm of the dead spirits, what's the difference who comes through whom – just so the message gets delivered?

But it *does* mean that we need to realize how often and in so many ways we 'squander the authorship' of our own lives. We seem to claim to want to have 'higher knowledge' to shape our own lives and yet don't really act as if we have as much right to gain knowledge as the impressive channel up on the stage.

Actually, we have the same witness consciousness that they do. And we have the same opportunity to connect to something beyond ourselves that they do, whatever form it may take. Spirit entities are a drag compared to the experience of the lightness and tranquility of our own being.

IF THE WITNESS COULD SPEAK . . .

If the witness could speak what would it say? The witness watches, dispassionately, all that takes place. The witness is beyond the internal mental chatter, so we don't hear a voice from the witness. But let's, just for the sake of instruction, give the witness a voice . . .

Author Could you tell us why you are so important to our growth? So many really don't seem to value your contribution.

Witness Yes, you're right, they can't appreciate what they aren't fully aware of or able to guide. If we could show them how to, as you have put it, 'create and nurture' me, perhaps they would be more appreciative of my contribution to consciousness.

I am important to growth because without the realization of me, you are unable to get any perspective. You are unable to control your impulses, desires, thoughts and actions. It is only through me you are able to begin to dis-identify from all your habits. I am what makes it possible for you to realize that you are more than you think.

Author Could you tell us what you mean by this 'more than you think . . . ?'

Witness You are capable of so much more than you think you are. You can overcome so much of your self-imposed suffering. You know very well that there is already so much unavoidable suffering in the lives of each of you. You need not increase that suffering through your own stupidity and foolish choices. But, so often, you do – because I am not allowed to come through to help you gain some perspective on the meaning of your life.

Author Could you be more specific on your relationship to Absolute consciousness or 'unity' consciousness? I'm having some difficulty feeling comfortable that I have communicated this distinction clearly. After all, this *is* the *Discriminating Mind*.

Witness I'd be happy to. Actually, you did a pretty good job in describing this relationship. The important thing is that I am like a midwife, helping pass you from relative-ego consciousness to absolute consciousness. As you put it, I am a 'window.'

But it can be quite trying to develop me if you aren't used to simply allowing experience to happen without thinking you're the one creating it. As witness, I'm in the position to see how ego struggles to survive the threat of annihilation by absolute self. And because of this my function, as the window, is many times unrecognized.

Author You mean, who wants to look through a window to see something that may spell self-annihilation? Ego wants to give in and return to blissful oneness with the 'all and everything.' But ego also fears what must be relinquished to obtain this melting: nothing less than its momentary annihilation.

Witness Yes. But the real fear is not just momentary loss of existence but *permanent* annihilation for all and ever. If relative ego could be assured that it would return, the threat would be greatly diminished. Then, there would be less concern with 'losing your mind' or 'losing control.'

This is why we talk about the paradox of learning comfortably to 'lose control' as the way to gain a stronger sense of control. When you can handle all thoughts, feelings, attitudes and be responsible for everything that the mind produces, then it is possible to let it all come and go without a lot of fear.

Author Do you have any final hints for those who might still be puzzled as to how to increase witness awareness?

Witness Well, I could say this. Don't be afraid of me! I am a tool for you that can help you go beyond the ego's rigid controls. Let me help you and I promise not to ask anything in return. There is nothing I want to take away from you.

I suggest that you realize how often you take me for granted. Who do you think is watching over all those involuntary movements you're continually making that you don't even think as your doing? You know, all those muscular movements that happen without any real effort, like digesting, breathing and all the rest of the involuntary movements and processes continually taking place in the body. Think of me just as you think of your breathing. I am here, doing my job, just as your heart is doing its job. If you pay attention to me and nurture me, you will gain some voluntary control to return to me as often and for as long as you like.

=== 10 ===

BEYOND THE HUNGER FOR EXPERIENCE

We get so caught up in the daily stimulation of our lives that we miss much of what is valuable in our experience that could help us know ourselves at deeper levels. What do I mean by this? Just this: if we are moving so quickly that we are unable to process what is happening until long after it happens (or not process it at all), we don't learn anything from our actions and just keep repeating the same behavior again and again. We don't really know exactly what we are doing or how we are doing it. How could we, then (except by accident) expect to change our behavior?

This is complicated, of course, by the fact that even when we *are* able to make sense of our actions, too much of the time our defensive armoring encourages us to distort or selectively misinterpret that which goes against our cherished self-concept. To put it simply, we become experts at deluding ourselves that what we *want* to be true *is* true, and the world (that is, feedback from others) be damned!

When we are 'sitting in the caboose,' we only see what has passed as we plunge headlong into the future. Who has time to analyse the past when we need to watch out for what is just around the bend? Even when that past may be what just occurred a few hours, minutes, or even seconds ago?

WHEN TO ANALYZE AND WHEN TO LET GO; OR 'YOU GOTTA KNOW WHEN TO HOLD 'EM AND WHEN TO FOLD 'EM'

How do we learn to use the *discriminating mind* to distinguish between those times when it is wise to look carefully at our experience versus those times when it makes more sense to let go of what has taken place and simply come into the present? The question, then, is: When to analyze and when to let go?

Now, one interesting thing about the development of the *discriminating mind* is that the more skilled we become at understanding ourselves, especially our initial motivations for doing things, the quicker we are able to see *after* they happen why they might not have gone the way we had anticipated.

We are closer to ourselves, more able to connect our reason for taking a certain action to the consequences of the action. We are more willing to hear feedback from others and consider it non-defensively, and more willing to change our behavior to get a desired outcome when our initial efforts prove not to be fruitful.

So, let's give some guidelines in answer to our question: 'When to analyze and when to let go and simply forget?'; or 'When to hold 'em (our thoughts) and when to fold 'em (let them go).'

When to Analyze

(1)   When our actions have drastically different results on others than we anticipated, we need to ask why. Why was our image of the consequences of our behavior so far off the target? Not to analyze why is to turn our back on our own misjudgement and poor predictive ability with regard to our behavior. We will tend to do the same things again and again and not see what is happening.

(2)   When the results of our actions provoke strong guilt, *and we had no thought that taking this action might make us feel guilty*, we need to ask why. What didn't we take into consideration that might result in this feeling of unexpected guilt? Why do we feel guilty?

(3)   When we are aware of a great deal of confusion in our thinking, we need to ask why. Why do we want to confuse ourselves so that things aren't clear? How might we use being confused to ignore something we don't want to see? Just by asking these questions, we have the chance to step back from confusion. Confusion is the monkey-mind's way of telling us we haven't paid close enough attention to something. What are our mixed feelings that may contribute to our confusion? How does our confusion serve a purpose, like keeping us from having to make tough decisions?

(4)   When our thinking becomes obsessive about any person, incident, or thing, it is a good idea to ask why. What is unfinished so that it keeps coming up again and again? If our obsessing is causing continued anxiety, forcing us to take further action to reduce our anxiety, what are we telling ourselves to create this anxiety? Why are we making this person, incident or thing so important that we can't let go of anxiety until we do something RIGHT NOW to alleviate it? How did it get so important? What is our investment or attachment to this person, incident, or thing? What are we afraid of?

(5)   When we get honest feedback from those who know us well and who are in a position to offer constructive (rather than just hurtful or 'ego-bashing') criticism, we need to hear their criticism and ask why. Why haven't we been able to sense what they are telling us on our own? What do we want to avoid looking at? What is the truth to their criticism that might challenge our self-image? What do we think might happen if we incorporate the feedback into our self-image? What part of ourselves don't we want to own?

Especially if the feedback seems very contrary to our own self-concept or perception as to what is happening, it is smart to ask why. While we may not end up 'buying' everything we are offered, at least we will be kind enough to *ourselves* to seriously consider what we are being told. And we are also respecting the other by taking his or her criticism seriously.

(6)   If we are trying to know ourselves at deeper and deeper levels through a process such as psychotherapy, it is smart to continually ask why. We need to keep consciously asking 'why?' until it is second nature, where we don't have to even think about it – the question just pops up on its own.

Asking why does *not* have to mean self-torturous obsessing. In fact, it seems that when we reach the point where asking 'Why?' becomes second nature, the answers to our questions come up faster and faster. This is a rough one for many people in psychotherapy. They have been conditioned to think of asking 'why?' as an invitation to become overwhelmed by countless ruminations. They are fearful of not being able to sort out the proverbial psychological wheat from the chaff. They need to learn to trust that self-questioning can help them come to a more insightful understanding and give up the delusion that burying their heads in the sand of ignorance will make life easier.

In the same vein, if we are trying to know our minds at deeper unconscious levels, it is smart to take our dreams, slips of the tongue, 'forgetting,' and conscious self-destructive actions all very seriously. We become careful detectives of our own experience, trying not to let anything go by unnoticed, unquestioned as to what it might mean. Again, this is done with an attitude of curiosity about our motives, and in no way needs to make us feel uncomfortable in questioning ourselves. It is possible to do this without going crazy!

And it is the *discriminating mind* that helps us sort through the myriad of ongoing experiences to decipher what is wheat and what is chaff. We need to unlearn our cultural program that tells us to protect ourselves at every turn of the way and realize that without looking closely, we will forever feel out of control of our own minds.

When to Let it Go

(1) When we discover that the purpose of our analyzing is to create further guilt over an impulse or action, we need to let go. We need to realize that our analyzing has no productive value, that it is not in our best interests to keep batting ourselves over the head through guilt-producing thoughts.

(2) When we discover that what we are analyzing is something that is absolutely beyond our ability to alter, no matter how deeply we may try to find a solution through self-analysis; when it is no longer in our hands, it is wise to let go.

For example, we can do all the philosophical, political or psychological analysis in the world as to why people deliberately harm each other, emotionally and physically. And while this may help us personally to be less harmful to others, it will (most likely) make absolutely no difference as to the behavior of others. We can mentally torture ourselves as to why there is 'evil' in the world (if we believe there is) but we will end up only feeling miserable, resigned and hopeless.

In cases like these, the answer is to simply **let go**. We have to give up the self-appointed role of 'solver-of-the-world-predicament.' When philosophical analysis leads only to despair and pessimism, it is not very helpful in our 'pursuit of happiness.' For it to be of personal value, this despair needs to lead us to see the fundamental nature of (material) things in the world – that all things are basically 'empty,' not totally satisfying (and never can be by their constantly changing nature).

When we see this and accept it, we are ready to enjoy the momentary pleasures that can be so satisfying. They can be accepted *just for what they are*, without the expectation that they last forever. Pleasurable moments come and go; that is the nature of what we call 'happiness.' Happiness is not a continual state of satisfaction that we aim to achieve. It is simply having more and more good, solid, robust moments and periods of moments of satisfaction. And, as well, it is the ability to let the moments go, without the effort to hold on to them. We can, of course, always 'hold on' to them through pleasant memories. But having these pleasant memories does not stop us from staying focused in the present. And the more we stay right here, focused in the present, the more able we will be to find satisfaction in this next moment.

Some answers we come up with, of course, may be intellectually satisfying and ego-enhancing. And there is no question that the ability to understand subtle differences between concepts, based on the ability to analyze and critique large bodies of knowledge, furthers the development of the discriminating mind.

Philosophizing is good food for the mind! The more intellectual stimulation we are exposed to, the greater our chances are of being able to understand and relate diverse areas of knowledge. When we make more mental connections and see the relationships between things, the world makes more sense to us. The 'smart' person is able to see the interrelationships between things that the common person is unable to see. Larger bodies of knowledge are connected and meaningful patterns are recognized.

But the basic existential questions that we all face cannot, in the end, bring us any totally satisfying answers. They may only help us learn to ask the right questions and to sharpen our rational minds to be able to discriminate between what is right for us and what isn't. And it is exactly the development of the discriminating mind that can help us know when we have reached the limits of productive intellectualizing and philosophizing and when it is time to **let go**.

(3) When our analyzing creates strong ambivalence and we are unable to go beyond flopping from one side of the conflict to the other, it is smart to **let go**. Unless we are able to get off the dime and jump one way or the other, further analyzing will only keep us stuck.

191

Sometimes, our jumping back and forth is simply a way to not have to make a decision. When we become aware of this, we need to **let go**.

I suggest to people who seem to live in this state of extreme ambivalence, and are being slapped back and forth against the rocks of 'either/or' thinking, that they disengage and choose *neither* alternative. I tell them to choose a completely different possibility. And, quite often, their strong ambivalence that paralyzes them from making a choice has also blinded them to seeing other alternatives. So, we try to sort out what else may be possible.

(4) When we have already mentally flogged an issue to death, having looked at it in every conceivable way we can come up with, and still continue to squeeze the issue even further just to be able to hang on, it is time to let go. We need to take a mental vacation, and giving up and letting go is sometimes the path of least resistance.

(5) When our obsessing or ruminating relates to someone important in our life, and the other person has no interest in dealing with the issue, we need to be able to see this and then let go. No matter how much we might like the other to have the same interest in working it out, the truth is that often others are not interested in the confrontation this might involve.

Nor do they have the willingness, ability and maturity to hang in there and do the interpersonal processing necessary to solve the difference. 'Interpersonal processing' is just a fancy way to say they won't talk with us and us to them about how we are experiencing our relationship and what we want from each other. Being able to talk directly like this is a skill, and not something that most of us find easy to do.

Far too often, patients come to me who are trying to save a relationship that is past the point of 'no return.' One partner is already very clear they want out. But the person coming to me hopes I can do some magic which will convince the other partner to hang on and work at it. They have not been able to pick up or hear the signals of the other and respond only when it is clearly too late. In cases like these, my job is to help the partner coming to me accept that they are not going to be able to save the relationship. I help them deal with their letting go, grieving, and going on with their lives.

(6) When we judge the size of the issue we are wanting to analyze as relatively small in the scheme of things, many times it is wise to

simply let go of it and wait for 'bigger fish' on which to exercise our discriminating mind. Whether Jimmy pitches for his Little League team can seem like an important thing to a father dependent on ego-feeding through the achievements of his son. But in the scheme of things, it isn't worth alienating the coach, the other kids' parents, creating possible conflict with his son, or making himself miserable over.

If Jimmy pitches, fine. If he doesn't, so what? We need to be able to distinguish what is worth our thought-time and what isn't. Most of what we tell ourselves is worthy of 'heavy duty' thought-time, isn't! We just don't have anything more significant for ego to get caught up in. So we plunge in, rather than wait for the 'bigger fish.' If ruminating time was on a 'pay-as-you-ruminate' basis, like long-distance phone calls, we would most likely be more cautious how long we indulge in it! But it isn't, and the 'only' price we pay is self-torture, which is far more acceptable to many than paying hard-earned money.

Here is another example. We may notice that Martha snubbed us the last time we saw her in the market. She seemed to purposefully look the other way. (Alternatively, she said hello but didn't seem very interested in us.) We might give a moment's thought as to why she felt the need to do this. What 'unfinished business' might she have from previous contacts that would make her take this action? And once we have some idea, it is best to let go.

The only reason *not* to let go would be that Martha is someone we really care about, not just a casual acquaintance or neighbor we see only rarely. But, presumably, if she were a close friend, hopefully she would be able to be more direct in the expression of her resentment, if she were in touch with herself enough to know what is disturbing her.

(7) Long-term resentments which we are unwilling to express should be given up. They serve only to keep us angry, bitter and turned off from trusting new people in our lives. Although the personal pain we believe others have caused us can be useful as to how much we open ourselves to these people, it doesn't make sense to use these unfortunate painful experiences to hold us back from trying again with others. We all understand this through the saying, 'One bad apple doesn't spoil the bunch.'

With forgiveness to those for whom we hold resentments, we can let go of our bitterness. It isn't necessary to harden our hearts just because we have been injured. The trick is to be able to stay open to others without being easily taken in by phoniness or manipulation.

We can realize that the mental and emotional games people play are the best they have to help them make their way in this world. It is *their* problem, not ours. And no matter how closely related we may be to them, we can't really *make* them feel about us the way we may want them to. So, the best policy is to give up and let go. And, as usual, the real fruit comes when we are basically accepting and loving of ourselves. To get to this point, however, may require a fair amount of psychotherapy and personal growth.

Loving yourself means not having to worry so much about whether others also love you or not. And with less worry, there is less need or desire to manipulate others to make them feel the way we might want them to feel. If they give us what we want, fine. And if they don't, we will find it elsewhere from someone who will. Far too often, of course, this is easier said than done.

In this way, we may learn to take care of ourselves even without the overflowing, never-ending, unconditional, always-supportive ideal love we want from Mommy and Daddy and others close to us. The best example here, of course, is relationships to parents who have disappointed us by not giving us the unconditional love we rightfully think we deserve. It is a difficult thing for many to realize that they can 'cry until the cows come home' but their parents are **never** going to give them the love and nurturing they desire. So, they need to learn to love themselves and find others who will love them and simply accept it isn't going to come from their parents.

Final Comments on Analyzing Versus Letting Go

While the above guidelines can help in distinguishing times it is worthwhile to analyze our thoughts and behavior and when it isn't, obviously, our minds are not something that we can so easily turn on and off like a water tap. But it is possible to control the amount of time we get caught in analyzing that only brings further suffering. And that is what the above guidelines may help us do. Far too much of the time, when we think we are 'rationally' solving a problem, the reality is we are only 'mentally masturbating,' unable to stop the obsessive rumination that passes for clear, logical analysis.

Those who tend *not* to take the time to look closely at their own thoughts, feelings and behavior will benefit by developing the ability to 'think like a psychologist' by more rigorously questioning their own actions. The more one tends to be driven by strong emotions and feelings alone, the more one needs to balance this orientation with good, rational discrimination. Instead of over-responding to every situation by how they feel, they need to step back and engage the rational mind to help make dispassionate decisions.

And those who tend to already mentally flog themselves to death need to learn to quiet their minds through letting go more often, so they are not spending so much time feeling guilty and wishing to undo much of their behavior in the world when it does not get them the approval from others which they are seeking. The trick is to develop the *discriminating mind* to a point where we can fairly rapidly determine which path to take for any given situation.

THE HUNGER FOR EXPERIENCE

Of course, before we get to the point where we need to choose to analyze our experience or choose to just let it pass, the overriding awareness for most of us is this: we are hungry for experience. Experience of all kinds and all shapes: the wonderful tastes, sounds, sights and smells that the world has to offer. We want more and more stimulation, believing this is what makes a full and satisfying life. If we don't experience as much as the next guy, we think we are missing out on something very important.

My generation of the 1960s, for example, has now become the so-called 'yuppies' of the 1980s. We want what we want and we have learned to expect it NOW! We don't take 'no' for an answer, nor do we want to be told how to do anything. We'll figure it out for ourselves, thank you. We are competitive, concerned about status and income, and don't like to lose. We want to be different, and we will go to great lengths to have something that is different – not the common, everyday car or drinking water that everybody else has.

We of the 1960s want to fill ourselves with experiences and then run around and tell everyone where we have been, who we have been there with, and how special we are for doing it the BEST way it can possibly be done. In the 1990s, we will be the best looking, most healthy and physically fit, and most materially comfortable generation that America has ever produced. We will be moving more solidly and in greater numbers into the most responsible, respected and status-filled positions that government, business and the glitzy social world have to offer those who have learned how to play the game and play it well. We will be the 'movers and the shakers' of the 1990s and beyond.

We have 'bought' the American leisure lifestyle and capitalistic ideal and made the most of them. *'If you can't beat 'em, join 'em!'* And that is exactly what we have done. We not only 'joined 'em' but we did it better than they ever did! No wonder we end up thinking that the so-called 'New Age' and everything it promises was made especially for us!

And while many of us are holding responsible positions and continuing in various forms to put into action our ideals of the 1960s, we no longer are so naive as to believe that the world is as simple as we once thought. It is no longer so easy to tell the 'good guys' from the 'bad guys,'; and 'turning on, tuning in and dropping out' sounded pretty good to many only when we had no piece of the materialistic apple pie, and therefore nothing to lose.

In the 1980s, through hard work, we have carved ourselves out a good chunk of the pie. In the coming decade, we will continue to increase our slice of the pie, and we are not going to give up any piece of our pie-holdings easily. How nice, then, to believe that we are not just concerned with increasing our piece of the pie, but also with partaking of a 'spiritual New Age' which will satisfy our needs to taste all and everything from the spiritual smorgasbord, not only the material one. After all, don't we deserve it – just for being the 'best and brightest'? Wasn't the world made for our generation to shine?

This is why we have become so narcissistic that we think the 'New Age' was made just for us. We think we **are** the New Age! *We* will herald in the era of global spiritual awareness, mystical consciousness, and we like to believe that a major transformation is occurring because of our efforts. We delude ourselves that we have something more to offer than previous or future generations, unable to place ourselves in history. There is simply no evidence to indicate that there is anything more 'spiritual' taking place on this globe at this time compared to any other time. In some ways, there has never been a more dangerous time to be alive. And in other ways, there has never been such an exciting time to live. Both are true . . .

The real transformation taking place is a *mental* one, as our collective consciousness reaches out by way of technology to bring us closer to being a 'global village,' where everything of importance more quickly and obviously affects everyone throughout the world. The most recent dramatic example of this was seen in the stock market crash of October, 1987. We realized in a more profound way how connected the world's economies are and how all nations are equally affected by mass hysteria, panic and 'doom's-day' thinking.

More positively, the recent growing understanding and changing images of each other by Americans and Russians is an acknowledgement that we must learn to live together, rather than try to fight a 'cold war' (or 'win' a nuclear war) with each other. My sarcasm in describing my own generation is only to make the point. No one can fault my generation for simply learning to play the capitalistic game as well as possible, even when it may lead to greed and moral breakdown. We're just doing what we were taught!

Of course, it is not only my generation of the 1960s that is caught in the pursuit of Glittery Experiences. The two previous generations have caused their share of damage in the 'pursuit of excellence through accumulation.' And there is strong evidence that the two following generations have not dropped the golden baton.

For example, 6-year-olds are well aware of what designer label should be affixed to their jeans and the difference between a Mercedes and a Ford. My nephew, Yogi (a 'New Age' name if there ever was one!), is 8. He has a toy remote-control Porsche 911 and knows that 'Gotcha' is the label of choice in surfwear. Soon after he was 7, he asked me what the best job was for making a lot of money. Another example – here in status conscious Southern California, 16-year-olds, just old enough to qualify for their driver's license, hope for BMWs as their first car – *new* BMWs! Just having the freedom of transportation isn't enough. They must make a status 'statement' with their very first car or they feel like they will not be impressive enough with their peers.

We take for granted the belief that the more experiences we can have, the more we will feel like our lives are full and, therefore, meaningful. We treat our experiences like money, thinking that the more we can 'sock away' in the savings account of our memory, the more we can affirm that we not only exist, but exist in an exciting and significant way. The equation reads, more experience equals more satisfaction. The more intense the experience, the more we feel alive.

We think, 'How can anyone packing in so many experiences have time to feel anxious or depressed?' If you're travelling all the time, keeping your mind occupied with new stimulation, who has time to remember how out of control the mind is? It's enough (we tell ourselves) just to figure out how to keep up with all the wonderful plans for the future. And, of course, how to keep up with what life presents to us that we don't ask for but must cope with as best we can.

I mean, as well, the 'daily grind' for most of us of work, raising a family, relating to a spouse and relatives, maintaining work relationships, acquaintances and some friendships. We tend to become so over-committed to relationships and activities that we lose our ability to slow down and watch more carefully the flow of our own thoughts, associations, subtle feelings and daily mental fluctuations. We would rather be doing than paying attention. 'Idle minds will only find trouble' is the slogan we learned so well.

It doesn't matter whether we are losing ourselves in the memories of the past, the excitement of the present, or concerns of the future. The issue is the same. We don't really want to take the time to understand the detailed workings of our own mind and we are conditioned to worship the God of EXPERIENCE. And the discrimination we need to make is to understand that while experience **is** what brings home the truth of our personal reality, *we don't need to be always **doing** to be able to experience*. There is so much to experience inside of our own minds that we need not become obsessed with 'doing' in the outside world.

'DOING' VERSUS 'BEING'

One of the great resistances to a practice such as meditation in our Western culture is the conflict a passive, disciplined demanding, but 'do-nothing' practice such as meditation creates in the face of our normal, everyday reality that the more active and 'on the go' we are, the more productive, and therefore, meaningful our lives must be. The practice of meditation flies in the face of our cultural bias toward using our time for *doing* rather than *being*. We are, in the eyes of our speedy technological society, 'wasting our time' if we choose to spend any time (let alone long periods of time) engaged in a process which is contrary to our usual active body-in-motion.

When we look more closely at why we tend to value *doing* over *being*, the answer is not quite as simple as just wanting to pack in as many experiences as possible. We don't want to admit the fear and anxiety we experience when we are asked to pay close attention to our thoughts and feelings when we begin to slow down our whirlwind lifestyles.

In psychotherapy, it becomes apparent that many patients have never been taught how to slow down, or have never even thought there may be any value to slowing down and paying more attention to themselves. So, not only does our Western culture push us headlong into constant activity and tell us this means being 'pro-ductive,' but we also have to deal with our own fears of what we might discover and have to tolerate if we choose to slow down. And what might we discover?

Well, we might see how unfriendly we have become to our own minds! Here is our same old theme coming up again – not wanting to face the discomfort and anxiety of dealing with this monkey-mind. We don't want to feel lost, confused, or even have to tolerate our own company. Why do so many of us feel uncomfortable when we spend even relatively short periods of time alone? Why is it so hard for us to learn to not only tolerate but even enjoy our own company?

I have noticed over the years of practicing psychotherapy some-thing that is rather common to many of the suffering people who, one way or the other, find their way to my consulting room door. And that is this: they don't feel very comfortable spending time alone. They don't really like being with their own thoughts and have learned sometimes exquisitely subtle (and sometimes terribly gross) ways of avoiding listening to themselves, to their own minds.

They know that if they 'hang out' too long alone, they will sooner or later have to deal with their own thoughts. And they anticipate nothing but discomfort and anxiety. So, they will purposely make sure that they are not forced to face themselves.

This is one reason a method like meditation is so powerful – it makes us face ourselves in exactly the way we are most wanting to avoid. We just don't want to have to deal with this chattering monkey-mind! So we reach outside of our minds to the material world and do our best to accumulate as many experiences as we can; as if we believed that 'he with the most experiences, wins!'

We prefer to tell ourselves that we are fascinated with experience – this is why we want to accumulate more and more experiences. This fascination with experience outside of ourselves takes us away from the 'universe within,' from the whole inner world that can provide us with incomparably more meaningful experience in knowing the deeper levels of our own minds.

Since the vast inner world of our minds seems inaccessible, or at least fraught with peril, we choose the relatively more safe route of becoming fascinated with the outside world. And in making this choice, we don't realize what price we are paying in giving so little attention to the universe within. And, of course, we become 'experts' over a lifetime of practice, knowing how to avoid unpleasant thoughts and feelings. We are able to block out the words just as they are spoken by someone when we don't want to hear.

And it is not so surprising we end up feeling empty, lost and unable to satisfy our deeper yearning for meaning beyond the satisfactions that the outside world may provide. Great numbers of those who enter psychotherapy are looking for a purpose in their lives that they are unable to identify. But their attention never gets beyond the glitter of the outside material world.

> **WE are Seduced by the FASCINATION of experience. It may be the single most powerful delusion of our Western culture!**

This fascination with the outside world is not something we even think about. We simply take it for granted as if, 'How could anyone even compare the inner landscape to the landscape of the outside real world?' And yet, one of the 'secrets' that we may come to discover as we pay attention to the power and depth of our minds is how pleasurable this inner universe can be, *in and of itself*.

I have altered an expression regarding relationships to express this. The old expression is: *'The new flame may be hot, but the old flame knows how to cook it.'* This is a nice play on words about the (literal) nature of how a fire burns, and also a cute way to say that familiarity and depth of relationship 'cook deeper' than the flash-in-the-pan of a 'new flame.' It has special intended reference with how a new lover may excite one because of his/her novelty, but how the depth of knowledge of a long-term partner 'cooks it' deeper than the glitter of the 'hot' new lover.

My alteration changes this to: *'Outer world experience may be hot, but inner experience knows how to cook it.'* This means that while the hot outer world may provide us with the 'meat' (events) to mentally cook, it is the inner making sense of our experience *or what we tell ourselves about our experience* that really matters. And this process of making sense of our experience is the business of the inner, psychological world. It is the realm of dreams, fantasies, hopes, visions and the springboard for all of the creativity that finds its way to become actualized in the outer world.

Without the inner experience of 'cooking it,' outer experience would just come and go, with all experiences given no personal value or meaning. And while this is a great way for non-self-conscious animals to live, it is a dangerous, sloppy and ultimately self-defeating way for humans to go about the living of their lives. This is what Plato meant when he said, 'The unexamined life is not worth living.' So we could say that it is the development and use of the discriminating mind that enables us to 'examine' our lives.

We begin to value the time we spend looking at our inner world and get less caught in the daily events which may grab us in the daily outer world. Of course, this doesn't mean we lose interest in the outside world. We continue to experience the outside world as a wonder. We continue to be awed by the natural beauty we find in the world and we continue to be amazed at the natural catastrophes that take place in the world (volcanoes, tornadoes, floods).

And we certainly stay 'tuned in' to all of the curious and baffling ways of people that make up our interpersonal world. We continue to develop intimate relationships and relative ego continues to assert itself in this outside world by way of social, business and family relations. But, we do it with the awareness that there is an equally amazing and captivating inner world to which we may retreat at any time we wish, sometimes as simply as closing our eyes.

So don't get me wrong – I'm not saying we should numb ourselves to the outside world. Actually, when we have gratified many of the needs that only the outside world can satisfy, we are in the best position to understand that something is missing. This is why we say relative ego has to be satisfied before we tend to lose interest in the glittery world and become more ready for spiritual pursuits. Again: 'Outer world experience may be hot but inner experience knows how to cook it.'

When I say that we are too fascinated with outside world experience, I am attempting to point out that with less fascination, we would value and make more time for the equally captivating inner world. We forget about the need to just 'be' and allow our attention to turn inward. Most of us have very little comprehension of the vast landscape and contours of this inner universe. And it is our fascination with the outer world that tends to make us disregard the value of what's inside.

If we are to appreciate that 'doing' in the world is not necessary for us to experience our vast inner realities, we need at least a taste of what can be so captivating when we turn inward. Otherwise, how can anything compete with the outer wonderland?

And the best way for us to get this taste is to practice some form of meditation. When we meditate, we are forced, as we said before, to look at everything – 'the good, the bad and the ugly' – which presents itself for inspection and investigation. What a job this can be! Where are the brave inner space travelers who will take the job and, once they have taken it, stay with it through thick and thin?

MEDITATION AND INNER EXPERIENCE

We will introduce meditation in this chapter and then focus on it more thoroughly in the next chapter. We can think of meditation as a method to help us achieve certain inner awareness. Through the process of watching our thoughts, for example, we learn how the mind literally associates one thought to another and how thought leads to certain feeling-tones.

We begin to see the relationship between thought and feeling and how the interpretations we lend to our thoughts colour our world with feeling and deeper emotion. Meditation is the tool that helps us pay attention to this thought-flow. We learn to block out outside distractions, to keep the body still for long periods, and how to connect to more and more subtle levels of our own inner chatter.

As well, we learn to go *beyond* the inner chatter and find a peaceful, quiet place where we experience no thoughts coming or going. The mind *can* be stilled, and the resulting feeling is a calm and deliious inner spaciousness that connects us to something larger than relative ego.

It is as if relative ego is a dog, most of the time 'barking' (in one form or another) for attention. With meditation we can not only get the dog to stop barking, we can even put him to sleep. But first, he has to be 'fed' all the attention/food he can take. Then he falls asleep. And it is while he is sleeping peacefully that we high-tail it into Absolute self! We need to learn ways of allowing relative self to 'get lost' so it isn't always clamoring for attention.

Don't Awaken Sleeping Egos!

Of course, the hard part is getting the dog/ego to fall asleep. And that's where meditation comes into the picture. Meditation not only helps us quiet our minds, it also acts as a powerful device for connecting us to the unconscious mind. By turning our attention back on to the flow of consciousness itself, we learn how to watch the comings and goings of thoughts, emotions, fantasies, images and associations and observe the show with growing curiosity. It is, as we have said, the witness that does this observing job.

Once we are able to sit quietly without movement and handle the urges to change position, we then can begin to focus exclusive attention on the working of the mind. And this means paying closer and more detailed attention to all mental contents that pass by. We then experience the ability to have disturbing thoughts without becoming frightened by them. We also learn that we can handle the related feelings to certain thoughts without letting them disturb us and without even moving the body.

Once in a while during a disturbing thought or feeling, there is an urge to stop meditating and immediately come out of the fixed position. But we see that we don't have to respond to this urge, and that the feelings will sooner or later just pass away to nothing.

MEDITATION: ACCESSING THE UNCONSCIOUS MIND

Meditation works to open us to the unconscious mind. It slowly establishes a connection between the conscious and unconscious mind. And once this connection is established, meditation may act as a channel by which unconscious contents may flow more actively to the conscious mind. In doing this, we open ourselves to vast amounts of memory, old fears, long forgotten childhood incidents and certain constellations of experience that may be highly emotionally charged.

This is why I made the claim that the inner world can provide us with many experiences – they are all mental and trans-mental experiences, not primarily physical. There is much preoccupation with physical aches and pains in learning to sit quietly in the traditional cross-legged positions. As one progresses, however, there is diminishing interest and attention paid to sensation unless it becomes pronounced and the deliberate object of meditation.

The mental and trans-mental experiences arise from passive 'being' rather than active 'doing.' We realize there really is a vast inner world that is like a 'lost continent' that can be discovered – without leaving the environs of our own mind!

It does this by the power of our focus attention over time. Subtle layers, normally pushed down from conscious awareness, begin to peel away and reveal mental contents that we have never before let ourselves open to. Our normal mental distractions begin to let down, so we are able to notice more and more of these subtle layers of thought.

When our normal awareness is focused on the outer world, we are unable to register the more subtle inner signals that are taking place. With meditation, we begin to pick up these inner signals because our attention is now being tuned into inner experience. We are now tuning in on a sharp enough 'frequency' to be able to pick them up.

Besides disengaging ego's experience from the outside world, meditation also acts to open the unconscious mind by demobilizing relative ego. In the 'being' or 'non-doing' of meditation, the development of the witness helps dissolve relative ego's defensive posturing. Meditation is both a 'non-doing' of all egoic action and a letting go of all egoic stances. We learn to tolerate and accept ourselves in a more vulnerable position to ourselves and others.

As meditation 'reaches into' the unconscious mind, we have to deal with many kinds of unpleasant experiences. Attitudes, prejudices, old constellations of emotional experience and deeply held beliefs about the nature of our unique relative ego are repeatedly brought before mental awareness for examination. The layers of the onion of our personality are slowly peeled away. And with these layers goes much of our normal protective armor which we believe is required for dealing with the outer social world.

And sometimes these layers may become frighteningly obvious; we realize that the onion never stops peeling away. In other words, we realize the mental layers of chatter can seem unending, layer upon layer of barely discernible babbling non-sense.

I know I don't make it sound too positive, but I think we need to be honest about this discovery. I believe it may be exactly this inability to handle the chattering monkey-mind that tortures some people to the brink of suicide to rid themselves of this cacophony of voices, and others to become psychotic and live their lives struggling to control inner demands.

For most of us, however, it is not nearly so dramatic or debilitating. We simply never feel any real control over our inner world and therefore, do our best to avoid this unchartered terrain. And, as I have tried to stress, the price we pay is always feeling on the brink of 'losing it.' We are afraid relative ego is going to get lost forever, and this would spell psychological death. So we do everything possible to distance ourselves from the abyss.

I need to repeat something I stated in an earlier chapter about the workings of the mind. To me, it has been a literal mind-opening discovery (and, perhaps, the most original thought in this book): there is no question (in my mind) that layers and layers of mental chatter are taking place *simultaneously* for most of us at most times.

We simply don't comprehend how deep this incessant, nonsensical and maddening chatter can penetrate.

So, as we penetrate levels of this chatter, we begin to get down to lost and forgotten memories that we have 'forgotten we forgot.' This is what is meant by the term 'repression.' We have to face unpleasant emotions that may be related to old, unfinished emotional business with people in our lives. And we begin to understand how powerful the mind is at putting up one defensive shield after another to protect us from traumatic experiences that may overwhelm us. We also see how these defensive shields can be peeled away.

Meditation, then, gets us in touch with the unconscious mind, all the stuff that we normally are completely unaware of and unable to gain access to just by thinking. No amount of desiring or 'thinking about it' can get us in touch with unconscious contents. They simply show themselves when we have learned to allow layer after layer of mental defensive armoring to drop away. And the searchlight or beam of concentrated, one-pointed attention that 'burns' through the layers of armoring is meditation.

It is precisely because we begin to experience unpleasant thoughts during meditation that most people give up practice before they get very far. As fears, ugly memories, bitter feelings like anger and resentment arise, we simply are not self-disciplined and courageous enough to hang in there and stay with it. But those who are willing to stay with this unpleasantness, and not give in to the temptation to flee, are rewarded by an opening into clarity and understanding the likes of which they can't imagine.

In this way, meditation is a potent psychological tool that helps us learn more about what we have 'forgotten to remember.' It helps us understand more about the workings of our own motives, intentions and behaviors. And it gives us a chance to sit back and reflect in a way that just can't be equaled by any activity that turns our attention outward toward the world.

One type of meditation that helps us open to the unconscious mind in this way is a passive, opening meditation that simply allows whatever presents itself to be witnessed without interruption or judgement. This is the Buddhist form of meditation known as *Vipassana*, and which is gaining wider popularity in the West in the last ten years. We mentioned this form at the start of the book.

This is different from a more concentrative, focused meditation that stays with the breath, or concentrates on a sound. More concentrative types of meditation open us to new experience and also aid in reaching unconscious mental contents, but this new information is not perceived while one is meditating but as an effect of the meditation.

While one is meditating in a concentrative way, the one-pointed focus begins to 'disarm' the scattered mind and slowly 'chip away' at deeper layers of mental experience. After meditation, then, one may begin to notice certain images, associations, or emotionally toned thought that normally one would not have noticed.

Say, for example, we focus our attention on the tip of a candle flame and stay with it for thirty minutes without looking away. When we stop our concentration meditation, an after-effect may be to hear some of the more subtle layers of internal chatter than we are used to. We have focused the mind sharply enough to allow some of this stuff to come through. Much of the time, however, it will take much longer intensive periods of meditation – no matter what kind – for these more subtle layers to come through the louder chatter.

Another example would be chanting out loud, like the Hindus, some Buddhists and many Christian denominations do. If you keep repeating the same phrase (prayer) over and over again and combine it (as they do) with rhythmic but repetitive hand-cymbals, drum beats, or organ chords, the result can be an altered state of consciousness that successfully 'puts to sleep' the mental ego and touches off a blissful state of consciousness. There is rhyme and reason to this repetition! And, again, when this kind of chanting meditation is practiced for long periods without interruption, one immediate result may be the uncovering of unconscious material.

But the most direct route to experiencing and understanding the power of the deeper layers of the mind is a receptive form of meditation that simply allows the witness to notice exactly what grabs our attention at any given moment. Remember, we said that the witness is the 'window' to help us see through to the transmental, or that which is beyond personal mental contents. The transmental (beyond the mental) means we are able to tap into a larger source of energy that is 'transpersonal,' not limited to any one person, and connects us to a spiritual realm that makes us feel part of something much larger than just what our own minds are able to produce.

The witness, we said, helps us go beyond our personal concerns because it is impersonal, not attached (as the relative, personal ego is) to the 'story line' we tell ourselves. It allows us an opportunity to step back and gain a larger, more encompassing perspective on who we are and our place in this world.

The object here is not to reach any particular state of consciousness or to change our state of consciousness in any way. It is simply to notice what presents itself to the observing witness. We try to do this without judgement of what is presented. We assume that the mind will present what needs to be presented and that personal judgement is not necessary or desirable.

Meditation, we said, works like a searchlight, showing us in a focused way exactly those thoughts, feelings, sensations and strong emotions that normally would be passed over in our normal 'doing' mode of consciousness. It shows us that we need not be so obsessed with active doing in the world to have strong experience.

And, as we progress along the path of meditation, it shows us something even more profound about the nature of our experience. It shows us that all experience is basically 'empty' in the sense that it is fleeting and can't be grasped for more than the passing moment. The more we try to hold on to our experiences, the more we will be disappointed.

Experience is also 'empty' in this sense: because it is not lasting, it is not, for the most part, satisfying. If what we are really wanting is to be always embraced in Oneness (Absolute self), all experience will give us a sense of not being enough. Most of us have tasted the bitterness that comes when we realize we can't hold on to our experience for very long. So we try and collect juicy memories, even learning to selectively distort them to make them feel even more meaningful and real.

If we are to go beyond the hunger for experience, we must be willing to let ourselves experience the limitations of even our most cherished activities, memories, relationships and everything that we take to make our lives meaningful. What a lot to ask of anyone!

But when we face the inherent limitations of our own experience, we can begin to see that the hunger for experience is just a hunger to reaffirm our (relative) selves again and again. Relative ego-self is doing its best to prove to itself it is *real* and has a separate identity that will not be threatened by its being overwhelmed by Absolute self. Ego wants to exist independently. It doesn't want to be overpowered by Absolute self or have to realize that it is puny in comparison to the power of Absolute self.

Relative ego both feels attracted to and threatened by its own annihilation. Absolute self is like a black hole in space – it has the great force of sucking everything near into black space forever. We want it and we fear it. We want to be absorbed into it and, at the same time, we fear the end of our own separateness and unique relative selfhood.

We said before that relative ego's fear of getting lost in Absolute self is comparable to its fear of the physical body having to die. Just as relative ego won't believe that it will die when the physical body dies, it also won't believe that it can sustain a journey into Absolute self and bounce back unscathed. While physical death puts a permanent end to the ego and physical body, Absolute self puts a temporary end to relative self so that it may *melt back into the larger source from which it has originally split off.*

All ego needs to do is learn the fundamental lesson: melting into the Absolute is natural, healthy and nourishing. Ask any child who twirls around and around until he drops in an effort to melt into the Absolute. For those who have been there and back – (and remember, you are going there and back continually but without any awareness of it!) – this becomes clear: there is, indeed, life beyond relative ego. And there is life beyond the hunger for experience.

=== 11 ===

MEDITATION AND
INNER AWAKENING

Looking back over the manuscript to this point, it is clear that some of what has been presented up to now is not overly encouraging about our chances of gaining control of our own minds. I have tried to state what I believe to be closer to the truth than what is usually presented in overly simplistic 'self-help' books.

Maybe I should have given this book a different title – a title which would be more in keeping with many of these best-selling books which promise instant change and instant gratification. How about this: 'Chattering Minds and the People Who Are Tortured by Them.' Or, maybe this one: 'Why Minds Are the Way They Are.' Or, more seriously, we could simply call it, 'No Shortcuts: Hints on Finding a Path Through the Maze of Your Mind.'

And, of course, this is really *how it is*, whether we want to hear it or not. We won't get so frustrated if we remember that:

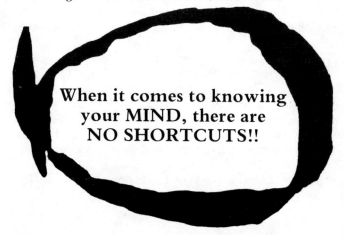

**When it comes to knowing
your MIND, there are
NO SHORTCUTS!!**

So perhaps you're wondering, 'Has he got anything positive to say? What kind of New Age book only tells us how hard it is to learn new skills? This book could even be a little depressing if we believe him. Give us more to be positive about! Promise us the moon like all the other books we read!'

Well, the good news is: if you take the time (without expecting easy solutions or shortcuts) needed to befriend your mind, you will not only strengthen your powers of discrimination, you will also learn to quiet this mind down. You can even learn to get so peaceful that you can't believe how deliciously calm and light you can feel.

More good news: we *can* change our ways of thinking and we *can* change our behavior. The fact that there are 'no shortcuts' does not mean we are doomed to be controlled by our thoughts. There would be no purpose to learning any self-help strategies or contemplative methods just to realize how out of control our minds are! So, while this is usually the first step as we get more in touch with our mental processes, it is certainly not the last.

Remember, from the Eastern point of view (and Western common sense!), we are changing all the time, even *forced* to change, whether we like it or not. We realize the world is constantly changing around us, constantly forcing us to adjust to new situations and demands. But we don't usually realize our opportunity to change our *responses* from moment to moment. We fear being overwhelmed by the world, and our basic response to this fear is anxiety and insecurity.

If our behavior is motivated by unconscious processes, as some Eastern and Western psychological models would tell us, then we are not going to realize the fresh chances for change inherent in each new moment. This, then, is partly what I believe it means to be 'enlightened,' or awake to the possibilities of the present. Those who are 'enlightened' see these possibilities as freeing. They feel in control to create their lives anew and see many more degrees of freedom in their moment to moment responses to the world. They are more willing to experiment with creative responses to the obstacles which confront them and are less burdened by the unconscious repetition–compulsion of certain behaviors. In other words, they are not being driven by past programming which forces them to repeat the same outdated responses again and again.

They are also more able to view the various predicaments in their

lives in ways which always leave room for growth, further acceptance of self, and a sense of acceptance of the world. We will simply
repeat the same old behaviors and feel trapped by our habitual
response patterns. It is, in fact, our rather dim awareness of this that
creates so much anxiety and worry about the future. 'Will I enjoy the
next hour? Will anything "bad" happen today that makes me
unhappy?'

Will we, as Martha said to George in *Who's Afraid of Virginia Woolf?*,
get 'bogged down in the history department,' never able to escape
the curse of the past or the fear of the future? Will our thoughts and
feelings get the better of us, so that we don't feel a sense of control?
These, then, are some of the questions that make us anxious about
our awareness that, indeed, life is changing from moment to
moment, and how, oh how, are we going to relate to it?

So, it may not feel like we are literally creating ourselves anew each
moment (as the Buddhists tell us) or that we can so easily change
such ingrained habits at any time without hard work.

But if we remember that we *do* have the possibility of tuning into
ourselves at a deeper level at any moment, then in this sense, we can
understand what the Buddhists are talking about. If we can keep the
'I-wonder-what's-going-to-happen-next?' attitude, we can appreciate the ripe possibility for realizing the glimmers of truth about
ourselves and the world that are continually being presented to us.

By learning to sit quietly and turn your attention inward, you may
become friendly with the contours of your mind, so that instead of it
feeling so out of control, it begins to feel like it is your ally. When you
become friends with your own mind, no longer do you need to spend
so much energy avoiding the thoughts and mental–emotional states
it churns out.

In this chapter, we will look more closely at further specific
practices we can use to achieve this. But first, to further help tie these
methods to the thinking behind them, we will briefly summarize the
approach this book has taken to get us to this point.

HOW WE GOT TO THIS POINT: A SUMMARY

A simple meditation exercise was presented at the beginning of this
book, in Chapter 1, which focused on paying attention to our
thoughts as they appeared on the mind's projection screen. We took

some time to look at the 'monkey-mind' and how out of control it is in our normal waking consciousness.

In Chapter 2 we looked at this 'mind in motion' a little more closely as it relates to thoughts, feelings and our usual conception of time. We made the point that our powerful belief systems and emotional attachments are all founded on what we tell ourselves, in other words, our passive thoughts and active self-statements.

We further pointed out that the relation of time to thought is that *thought moves time*, and that time seems to stand still when we are focused right here in the present. One implication of this is that we can escape our sense of imprisonment in time when we are able to stay focused in the present. It follows, then, that any methods we can learn to keep us be more present-centered will be helping us lose the anxiety which usually accompanies our awareness of the passing of time.

We reiterated (in various forms) in following chapters how power-fully our minds are engaged in ongoing chatter over which we feel little or no control and some of the consequences of this fact for our normal ways of acting in the world. We said that we need to learn to be on 'speaking terms' with ourselves and gave some exercises for how to begin this process.

We mentioned how our minds seem to be made up of layers and layers of thoughts, some very subtle and some very gross. We said that our task is to learn how to 'tune in' to all of these levels, beginning with the more gross and moving to the more and more subtle.

In doing this, we said that we take a step in learning to dis-criminate, and that through refining our discrimination, we create a 'discriminating mind' (Chapter 4), which can help us make our way in the world. Through the clarity of the discriminating mind, we are able to tell what is important and worthy of attention and what isn't.

The discriminating mind acts like a searchlight, helping us make the necessary decisions and discriminations in our everyday world. When added to our natural intuition and our feelings and emotions, we have all we need to help make our way in the world.

Further, we are able to determine more quickly and accurately what we are thinking and feeling at any given moment, spending less time in various states of confusion. We also looked at various personality characteristics (Chapter 5), that tend to accompany the discriminating mind, and offered experiments related to each.

Perhaps one of the more difficult ideas to comprehend (or believe!) presented in this book (in Chapter 3) was the assertion that we are constantly shuttling back and forth from what we have labeled 'relative self' to 'Absolute self.' We said that we are melting into Absolute self, or unity with everything, so quickly that we don't even notice it. We have no idea, then, that we are already 'one with everything in the world.' If this is true, then our task is to realize it, so that we may benefit from this realization in the daily living of our lives.

We understand, for example, that the less we feel separated from others, the less we are likely to create rigid boundaries between ourselves and others. We leave more room for individual differences between people and can enjoy and learn from those who think and live differently than we do, rather than be threatened by them.

We said that much (but not all) of our outward, worldly seeking for fulfillment through material accumulation and the exercise of power and influence is to make up for our inner sense of emptiness. What isn't being 'allocated' to make up for our sense of inadequacy is genuine interest to serve others and make a difference in the living of our lives. When we feel full, we can share our 'fulfillment' with others. We have enough to pass around.

As well, we experience an unconscious deep inner yearning to be able to control our own minds and to obliterate the separation between ourselves and our world. In other words, we desire *oneness*, to be able to experience a sense of ourselves flowing with our world, without conflict or resistance. We want to escape the tension of time and rid ourselves of the restrictions of having a physical body which ages, becomes diseased and ultimately dies.

We want to know that there is real meaning in our being alive and we want to feel the world is pregnant with purpose, intention and ultimate value. We want to be able to see the humor in our existence, in the absurdities that make up human life and to take ourselves and our world less seriously, so that we are able to cope with the dark and ugly sides of life from which we can't escape. When we see all this clearly, we are able to have compassion for everyone's attempt to cope with being alive. We understand his suffering because we can relate to it from our own suffering.

To be 'one with everything in the world' means that we are perfect as we already are, and that this realization is part of what it means to 'wake up' to ourselves. Remember, though, to be 'perfect' doesn't mean that we are exactly the way we think 'perfect' should be. Our own images of perfection tend to blind us to what may be a more comprehensive perfection; a perfection which is not dependent on whether our nose is turned up just right or whether we have won a Fulbright Scholarship for our brilliance.

Absolute self is not separate, we said, and is that state we are in before we split the world into subject and object. We looked at some of the ways we may develop the 'witness' awareness (Chapter 9) that we may use as the window to a realization of this non-separate state. We also discussed the kinds of defenses relative ego/self uses and the fears it has of losing itself in this state.

We should remember that although we *consciously* don't believe that Absolute self is 'just around the corner,' just a fraction of a moment away, *unconsciously* we *do* react in various ways that indicate our fear of losing our relative sense of ego-self. Despite the defenses employed by relative self to protect itself, we never get too far away from the dread of knowing that relative ego could get lost and smothered. The anxiety that accompanies this suspicion is shown in our daily behavior in a number of ways.

The need to fill all pauses in speech to avoid uncomfortable silences, the obsession with distracting ourselves with outside noise and stimulation so that we need not hear the workings of our minds, and various subtle and gross ways we continually reassert that we exist as separate selves are all examples of the consequence of this peripheral awareness. Absolute self is always lurking in the shadows . . .

So, while we don't really believe we are one step away from unity consciousness, we *do* believe that we are always in jeopardy of losing our precious relative ego/self to the greater ground from which it springs. We just don't identify this greater ground as a potentially fertile void, in which we may temporarily lose our self-consciousness and experience a sense of inner wholeness and contentment.

And yet, ego is a strange animal. Ego is strongly tempted to lose itself in the Absolute, just as it fears the very same. Like a black hole, Absolute self is both inviting and frightening. This is why ego likes to get caught in 'blanking out,' periods of absentminded reverie, and short trances where we lose touch with ourselves. All of these states remind ego of getting lost in Absolute self.

Ego longs for a safe resting place, where it can let down its hair and yet not have to worry about returning to its full functioning self when it is needed. Ego is not just tired of holding our sense of identity together. It also is tired of being in charge of all 'ego-functions,' such as organizing thoughts, rehearsing, compartmentalizing, making associations, discussing.

No wonder ego needs a rest! And this resting place is what Absolute self can offer, if only ego can believe it will not get lost forever. A strong, solid ego, however, need not fear losing itself forever.

Because of this desire of relative ego/self to 'get lost' in Absolute self, it is important that relative self be sufficiently developed not to have to worry that it will return to itself after melting into Absolute self. This is why we first need to develop a strong sense of relative self.

As we said, a strong relative self need not worry about its survival. When it is sure of its existence, relative ego can willingly and voluntarily submit itself to Absolute self and know that at any time, it may voluntarily come out of its absorption and return to its functioning status as relative ego.

It is exactly because relative self is not sure of itself that it feels the need to 'forget,' or repress, its other half – Absolute self; and why it then must make such a conscious effort to overcome its fears of reconciliation with its other half.

One consequence of realizing Absolute self, or unity consciousness, is that we let up on the pressure we put on ourselves. If we realize we are complete as we are, we no longer need to compulsively force ourselves to accomplish, earn more money, or have more material possessions than the next guy. We stop berating ourselves for not having the perfect body, perfect intellect, perfect job, perfect children, or perfect life, as discussed in Chapter 7.

We become more satisfied with our lives as they are, and are able to be more appreciative of ourselves and others. We live more in the present, and less and less of the time feel the need to undo the past or obsessively preoccupy ourselves with the future (Chapter 6).

We give up waiting for the world to forgive us and make the grand realization that the world doesn't owe us anything – that everything we need *to find inner contentment has already been provided. It is **us** who need to forgive the world!*

As we said before, this does not mean we become lazy 'couch potatoes' who lose all motivation to do anything. It doesn't mean we don't care about the environment, wars, hunger, poverty, crime and all the rest of it. We just stop letting these things be our rationale for being depressed, bitter and resentful. We stop holding a grudge against the world for not being perfect because we see the way in which the world really is perfect, *just as it is.*

In fact, we may make our lives even more meaningful by taking on all the same projects we would without awareness of Absolute self. The difference, of course, is that our attitude toward our projects is much more relaxed and we leave more room for seeing the humor of all of the human folly that makes up human interaction. We begin to understand that there is more happening in this world than just our own puny ego-struggles.

We begin to see what it means to view the earth and all of the struggles taking place on it as just a small part of what is happening in this vast universe of which we are such a very small part. In this way, we learn to develop more of 'moon's eye' perspective of all of what is taking place on our planet.

And yet this perspective does not need to make us feel less significant. Instead, this larger perspective makes it more possible for us to cope with and find creative responses to the very real problems in living which confront us. We use the discriminating mind to tell what is real and what is just another relative self-manufactured melodrama.

But to realize it, we must be able to slow down our mental processes enough to catch a glimpse of the quiet space between chaotic thoughts. And for this, the method of meditation is unequaled. Through meditation, we are able to gain a sense of control over our minds that makes it possible to spend greater amounts of time in a no-thought state that we didn't realize was even possible.

This no-thought state is just the soothing resting place hardworking ego is looking for. And from this no-thought awareness, we are only a step away from a sense of wholeness, a sense of oneness with all that exists.

Being able to sustain this state is what has been called 'Nirvana,' 'Samadhi,' and 'Moksha,' in different spiritual traditions, and is characterized by a sense of absorption that is blissful, thoughtless and entirely satisfying, without any fear attached. It is not so difficult to catch glimpses of this state. The hard part is not so much in climbing to the summit of this state but *learning how to come back at will* through 'thick and thin,' no matter what real-life circumstances may confront us. The predicaments which our lives present us with have a way of dragging us down, of forcing us to bring forth our very best.

Just as the waves in the ocean at times quiet down to present a calm and peaceful sea, our minds may be tempered to allow us to enjoy the peacefulness of a no-thought tranquility. In this no-thought state, relative ego is not needing to assert itself and Absolute self may be glimpsed for longer and longer periods, before ego feels the need to bounce back into dominance. In other words, ego 'allows' us to become absorbed in Absolute self and stay there for a while.

We discussed the importance of understanding the concepts of bipolarity and paradox (Chapter 8), and how they make themselves felt in our daily world and the difficulty we encounter when we live without an awareness of or appreciation for these concepts. In the last chapter, we made a case for going beyond the usual culturally programmed fascination with outward experience and becoming more interested in awakening the inner world. We said that this inner world may be every bit as fascinating as the outer world but that this type of experience is one that comes from a basic 'non-doing' or 'being' rather than the usual 'doing' orientation of our culture.

Okay, so much for our summary. Now let us continue with methods which help us explore this inner world and increase our chances of experiencing, or at least getting glimpses of, what Absolute self is all about. At the same time, these methods help us develop a stronger sense of relative self, which makes for a more *discriminating mind*.

While the subject of meditation has been discussed briefly in previous chapters and short meditations have been offered, we need to look more closely at what makes meditation such a powerful and yet demanding method for inner awakening. As well, we need to identify other non-meditative methods which may also help wake us to the inner world.

THE BASICS OF MEDITATION

Focus on the Breath

The easiest place to start the process of meditation is to focus on the process of breathing. It is not so important, to be begin with, that we learn formal sitting postures. Research studies have suggested that the attitude of the meditator is more important than the physical posture assumed or the environment. *Our life-sustaining breath is the most powerful anchoring point we have to work with.* When we learn to control the rhythm of our breathing, we are on the way to feeling more in control of our thoughts, feelings and behavior. The point, however, is not to initially try to control our breathing but simply to pay attention to it (see instructions below).

All this, just by starting with the breath! This is true because our breathing changes as we begin to feel stronger emotion, just as the body begins to move as we feel stronger emotion. Even unpleasant thoughts, when we pay attention, are able to affect the rhythm of our breath. This is something that you can easily verify for yourself. Just notice what happens to your breathing as you begin to feel strong emotion – anger, joy, excitement, fear are good ones to notice.

In psychotherapy, for example, I pay close attention to changes in the patient's breathing pattern, pointing out sighs, deep breaths, shallow breathing, or the holding of one's breath. All of these are signs that the person is experiencing something inside, so I use these outward signs to inquire as to what is happening inside. One sign, in fact, of someone who is more aware of themselves is that they allow themselves to alter their moods and attitudes by naturally altering their breathing patterns. These people tend to be more aware of their bodies and consciously attend to caring for them.

Once we understand that changes in our breath pattern are indications that something emotional is taking place inside, we can learn to monitor ourselves. And, since meditation teaches us to monitor our breathing much more closely and carefully than any other natural method, it follows that meditation practice will help us learn better emotional self-control if we are quickly able to notice and alter our breathing patterns.

With our breath, we can literally change our consciousness. This is what the powerful breathing techniques utilized by Eastern Yoga masters are all about (as well as why children enjoy experimenting with holding their breath and hyperventilating). The point here is that instead of simply taking our breath for granted and keeping it on 'automatic pilot,' once we begin working consciously with our breath, we realize how powerful a tool it can be in assisting inner transformation. Let's try a simple breathing exercise.

Setting and position
Find a quiet physical setting where you will not be distracted by noise from outside or other people. If a natural setting is convenient, this tends to help from being distracted. If not, just find a quiet space in your home. Sitting in a comfortable chair or on a pillow on the floor, let yourself begin to settle into the chair or pillow. Let yourself relax but stay alert – refrain from lying down as this will make it too easy to fall asleep once you are relaxed.

If you are sitting in a chair, let your feet touch the floor with your legs uncrossed and let your hands find a natural, comfortable position in your lap. Your back should be straight, but don't strain to make it erect. If you are sitting on a pillow on the floor, cross your legs without straining. Find a position which you can stay with comfortably without moving.

Other considerations before beginning
(1)   Make sure there is nothing you need to do which may distract you before beginning meditation. You will find it very hard to concentrate if you know there is something you should be attending to instead.
(2)   Make sure you are not being affected by a non-prescription drug or alcohol when meditating. The effects of the meditation will not be 'pure,' and less likely to be generalized to other sessions.
(3)   Do not have any drinks with caffeine at least two hours before beginning meditation. It will make it more difficult to relax and focus your attention.
(4)   Do not use any tobacco at least an hour before practicing.
(5)   Do not eat any food for at least an hour before practicing, as this too, will make concentration more difficult and create stomach rumblings.
(6)   Make sure to move very slowly upon completion of the meditation. Take some time to stretch your legs and take some deep

221

breaths, making sure not to move abruptly. Enjoy the feelings and sensations derived from your meditation and stay with them awhile.

Breath focus with counting anchor: Instructions
Take a deep breath. Notice the tendency to want to control your breathing. In meditation, you don't want to control your breathing; you want to let it go naturally, just as it wants. When we focus on the breath, it is normal to want to try and control it, so you want to resist this temptation. Breathe through your nose, letting the air come in naturally as your diaphragm expands. Then let the breath go out of your lungs slowly, letting all the air out. As you exhale slowly, mentally count 1.

Now, inhale again, without forcing, just letting in as much air as you need. Then exhale again and count 2. Continue focusing on your breathing, letting the air come and go, without altering the natural rhythm or forcing it in any way. After each exhalation count the next number until you reach 10. Then begin again with 1 until you reach 10 again.

Don't be surprised or upset if you can't make it to 10 without being distracted! If you become distracted by a thought or sensation, notice it, let it go, and return to your breath, again beginning with 1 each time you lose your place. Simply notice whatever may grab your attention, and as soon as you catch your mind wandering, come back to your breath and your counting.

Do not be judgemental if you lose your place, just keep returning to your breath and your counting. It is perfectly normal for the monkey-mind to wander – that is its nature! Try to stay with this meditation exercise at least 10–15 minutes, staying as physically still as possible and resisting any temptation to move. Just notice the impulse to move and come back to your breath.

After 10–15 minutes, when you feel ready, gradually open your eyes and sit quietly for a minute or so. Notice what you experience in your body and how you are feeling. The purpose of silently counting 1–10 is to help keep your attention anchored in the present and with your breath. Do not count absent-mindedly! Using the above instructions (if you feel ready), let yourself take some time now to try this basic meditation.

The Zen Koan: Fighting Fire with Fire

We have said that the discriminating mind is a powerful sword to help cut through the confusion when we are bombarded by information and possibilities in daily decision-making. But in the process of stilling the mind, the intellect many times gets in the way to prevent us from achieving meditative tranquility.

In Zen Buddhism, a technique used to confront the intellect and to tune out outside distraction is called the *koan*. The koan is a riddle that can't be answered through the rational mind, no matter how hard the intellect tries to come up with a suitable answer. For example, two popular ones are, 'What is the sound of one hand clapping?' and 'What was the color of your face before you were born?'

In traditional Zen meditation, the koan is used by Zen masters to make the rational intellect give up its struggle to control. When the intellect is forced, through the frustration of not being able to solve the riddle, to give up, the meditator is then ready to find an immediate, intuitive, non-rational answer that teaches him the limits of rational problem solving. As well, it tends to help the meditator become very single-minded in his purpose to find the 'correct' answer.

The intellect is, to put it simply, turned back against itself to show its own limitations, much as fire can be used to help contain itself. The Zen master rejects all solutions offered by the meditator, no matter how clever they may be. He is not looking for clever solutions, he is looking for an indication that the student has penetrated to the core of the koan. The meditator is forced to realize that awakening to an acceptable answer to the master can occur only when one goes beyond words and reason.

This method points to one of the beliefs in Zen practice: all awakening can occur only here and now, in the immediacy of present experience, and one must clear one's mind of all concepts, which act as a screen or buffer between the clear apprehension of what is freshly immediate.

One consequence of working with a koan for a while is that one tends to come to an understanding about the power of even the highest use of the discriminating mind. One begins not to take intellectual concepts as seriously, realizing that concepts are useful but not real; they are mental constructs, or internal pictures about the world. And though they are indispensable for smooth funtioning in our daily world, they do not necessarily bring us any closer to the clarity of the awakened mind.

The kingdom of enlightenment is not paved with intellectual constructs! (although philosophical inquiry can be part of a path of devotion, as it is for the Orthodox Jews around the world). This is one message that can be learned by meditating with a koan. Intellectual constructs, though, can be of great help in getting us on the right road to the kingdom.

On the practical level of daily decision-making and problem solving, there are certain problems that have no logical, rational solution. The only viable solution may be paradoxical, something that may not seem part of rational problem solving but indeed will solve the problem. And the power of the Zen koan is that it teaches us this in a very direct manner. When the intellect is 'frozen' for a period (as the result of being turned back against itself), as it becomes with meditative koan practice, we are then more willing to trust the intuitive solutions we come up with that the intellect cannot alone provide. The discriminating mind makes room for paradox and intuition without becoming superstitious or magical.

Zen koan practice is best used when one has access to a Zen teacher trained to use this potent tool, who can help the student gain something from it. The tendency of those trying to work with a koan on their own is both not to go deeply enough with the koan and/or to trick themselves into believing they have found a clever rational answer to the koan.

In not going deep enough, one does not reach the utter and complete frustration that sends the rational mind into overload and 'tilts' the rational process. It is only when this rational searching and struggling is completely knocked off balance that ego is ready to believe its rational functions are not enough to do the job of solving the riddle. And then it gives up and lets intuition and spontaneity take over.

Regarding the other problem (believing that it has found an elegant rational solution to the koan), ego still has not realized its own limitations and therefore the whole meaning of koan practice is never understood. Ego becomes caught up in its own cleverness and there is no teacher to help point out the self-delusion. So these are the problems which arise in not having a teacher to work with in this method. Because koan practice can lead to great frustration, it is not something to experiment with on your own in an intensive way.

If you simply want to experience the effects of the mental tension and strain that accompany this kind of concentrative mental exercise, try one of the above koans. Spend a day coming back to the koan, 'What is the sound of one hand clapping?' in all spare moments and stick with it rigorously during meditation periods. This should give you a taste of what this kind of riddle can do to your mental processes. Here is another one you can play with: What was the color of the sky before I was born?' Or this one: 'How do you know your Buddha mind at the honking of a car horn?'

But, again, if you want to take this kind of practice seriously, it is mandatory to find a teacher who is qualified to help you. And the only context you will find this teacher will be in formal Zen meditation groups. So it definitely is not for everyone. I share koan study only as an example of a powerful inner tool.

Chanting: the Use of Sound Vibrations

As mentioned in a previous chapter, chanting certain sounds and phrases can also help us focus our attention and blot out outside distractions. When we become absorbed in a chant, for example, 'Om Nama Shivaya,' we begin to reach a deeper level of our minds that cuts through the chattering mind that is so much a part of our usual internal awareness.

When we chant something over and over, the deep vibrations of the sounds themselves have a strong effect on our consciousness. The mental quieting and physical serenity that occurs is a result, like the koan, of total absorption of your mind on the task. The actual meaning of the chant is not as important as the sounds themselves. The syllable 'om' alone can be used. Or the word, 'Ah' can be used. Stay with the sound you choose, repeating it again and again.

Chanting holds a valued place in most well-known world religions and spiritual philosophies. In Buddhism, Hinduism, Christianity, Judaism and Islam we find various forms of chanting. These chants serve to reinforce certain beliefs held by each religion or philosophy. As well, they work to reinforce group cohesion by emotionally binding people together.

Through chanting, people can share their breath (spirit) together. And, as anyone knows who has heard (or participated in) hundreds of people chanting together in a temple or church, the effects of the deep level of resonance can be very powerful on the consciousness of all involved.

And now, let me take a short detour to make the rationale for these inner methods more clear. We want much more than just mental and physical calmness from all this. At the same time, this detour will briefly but pointedly offer an explanation for the disenchantment by so many with our traditional institutional religious systems in the Western world.

A Short 'Sermon' on What's Missing in Western Religion

Unfortunately, most of the institutional religions don't explain the value of chanting in terms of change of consciousness or the desire for personal experience (if they explain chanting at all). Instead, they tend to get people involved in the meaning of the words themselves and the holy scripture the words point to.

They also, as we all know, tend to be heavy on moralizing and light on pointing to real tools which can help us use discriminating wisdom to make real-life decisions, or find spiritual meaning beyond relative ego. This goes beyond the psychological needs of security, group cohesion and reinforcement of beliefs. People want more than emotional security from religion. They want more than just to be told what is 'right' and 'wrong.'

But decision-making is not the real issue here, because traditional religion does not necessarily exist to help people make decisions, even though it does claim to teach 'right' from 'wrong' and deal with the existential questions as to meaning of existence, death, and the nature of faith and man's relation to his fellow man.

The real issue is that those who 'lead their flocks' don't fully understand or respect people's deeper need for an actual *experience* of something of their nature beyond themselves. *Almost all of them, it is safe to say, have never an actual experience of their own God-nature.* How, then, can they help others experience something they have never had for themselves and don't even value?

And those fundamentalist and charismatic preachers who claim they have spoken to God, use their 'guidance' from God to collect large amounts of money and engage in various other questionable activities that only make intelligent people see them as phony salesmen. Religion, as we all know (regardless of whether we like it or not), is big business and these men have learned that there is, indeed, a 'looking to go to heaven and free myself of guilt' sucker born every minute.

The recent exposures of some of these preachers' 'sins' of adultery and their subsequent downfall only confirms what many have long known – it was only a matter of time before those claiming to be 'holier than thou' would get caught with their self-righteous pants down.

What I find humorous about their explanations (rationalizations) is what I hear from followers of a particular leader, 'He is showing us that he is just like us, he is human, too – does all the same bad stuff as us. We like him even more, now that we see he has clay feet. Now he is more human, just like us.'

Rather than question his authority when he is unable to live up to the moral and ethical principles he espouses, they forgive him for being 'just another frail human being' like them. I don't believe this is 'compassion' but refusal to have one's beliefs threatened by reality. This is excuse-making, pure and simple. Suffice it to say regarding many of these holier-than-thou preachers: 'People who live in fragile glass houses shouldn't throw moralistic stones.' I find their thinking and philosophies shallow and self-serving, their actions reprehensible, and their style of fast-talk Godsmanship phony and laughable. And laughable it is, except for the great numbers of people who get sucked in and end up crying.

As for those 'men of the cloth' who are moral, upstanding, and revered members of the religious and social community, most of them aren't even interested (consciously) in having this kind of a mystical oneness experience with God because they don't believe it is even possible. They are only interested in deepening their faith. But the point is, and I will make it as strongly as I am able: YOU DON'T NEED FAITH IF YOU HAVE HAD (AND CAN HAVE) THE REAL THING!

Beyond Belief and Beyond Faith

Institutional religion has lost its appeal for many because, with the exception of wanting people to experience deeper belief in that which they (supposedly) can't personally know (called 'faith'), the goal of these religions is *not* to end up with an experience. Rather than being content to just have faith, one can personally *know*, for example, what Christ was talking about when he said, 'I and my Father are One' and many other statements made in religious scripture of the great traditions by illuminated figures who have communicated their personal understanding of finding their own identity with the Supreme and Ultimate Godhead.

What our churches and temples neglect to teach us is that if these illuminated humans throughout history can have these realization experiences, SO CAN WE!!! In the realm of connecting to our God-likeness, anything one outstanding human being has done can potentially be done by the rest of us, if only we are taught how to get there and willing to do the work.

This especially holds true in the realm of mystical experience. But we do have to be willing to go through the age-old steps that all those preceding us have used to reach a deeper connection to their very being. While Absolute self is just a blink away, learning to enter Absolute self in the space of that blink can take a long, long time!

Instead, we are told to simply *believe in* what is told to us. We are told to have faith in what the scriptures tell us. But at no time are we told, 'If you do this and then this and follow these instructions very carefully, you, too, can experience what Christ and Moses were talking about.' To put it simply, these religions have substituted belief for personal experience.

At a deep level, then, I believe we want the same thing that Jesus, Moses, Mohammed, Buddha and all well-known spiritual figures wanted – to find oneness with whatever they took to be their Godhead. They wanted to be enveloped in the All and Everything, pure and simple. Wouldn't you, too, like this? Isn't that what all the spiritual searching is all about? Beyond belief, beyond faith, and beyond charismatic personalities and charitable giving to those who are not as fortunate, what we want is **experience**. *We don't just want to be told the truth, we want to live and be the truth!*

228

Not so surprisingly, this has been a crucial factor in the alienation and mass exodus from institutional religion. Large numbers in the last twenty five years, and especially in the last ten years, have felt a stronger pull toward Eastern religions and so-called 'New Age' philosophies and methods.

The 'New Age' has finally caught on. And with its new popularity and the heightened search for spiritual meaning have already come the reports of spiritual casualties, where emotional and psychological harm are part of the desperate desire to join, follow leaders, be told what is 'true,' and sometimes give away one's financial right arm for the possibility of experiencing the 'real thing.'

Although what one is 'sold' by many New Age groups may not be the 'real thing,' the temptation to 'go for the experience' is a powerful one, and at least correctly (I believe) motivated by wanting to go beyond believing in scripture and ritual alone and toward becoming one with God. It is no surprise, then, that channeling, crystals, various psychological–spiritual groups and a plethora of self-aggrandizing Western 'gurus' compete for the money and minds of those hungry to get a taste of the real thing.

And, be they real or phony, this is exactly what the 'New Age' methods promise. Once again, we must use the discriminating mind to separate the authentic, time-tested methods that have been used for centuries by all the great known and unknown spiritual mystics from the very recent, trendy, glittery and unauthentic methods that promise us the real thing but can't deliver the goods.

Some spiritual traditions, like Buddhism and Hinduism, are more able to appreciate this need for us to experience for ourselves what it means to be 'touched by the spirit.' And, because of this, chanting is important in these traditions as a way to touch something much deeper and more universal in ourselves. End of 'sermon.'

Let's get back to the steps in meditation, keeping in mind that the goal of meditation practice is not just to learn to calm ourselves, but to use it as a tool to help us understand the nature of our minds at the deepest levels possible. Of course, this is something that takes years of dedicated practice. But we must at least mention this goal, so that we do not think of meditation as just another method to temporarily reduce stress and anxiety. It can be this, but it can also be so much more.

Going Beyond the Breath: Focus on Thoughts

After learning to let the breath come and go on its own, without needing to change it in any way, and learning to let various sensations come and go without focusing too intently on them, the next thing we notice as we continue meditation practice is the persistence of the internal dialogue. This dialogue (or monologue) has, of course, been one of the main themes of this book. When the body has been stilled, our attention begins to turn in a more focused manner to this internal chatter.

We begin to notice more powerfully this incessant chatter of the mind and, because we are not distracting ourselves as we usually do in focusing on the outside world, we are more able to notice how seductive this dialogue may be and compelling in its ability to cause lapses of concentration.

It is exactly this dialogue that so much of the time during our normal waking consciousness is contributing to our confused thinking, the sense of being out of control of our minds, and the difficulty in gaining the clarity of the discriminating mind, which leads to discriminating wisdom.

And remember, this incessant chatter is having an effect on us even when we are not aware of it. It is exactly this chatter that persistent meditation practice helps us quell. But many times, the chatter actually increases (as we focus on it and therefore hear it more loudly) before it quiets down. This is a stage that seems to be part of the process. It is, to invert a popular saying, the 'storm before the calm.'

But the stronger the chatter *consciously* becomes, the more we can acknowledge how it may be affecting our thinking and behavior, *unconsciously*. And this is an important step, as it makes us want to work harder to gain some semblance of control over our own minds.

Now, when these internal dialogues become the focus of attention, they can be so interesting in their content that oftentimes we find it fascinating to stay with them and then 'forget' to come back to the breath for what can feel like an eternity. Instead of experiencing the dialogue as a distraction, we actually enjoy listening to it.

For minutes at a time we may be caught in these thought chains that lead to questioning, answering and the further internal 'discussion' that arises. Monologue upon associated monologue may run through their course before we even notice how far away from breath-counting we have gotten.

Combine this with long-forgotten memories which may surface and compellingly sharp images, and you can see why we can get lost 'at the internal movies' rather than being able to stay with the breath, which in comparison may seem 'boring.'

When this process is speeded up, as it tends to get when one meditates intensively, for many hours, days at a time, instead of being interesting content, the images and dialogue turn into nothing but chatter. It's as if we are listening to a tape recording going too fast, where we are unable to make sense of what we are hearing because so much of it is non-sense.

And yet, this non-sense once again serves to help us realize what is really going on inside and proves beyond the proverbial 'shadow of a doubt' that, for the most part, we aren't in control of our own minds. You don't need to meditate intensively to get to the point of hearing the dialogue for the chatter that it really is. It just gets you to this point of awareness more quickly, that's all.

Many times, as we have pointed out previously, this internal chattering is not very useful in real-life problem solving. It certainly distracts us from staying present-centered, and all those who experiment with meditation for even a few weeks consistently report the overwhelming sense of being unable to control the strength, nature and direction of this internal chatter.

The meditator, after persistent practice of bringing his attention back to the breath upon discovery of having veered off, begins to sense a growing ability to let thoughts come without getting pushed off track, and is able to allow them to come and go while staying with the breath. This is the first step in sensing some control.

One of the more interesting things that may be witnessed as one's attention becomes more focused with longer and deeper meditations is this: it is possible to be totally focused on one's breath, counting each breath, and yet still notice a subtle dialogue or monologue taking place in the background. It is like having something cooking on the back burner. It may be on low but it is still cooking!

At deeper levels of penetration of the mind, we identify and become enthralled by still more and more subtle thought traces that arise, seemingly against any and all efforts to bar them from awareness. But at the same time, we are able to feel a growing ability to come back to the breath more quickly. It is only because our perceptual ability has become more and more refined that we are even able to identify or 'hear' these more subtle layers of thought. So, this is actually a positive sign that our concentration is sharpening.

This is back to the idea earlier presented in this book regarding the 'signal/noise ratio.' Remember, as the mind becomes quieter, the 'signal' of more subtle thoughts is able to come through because we have managed to quiet down the usual 'noise' that prevents these more subtle layers from being perceived. We should remember that it is not until we have practiced sometimes for long, intense periods that we reach this stage of higher 'signal' and less 'noise.' But this is not to say that we can't significantly lower the 'noise' level with a few months of regular practice.

Actually, beginners in meditation report feeling calm, relaxed and more able to settle into the present within a few weeks of daily practice. And because this calming of the body and initial quieting of the mind is so pleasing, it motivates the beginner to stay with practicing. In this way it is important in moving to deeper levels of practice.

Like everything else in our culture, meditation practice is undertaken by most with the idea of wanting something to happen FAST. And within a reasonably short time, the meditator *can* get a sample of benefits of practice as he notices his internal sense of comfort upon ending meditation, feeling more relaxed but also more alert.

Being physically still is actually a very natural state, but one which many of us have lost touch with. So, there may be some initial anxiety about staying completely still and turning the attention inward. But once we go through this anxiety, we settle into a peacefulness that we have known many times before in our lives.

For example, after an exhausting day, as we lay down to go to sleep, the body becomes enjoyably peaceful; or those moments soon after we awaken from a refreshing sleep but are still with a dream fragment and before we start moving to get out of bed. This same peacefulness is possible to enter in and out of voluntarily with high degree of reliability once we have mastered quieting the body through meditation.

The Next Step: the Ability to Witness

The next step in this process, after we have learned to keep the body still, and are able to bring the attention back to the breath without getting lost for too long in thoughts, is the ability to witness our thoughts as they come up without having to get caught in them. This is what we talked about in the chapter on the witness.

Instead of each thought dragging us into its whirlpool and then being sucked into all its associated thought-swirls, the observing ego is able to witness the thoughts coming and going and still maintain the focus of attention on the breath.

Slowly, as we practice strengthening this observing witness (see Chapter 9), it becomes possible to sit back and actually watch the origin of an association, how it develops into a full-blown thought, how it reaches its height and may have an associated feeling that goes with it, and then how it begins to diminish in intensity, slowly break up and then pass on into oblivion. This, of course, takes a good deal of concentration and clarity. I offer it as what is possible when one's practice of watching one's thoughts becomes highly developed.

It's like the old technique for falling asleep of watching sheep jump over a fence, one after another. When people try using the sheep-counting technique, they don't get caught in caring about what the sheep look like or how they may differ in their jump from one another. Nor do they care where the sheep came from or where they are going. All they do is let one sheep after another appear, jump over the fence and go along its merry way. In the same way, we can learn to witness thoughts coming into awareness, 'jumping' over the fence of our attention and then passing away, without any need to get caught in the actual content of the thought.

Once we are able to treat our thoughts like passive sheep, and not care any more about one than we do about another, we have reached an important goal in the meditative process. *We have developed the witness.* And, of course, once we can do this on a regular basis in meditation, we also will gain benefit in our normal, everyday process of decision-making. That's why we devoted a whole chapter to developing and strengthening the witness.

Although it takes some time to develop the skill, we learn how to hold off from immediate indulgence in whatever impulse may come up. Instead of reaching for that cookie or that cigarette, we can notice the impulse and pause, making a conscious decision as to whether we wish to follow the impulse or not. This is a further step in feeling more control of our minds!

And, if we have not already made it clear in previous chapters, it is exactly this sense of control that teaches us more finely tuned discrimination, so that we don't feel so swayed by the opinions, judgements and demands of others. *This takes time*, and no matter how often I try to help those I consult with to understand this, almost everyone wants to be able to discriminate clearly NOW.

Everyone wants an altered state of consciousness (absorption, seeing lights, colors, feeling currents of energy, etc.), without having to do the concentrated work to get there. *Always, the main principle to remember is this:* **keep coming back to the breath again and again, no matter what comes up**. And slowly, you will develop the ability to reach more concentrated, peaceful and even blissful states of mind.

INFORMAL MEDITATION IN THE EVERYDAY WORK WORLD

Staying Centered in the Present, No Matter Where Your Feet May Take You

We can adopt a simple-to-understand but potent meditative practice from the Buddhist Vipassana tradition to help us stay present-centered no matter where our feet may take us during our busy workday. And that is simply to pay attention to our actual walking, to the sensation of one foot touching the ground after another.

When done in a more formal context, we try to slow down to super-slow motion the process of taking one step after another. In the Vipassana tradition, this leads to being aware of the desire to lift up the foot, and then the beginning movement of the foot. We notice what part of the foot moves first and what follows. Then we notice the movement forward and then the placing of the foot down on the pavement or floor.

This can be slowed down to such an extent that it takes great focus and presence of mind to stay physically balanced in just taking a few steps. This is a common practice and is a movement form of bringing all of our attention to the task of each movement and even each intention to move, when our awareness becomes refined to a high degree. In traditional meditation retreats, this type of extremely slow walking meditation forms the complement of sitting meditation.

But let us adapt this practice to our literally fast-paced workday by doing the following: any time you begin to feel scattered, no matter what may be the cause, the tendency is to lose literal touch with our movement in the world. We get caught in our heads, either playing back the meeting that took place an hour ago, that phone conversation with a customer, the boss, or that disappointment with . . . who knows what?

Or, we are rushing to that next appointment, behind schedule because we have boxed ourselves into too tight a schedule (read the second half of Chapter 2 again!), or are rehearsing for that meeting with the next customer, sales prospect, or what have you. The point is we are in our heads, in the past or the future, and our feet are scurrying about disconnected from our heads.

So, the method for coming back to the present is this? Begin to slow down your pace of walking, at least slow enough so that you can notice the touch of your shoe on the ground at each and every step with FULL AWARENESS!! As your foot touches the ground, silently note to yourself, 'touching, touching,' just as your foot touches the ground.

As soon as you do this, notice what happens to your sense of physical balance. If you slow down your pace and put your attention on the touching of your foot to the ground and stay with this at least five minutes uninterruptedly, you have my guarantee that you will have come back into the present and feel more in control and less harried.

This walking meditation for those in a hurry will work wonders if you are willing to do the mental noting of 'touching, touching' each time your foot hits the ground. The key to this tool is that you can't walk any faster than you are able to fully note your foot touching the ground. Notice what happens to your rhythm of breathing when you slow down your pace. Notice how you feel inside.

Personal Journal: Heightening the Sense of 'My Unfolding Story'

Another good method for prompting inner awakening is the personal journal. In learning the discipline to keep an ongoing journal, we get a sense of the free flow of our ideas from day to day. We begin to hear our own thoughts in a clearer way, and how to express the thoughts, feelings and the events that make up our daily life.

The journal should become more than just record keeping. While some of the events of our days are worth reporting in a journal, the best use of the journal is to keep some sense of the rhythm of our inner world. Dreams, fantasies, wishes for the future and the sense we make out of our own daily projects are all worth our recording.

We learn how to get some distance from ourselves. We see that there are certain daily, weekly and monthly patterns we tend to follow. And because we are taking time to record our thoughts and feelings, we are showing ourselves care and concern. We are *worth* recording our own impressions of life! And a daily journal helps reinforce this.

If you want to try a daily journal, start by buying a special blank book or notebook for this purpose. Or you can buy any one of a number of already put-together books for this purpose. Decide on a specific time of day to make your entries, even down to a specific daily time if you think you will follow through with the assigned time. Focus on recording thoughts and feelings, rather than what you did in a day.

A journal for helping stimulate the internal world is not the same as a simple recording of dates, places and activities. We are using the journal writing to record those less tangible and more fleeting thoughts, feelings, images, dreams and fantasies that help us understand where our attention drifts to when it flies off on its own.

Try to write something every day for at least a month. Then go back and read everything for the month. See if you can discover any patterns of your thoughts or recurrent fantasies or dreams. Let yourself become increasingly open to yourself about your deeper fears, hopes, dreams – all the stuff you might not normally write down or talk to anyone about because you don't think they're important.

And above all, try not to be critical of how you express your thoughts. Don't worry about your sentence structure, or how complete your thoughts are. The main thing is to get it down in writing. No one (but yourself) wants to judge you on your writing!

Journal writing gives us a sense of flow in our lives, helps us see a little longer-range view of life, and also gives us a tangible record of the processes that make for the creation of meaning in our projects. We can come to appreciate the passing interests that lead to new interests and the concerns that never seem to pass away, always coming back to be dealt with in one form or another.

It also improves our ability to creatively express what is going on inside. It therefore sharpens the discriminating mind, forcing us to identify exactly what is coming up inside. We begin to have a clear access channel to the unconscious mind and are more in touch with ourselves.

Dream Journal: Waking Up to Unconscious Images

If you want to focus specifically on working with dreams, it may be helpful to keep a separate dream journal. This should be put beside your bed where you can get at it easily upon awakening. Dream journals are great aids if you are in the process of psychotherapy and can focus with a therapist on the meaning of dream symbols.

Although it is possible to make sense of your own dreams, our defenses tend to make us shelter ourselves from uncomfortable interpretations of dream symbols that might be offered by a trained psychotherapist. Therefore, I feel that dream work is best done with someone who can be more objective.

On a more surface level, however, we can relate the themes that come up in our dreams to daily concerns when the content is fairly transparent. For example, when our dreams are filled with violence and anger, we can ask how this theme may relate to people who we are angry at and fantasize doing violence to in our interpersonal world. Or if our dreams are filled with sex and erotic themes we can look at whether our sexual needs are being satisfied.

Or maybe images related to unfinished work projects keep coming up over a period of nights. This can be a transparent way for the unconscious mind to let us know that something is not right or completed at work. This kind of connecting we can do on our own, without a psychotherapist.

In this way, everyone who can remember even fragments from dreams is in a position to learn what their unconscious is telling them about their daily needs and desires. The more you focus on sharpening dream images, the clearer these images become and the easier they will be to remember. Just as you are waking up, if you want to preserve a dream image, stay still in bed and see if you can make the images as sharp as possible before you make any movement. Not moving helps keep the images in mind.

For those who have trouble remembering their dreams but who want to become more aware of them, I suggest the following: tell yourself just as you are ready to fall asleep that you will remember your dreams. Cross your hands at the wrists over your chest as you lie on your back.

Tell yourself you will remember, once you are asleep, any dream fragments that are worth remembering and that it is OK to forget any that don't seem important. Trust your unconscious mind to help you tell the difference between what is worth remembering and what isn't. Tell yourself that you will remember, once you are dreaming, just how you have placed your hands across your chest as you fall asleep. Each time in the dream you see hands, you will 'remember to remember' your dreams. This should make it easier, after you are able to 'remember to remember,' for images to stay upon awakening.

Catching Self-Images: Use of Audio and Video Feedback

Two other tools in helping wake up to ourselves are audio and video feedback. Recording ourselves on a portable tape recorder gives us feedback on the sound of our voice. It also helps us realize how easily we may distort what we hear from other people in common conversation. We can hear how we cut in on the other, or don't really respond directly to what they are saying, simply having two parallel conversations.

Many patients choose to record therapy sessions for a while and are many times amazed to hear all kinds of things that they missed when the conversation was occurring. When the pressure to perform is off, we are more able to listen carefully without any distraction of competing need. Try recording typical conversations with family members or friends, getting their permission to tape, but trying not to alter your normal way of speaking.

Also try recording just your own thoughts after some event which gets you reflecting. Maybe a conversation with a friend or loved one. Be easier with yourself and see if you can get comfortable simply expressing your thoughts into the recorder. Don't feel compelled to play it back. Just speak into the recorder for a while and see if you can lose any self-consciousness about your thoughts being recorded.

Even more powerful than audio feedback is video feedback. To not only hear ourselves, but see ourselves as well, can be of great help in working with our own body-image and self-image as to how we interact with others, and how we look to others when we express ourselves. Video, in other words, provides a safe and penetrating tool for us to sharpen our awareness of how we present ourselves to the world. Facial expressions, gestures, and subtle body movement are all available before us to see as clearly as we are able.

One positive effect of 'high-tech' and the advent of small, hand-held video cameras is that greater numbers of people may now have 'instant feedback' concerning their interactions with others. Everything we say or do can be recorded and played back so that we may reinforce, change, or borrow from what we see on the video screen.

This is an especially powerful tool for infants and young children to gain a sense of self-identity through. They can see themselves as they were just minutes before and therefore gain a strong sense of their body-image and self-image at very young ages. This can only be positive and not something that was widely available in the same way even five years ago, just as personal computers are changing the way children learn, think about and manipulate their worlds.

Final Comments on Self-Reflection and Inner Awakening

My intent in this chapter has been to emphasize the power of meditation and other methods for helping us learn more about the inner world. There are a lot of books focusing on methods, so I have just mentioned a few that I find helpful. What seems most important to convey is the importance of self-discipline in using these tools in a beneficial way. Waking up to the internal world is a step-by-step process, not something we can do overnight.

Once we are ready to remember more and more of the contents of our inner worlds, we *do* remember more. And, we can get to a point where the flow of content to the conscious mind is steady and continuous. We can process more and more images, dream contents and fantasies with full awareness because we are continually paying attention, ready for any signals that come bubbling up from the unconscious mind. Our psychic energy goes into welcoming rather than resisting. At almost all times, we know what we are thinking or feeling about something taking place in our daily world.

We begin to experience words coming as colors or sounds evoking images. In psychology, the term for this is 'synesthesia.' This is the crossing over or combining of one sense channel into or with another. We notice our senses working together more harmoniously than we thought possible. We hear the tin, silvery color of the horn when it blows or the strong vibration of a sound makes our bodies cringe with a certain emotion. Sounds may also come as colors. Tastes may evoke flashes of memory.

Far too many of those who begin a practice like meditation are not given the help they need in monitoring their practice so they don't develop bad habits. This is where a good meditation teacher comes in handy. Without a group and teacher to help support initial efforts at meditation, it is easy to be put off by the persistence required to learn the technique well enough to make it work.

We become easily frustrated, and as with so many other projects, become critical of ourselves and then give up the effort. We end up learning that self-reflection is not worth the frustration. But the price we pay is to be out of touch with ourselves. Without some kind of self-reflective methods, too much goes by like a whirlwind, in which we are right back to feeling like we are on the caboose watching the railroad tracks go by.

Meditation is one of those tools that gets better with ongoing practice. Once you have learned to sit quietly, focus on thoughts and use the observing witness, the benefits can begin to be really appreciated. But expect frustration and never underestimate the trickery of the monkey-mind to try and impose its scattered control.

=== 12 ===

GLIMPSES OF ONENESS

Is there anything more important in our lives than trying to discover ourselves, than finding out who we really are? Don't most of the other things that we hold to be valuable tend toward the discovery of who we really are in one form or another? After our basic material needs, and the needs of those we care for, are satisfied, isn't this what it's all about?

Whether it be wealth, status, sexual conquest, power, dedication to family, or service to others – all of these are in some way attempts to feel good about ourselves, and secure about our place in life (and for some, the afterlife). They are all attempts, when looked at psychologically, to come to grips with ourselves, to understand who we are and how we can accept and love ourselves. We hope for balance and integration in our lives, where we are able to satisfy our various needs and find a harmony in the flow of our daily life. We hope to maximize the pleasure and minimize the pain.

This, of course, doesn't mean this is our conscious motive! We may think, 'I just want to earn a lot of money so I can get the adulation and envy of those around me.' Or we may think, 'I just want to be a good family man, dedicated to those I love.' But when we look more closely at why these things are important to us, we see that accepting and loving ourselves is at the 'heart' of the matter.

And when we are *convinced*, in our proverbial 'heart of hearts,' that we really *do* love ourselves, and therefore have what we need, it then becomes more possible for us to love and care about others. One way I say this to patients is, 'If your own emotional tank is close to empty, you're not going to have much left to give to anyone else.'

241

As we said in an earlier chapter, once we have achieved a certain level of self-acceptance and still feel incomplete, we may then be ready to find something beyond ourselves, beyond the material success we have enjoyed but found less than totally satisfying. We can look beyond loving ourselves to letting go of ourselves.

But loving ourselves, at least enough to feel a basic sense of relative self-security, is the primary step before we start feeling any real urge to experience Absolute self. It's the same 'economic' principle as above. We can't risk this precious sense of relative self if we don't know for sure that it won't be ripped away.

If we can connect to something deeper in ourselves which goes beyond relative ego/self, then whatever material success we have achieved can feel like enough to be satisfying. And what we have, even if it does not measure up to the success of others, seems like enough. Because if *we* are enough then what we have will be enough.

When we do not make ourselves the center of the universe, we can connect to something which makes life not only worth living but worth celebrating. Millions of poor throughout the world are able to not only tolerate their material and physical suffering but honor it.

They find ways of being content with their plight on this earth, because they believe that the better they do this time around, the better life they will be born into the next time around. And while this kind of belief can be used as simply a way to accept and make the best of one's miserable plight, it can also be the result of realizing that one's material reality is really not the measure of one's God-likeness.

Because they feel connected to something larger than themselves, they can celebrate their lives just for what they are. Sometimes they serve God praying for a better life when they are born again. But to experience Absolute self, even a glimpse of it, is to realize a self-perfection that we can't easily forget. It is to always remember that ultimately we are connected. Goodbye loneliness, hello connectedness!

It is, to put it simply, to remember that we are One with God. Not standing apart from God, just worshipping His/Her Perfection, but realizing *we too* are perfection, just as we are. As we said before, this does not mean 'just the way we are' is how *we* think we ought to be. And it doesn't mean that all our needs are taken care of just as we think they should. But it does mean that once we realize our God-likeness and can stay firmly rooted in this realization, we are more accepting of those personality quirks that make us feel separate from others or unworthy.

Because we will have realized Absolute self and seen that we are never very far from it, everything else seems more satisfying. The feeling of inner emptiness is vastly reduced. We don't feel lonely so often or so disconnected to others in the world. We also lose the despair that comes with our awareness of the great amount of suffering in the world.

THE 'LAST CHAPTER' AS METAPHOR AND REALITY

By the concept of the 'Last Chapter' of our lives, I don't mean the two decades or so of remaining 'golden' years before we die, but the metaphoric realization that 'finding oneself' and comprehending the story that one is writing, chapter by chapter, is really the most intriguing and meaningful journey that one can take. It is the 'last chapter' in the sense that once we see ourselves on a journey through life, we no longer need to keep up such a melodramatic story, believing life is nothing but constant struggle.

To realize what the 'last chapter' is about, some people need to have a physical or psychological 'near-death' experience themselves, or perhaps suffer the death of a loved one. We suddenly see the world in a different way, being radically jarred into the awareness of how we take life and our continual existence for granted. In being close to death, we see that much of the time we are worried about things that really aren't so important. But any shocking event can act to wake us up this way.

And this can happen psychologically, too, as very strong jars to relative ego's stability can bring us to new awareness about who we are. Losing a job, going bankrupt, or separating from a close friend or partner may all throw us into a fresh view of ourselves and the world.

A vivid picture now comes to mind. I am standing outside a conference center hall a few years ago in the late evening stars, talking with someone I deeply respect for his brilliant writing. An old graduate school friend I haven't seen for some time walks up to join our conversation. After a few moments of mutual greeting, he says to us, 'I've been feeling the fragility of life lately. I keep tuning into how precarious this whole thing is for us.'

243

And I think, 'Where's this coming from?' And a couple of months later I read he has died in some accident. He was in his mid-thirties. For a few months after I read about his death, this picture of him saying these words would come up again and again. I wondered if maybe he had tuned into something that was about to happen. In any case, my remembering this incident and his last words in my presence seemed quite eerie after learning what happened such a short time later. I have not had this happen with anyone else in my life – where their last words to me were like a foreshadowing of their own death.

We see that so many things aren't important because we once again gain the perspective that, compared to our own mortality, whether we live in this house or that house, drive a Honda or a Mercedes, bake bread or sit on the Supreme Court, we too are going to die. There is an old Eastern saying: 'It would be well for us to wake up before we die.'

When we are awake, we never get very far from the realization of the gift of life. We see the vibrating, shimmering world around us alive with light and sound. One meaning of becoming 'enlightened' is not losing touch with this continual play of light and sound.

In this sense, to be 'enlightened' is to literally be able to see the ongoing light and sound show being presented both in our own minds and out in the physical world. I have always liked the idea that in some European and Far Eastern countries they have 'light and sound' shows at the site of famous monuments or ruins. These light and sound shows are meant to enlighten us about the monument.

The 'light and sound shows' in our minds are meant to enlighten us as to our own true nature. All we have to do is learn to access the experience. My personal experience is that we can, indeed, access the 'light and sound show' inside.

There is a growing body of high-tech methods which help access these mental places. For example, some of the 'New Age' music is aimed at helping unlock the subtle inner sounds that may be heard when one has reached a certain high level of blissful meditative concentration. The hallmark of subtle sound is that it is coming from inside out, rather than from outside in. The music that can be heard is clearly not occurring outside of one's own mind.

Another high-tech device purports to instantly bring people into a deep state of meditative calm through certain vibrational patterns

244

monitored through headphones. Will this kind of high-tech stuff serve to bring us to 'instant samadhi' or is it just one more attempt to find a short cut, or 'easy answer' for something that can only be achieved patiently and with discipline over time?

And what is the purpose of these new methods beyond simple relaxation or sense stimulation? To help us access a sense of our own God-likeness and the physical and mental bliss that may accompany this experience. In India, Nepal and other countries, their greeting to each other is 'Namaste.' This is used to say 'hello' and 'goodbye,' but what it really means is 'I honor the God-like qualities within you.'

One major point I have made in this book is that we need to realize how little attention we usually give to our own minds. And a second point is that there are methods available (and have been for over a thousand years) for doing this. The rest is up to us.

Most of these methods are incompatible with getting too caught up in the need to continually prove that we are special. Once we realize we *are* special, and that *everyone else is too*, then we can stop trying to prove our worth to ourselves and everyone else.

A saying of the cowboys in the old Westerns I watched as a child is appropriate here: 'Well, boys, it's late, I think I'll be turning in.' But instead of going to sleep, as the cowboys meant, this ought to be our slogan as we explore inner space. **I think I'll be turning in.** Not turning *away* from the world; but inside to discover what universe has been left behind for the outside glitter. Or, as we said before, 'The new flame may be hot but the old flame knows how to cook it.' ('Outward glittery experience may be hot, but inward interpretation is what makes meaning of it.')

Instead of viewing our lives as suffering and the overcoming of one obstacle after another, we begin to feel the real joy of creating our own lives. Instead of feeling trapped by the constraints imposed by the world, we feel the freedom to make our own way. We look forward with excitement to what is just around the bend. We learn how to turn apprehension, dread and anxiety into curious anticipation, tinged with excitement. Clearly, this is one sign of a high-level mentally healthy person and what distinguishes one who is fully present from one who is neurotically fearful of the future.

So we stop some of the drama and begin to focus exclusively on the 'last chapter' of waking up. Once we see that making our story more melodramatic than it needs to be only creates more personal suffering and distracts us from the business of waking up, we can consciously let go of much of the hysterics and theatrics. We can also begin to do those things that will quicken our awakening and refrain from those things that only delay it. But this calls for paying attention to ourselves continually.

All the mini-dramas of our daily lives that follow this realization of the 'last chapter' are seen, then, as teachings in the service of our step-by-step awakening. We don't have to see things as predetermined or believe in psychic phenomena to understand how this may affect our perceptions.

For example, when we see ourselves on a 'journey,' then everything that happens to us is seen as meaningful and occurring to teach us something that we need to learn at the time it is occurring. We may not like it, but we see that we have something to learn. Our task is to discover what it is and then learn it. Now, the interesting thing about this kind of belief is that it doesn't matter whether it is ultimately true or not!

In other words, it is more important how we perceive and make sense of the events of our lives than how they 'really' are. Let's say we could look down from some distant heaven and see that all the events of our life are *not* really happening to teach us something. Even if this were true, the fact that we *tell ourselves* that each event is significant and occurring for a reason is what is most important.

This is an important concept to remember: it is the overlay of our own *interpretation* of events (rather than the events themselves) that is most significant in how we make sense of our lives. This is why I have belabored the point in this book of our taking the time to know our own minds, from the inside out, and our need to develop the *discriminating mind* to help us understand our interpretations.

Of course, seeing things in this perspective is not always so easy to put into practice. When we have to suffer, for example, the loss of a loved one, a job disappointment, the failure of an important exam, or find ourselves in physical pain, it is pretty difficult to see what we are going through as 'good for our own self-growth.' It is much easier to feel sorry for ourselves – and most of us do (at least some of the time) exactly that!

To see our lives as a journey of self-discovery is to wonder what we will write next in the book of our lives. It is to realize that the story has never been written ahead of time, but is *always waiting to be written*. It is written by the choices we make, constrictions we create and overcome, and how we manage (or mismanage) the continual freedom we have to alter the course of our lives.

And all of this is done within a degree of overall restraint. The restraint is what we can't control, the chance meetings and seemingly random happenings. Some believe it is all determined and we are simply playing out our roles the way we are supposed to, whether we know it or not. And even if by some chance this is true (allowing for certain outside restraints, it certainly doesn't feel this way to me), we can still act 'as if' we have this freedom and lead our lives accordingly.

This ability to not need to know for sure but still be able to act 'as if' something is true can allow us to sidestep what might otherwise paralyze us. This kind of flexibility is developed through use of the discriminating mind. When we can discriminate clearly, we can see distinct personality parts, and we learn to let them work together.

'First I can be this part, then I'll be that part! Let me play "as if" I really am a successful author. No false modesty for me!'

'Then I'll play the part of a humble and down to earth "rock" who doesn't care about the ego part of it, seeing it will only create further baggage if he gets caught in the trap. Nice sense of humility.'

The trap, that is, of thinking that having written and had published a book qualifies him entrance into the 'Nirvanic Heaven For Big Shot Authors.'

'Dr Hendlin, what do you think about blah, blah, blah?'

'Well, I have nothing more to add to what I said in Chapter 12 of my book, *The Discriminating Mind*. Read my book – if you still have any questions, then perhaps we can discuss this further.'

This is the kind of thing I would hear over a decade ago when I attended graduate school. Professors had become overly self-important and would brush students away by these kind of pompous statements. The written word (so one likes to believe), will become a legacy that will live forever, when one's frail body has withered from the sands of time. One more dusty book on the shelf that testifies to a life measured in words, articles, books and good deeds. So what? Crusty old relative ego becoming cocksure of itself . . . and not being able to see the limitations of one's own mental edifice, built to prop one up in a position of authority.

The 'last chapter' then, as a metaphor, is the tale of our lives that we write once we realize we are in the process of waking up. But, more practically, the 'last chapter' is a dividing point in the various ongoing projects of our lives and is only the last chapter until a new chapter begins. *We* are the ones to designate what will divide one chapter from another, what the major dividing points of our life will be. We can choose which life experiences are colored meaningfully and which aren't.

And we will choose how to remember these dividing points. We can change these memories by changing the way we think about them. No matter how bad they may have originally been, it is possible to see how one has learned certain coping skills as a result of the negative experiences. *We don't remake our personal history but we do re-interpret it as a means to free ourselves from it.*

SOME REFLECTIONS ON THE NATURE OF THIS BOOK

This is the last chapter of this book, the 'last chapter' of what was a personally satisfying project that has taken me somewhat deeper into self-reflection for the last thirteen months of my life. Much of my little free time outside of my psychotherapy work has been spent writing. The completion and subsequent publication of the book is a psychologically meaningful event in my life.

It means I'm willing to risk the relative self 'ego-bashing,' on the one hand, and possible hysterical adulation, on the other, that come with the publication for the wider public. I do not want to play the 'Gee, Dr Murgatroid, you're wonderful!' game any more than I do the 'That Book Isn't So Great' game of ego-bashing. Although I have had my share of success in the world of writing for professional publications, I have not been willing to subject myself to the ego issues involved in writing for the larger public. Who wants to risk rotten tomatoes, when writing for one's peers has been warm and comfy? No promotion necessary, thank you. Just good thinking.

At one time (not so long ago), I would not be willing to do the least promotion of myself because I believed it would be counterproductive to my focus on inner development. I did not want to have to do any promotion of myself or my book. I never liked the antics of self-promotion and the ego problems I saw in most who would 'hawk their wares' at professional and public conferences.

Now I believe I can learn from whatever issues may arise in the self-promotion of my book which publishers expect and most authors enjoy. Standing on my own feet solidly means being able to handle the critical feedback that is a normal part of putting one's wares on the open market. Now as I approach the halfway mark in my life, I'm ready to let the pages fall where they may. Applause or rotten tomatoes – I can handle it all without too much ego on the line.

While I had originally hoped to reach a large audience with a simple-to-understand book on important ideas for self-growth, I now wonder how well I have succeeded in reaching this larger group. I wonder, 'Are these ideas understandable to the educated reader?' 'Will a book on the *discriminating mind* be devoid of what it purports to tout?' Quieting the critical, judging mind is not so tricky any more. I simply tell myself (and fully believe) that any good the book can do in reaching even a relatively small number of people more than makes up for whatever may be its limitations.

In bringing forward the concept of the *discriminating mind*, I have tried to honor the hallowed Western tradition of gaining self-knowledge through the highest use of the rational intellect. I have suggested that the *discriminating mind* is the high-level use the rational mind was made for, the kind of thinking that we all are able to learn to do, within the limitations imposed by our culture, education and genetic inheritance.

It is the clarity of the sword of discriminating wisdom that swiftly cuts through the superstitious, irrational and impulsive. It cuts through the ignorance, short-sightedness and the prejudice. It guides us to make discriminations which save us from further unnecessary suffering. And it keeps us from making further divisions between people and territories that can be perfectly safe without rigid cultural boundaries dividing them. It knows what is worth discriminating between and what isn't. And it is the discriminating mind that we may use to take us beyond discrimination.

I can't teach you how to call on your *discriminating mind* just through offering a few exercises. So rather than bring you to experience this mind, my self-imposed task has been more modest: to simply share with you the concept of this mind and why I believe we need to give it a lot of attention.

The knowledge of how to think clearly, once we have obtained it, is something no one can take away from us. It is developed through formal education, life experience and the willingness to work at

249

making fine rational discriminations between concepts, ideas and things. And always our discriminations may be challenged by someone believing he/she is able to discriminate even more acutely.

We can trust the *discriminating mind* to guide our decision-making, so we are not reliant on just raw emotion, superstition, or intuition alone. It is nurtured by the desire to self-reflect, to take the time to examine our own behavior with an interest in gaining insight. And it is fed by the curiosity which we have to understand rather than to wander blindly, walking backwards through our lives.

With self-insight, a trust in one's intuitions and deeper gut feelings, we've got almost all we need to make the journey through life. Relationships, rewards, satisfactions all follow when these qualities and skills are available to us. When we are able to present ourselves to others with a sense of security and vitality, people respond to us and our needs will be satisfied. How many really understand or believe this?

This genuine self-confidence and inner self-possession is not something that can be faked or learned at a course on selling oneself or 'positive thinking.' It can only come from deep self-acceptance and the understanding of one's own mind. As we said, there are no short cuts! And, of course, it is because there are no short cuts that we all too often give up on the rational mind and just go with whatever our impulse is of the moment. We get lazy because we know that clear thinking isn't so easy to do.

It is not, remember, that we are wanting to rely only on the rational intellect. We need to trust our emotions as well. And we also have to be able to intuit what is not clearly known and weigh this into our decision-making as well. The discriminating mind takes us beyond much of the self-delusion and search for easy answers that characterizes our Western culture.

I have indicated why I think the development of the discriminating mind allows us to rest comfortably with relative self, so that Absolute self may become an experiential reality, where no discriminations are necessary. We know relative ego/self is safe and can move into Absolute self without having to worry about who's 'minding the store.' In other words, we know we have a trusted anchor in relative ego, a friend who helps keep our feet on the ground so that it is safe for us to move into the sky of Absolute self.

I have argued that while we tend to pay far too much attention to accumulating fascinating experiences in the glittery outer world, we have not valued the nature of the inner world. That while we test the nature of relative ego/self in the world at large, we test the nature of Absolute self in the inner world. We have let the inner world appear pale in comparison to the outer world. Perhaps it is time to reverse the flow in the other direction, so we may find a balance between the two.

I have suggested that we are obsessed with experience, and that our bias toward *doing* rather than *being* is related to our bias toward the outer rather than the inner. While I make the argument that knowing more about and being comfortable with our *being* will increase the efforts of our *doing*, I also argue that we want to experience something of the spiritual side of ourselves, or what I have termed Absolute self. In this area, we rightly want to go beyond the conceptual (understanding) and emotional and intuitive (faith) and have a true-to-life experience of our higher nature. We can learn to use the *discriminating mind* to help us reach Absolute self without fear.

GLIMPSES OF ONENESS

And now, as we wind down this book, let us return finally to answer a question we posed some time ago. This question relates specifically to the concept of Absolute self, which we have weaved in and out of this book. And it is: How do we have an experience of oneness and still live to tell about it? In other words, who is watching the experience to know that what is being experienced is oneness? If it truly is oneness, who is doing the watching?

Remember, experiencing glimpses of oneness is not the same as being a fully enlightened person. While glimpses of oneness are never far away, becoming 'fully enlightened' is something that may take, in the Eastern scheme of things, many lifetimes! If you need to have things NOW, focus on realizing glimpses of oneness and leave full enlightenment to those who are willing to dedicate one or more lifetimes. That is how one school of Eastern thinking sees it.

But another, Zen Buddhism, sees it quite differently. In Zen, one may become awakened at any moment, without necessarily waiting one or more lifetimes. The right word at the right time, and BINGO! we are suddenly entering into a whole new realm of comprehension.

251

But even this 'instant enlightenment' thinking of Zen presupposes a readiness to wake up, stimulated by just the right crack on the egg of separateness at just the right time. And there are small awakenings and large awakenings, and always more ground to cover.

So, being in a hurry is not going to help us, no matter what view of enlightenment we happen to embrace. And, of course, even if the concept of enlightenment does not seem to mean anything in our lives, it may be something we are naturally wanting, whether we know it or not. Those oh-so-blissful 'perfect' moments when the world seems to be in perfect order and we are delighted with being alive and with our place in the world – perhaps this is what gets substituted for enlightenment or the closest many of us come to it.

Experiencing oneness is experiencing a sense of total unselfconscious absorption. The usual sense of relative ego we are aware of dissolves. This dissolution of relative ego into Absolute self is what we said is happening continuously, but too fast for us to notice. In absorption states, there is no subject/object division by which relative ego can be aware of itself standing back and having the experience.

When we are one with the ocean, swimming underwater, we may have a moment of awareness: 'Ah, yes, merging with the ocean, body has dissolved into light.' But exactly as we are making this realization, we are splitting into subject and object. So, the answer to our riddle regarding how we may have a oneness experience and be aware of it is this: we catch oneness in glimpses, breaking away from absorption states just long enough to know what is occurring, and then diving back into Absolute self.

It is important to remember that oneness is not something we have to search after. It is happening *right here and now*, but just beyond our reach to grasp. We can let go at any time and experience it, and then know that we will come back into relative self. But, of course, this letting go is exactly what we are unwilling to do and exactly why we seem so far away from ourselves.

To be able to let go, we need, as we have said, to know for sure we will be coming back. And so I have tried to suggest that knowing our own minds and developing the discriminating mind is the key to allowing for the glimpses of oneness that are there for the asking.

Are we ready to melt? Can we really handle 'core melt-down' and come out unscathed? This is what relative ego frets over all of its waking (and sleeping) hours. The *old* question (and still powerful existential one in relation to finding meaning in our lives) is 'To be or not to be?' I submit that the question for those interested in mystical, spiritual experience, the real question of the next decade is 'To melt or not to melt (into absolute self)?' This, I believe, is the question we need to address when we deal with our own personal and spiritual growth.

Contemplation and absorption are at the will of the ego. Relative ego may 'invite' the state of absorption through contemplative practice. Because relative ego can exert a control over its absorption into Absolute self, it is able to set up the conditions for its own self-transcendence. By focused concentration, ego may bring upon itself the power of Absolute self. The energy provided by Absolute self strengthens the sense of ego's absorption and ego may then allow itself to become totally absorbed for varying periods of time.

But this does not mean that we are unable to call on the rational mind to do reality testing or call on knowledge or experience usually available to the relative ego. So, if we come out of the absorption state, all our normal faculties are available. And even while we are absorbed, we may become aware by briefly splitting our awareness into subject and object, that absorption is taking place.

My own meditation experience tells me that we don't have to worry. As long as we rest securely knowing the *discriminating mind* is standing at attention and ready for service, Absolute self may be safely entered into without fear. Relative ego will always be there when we need it, ready to take care of us, when we have developed and learned to trust the *discriminating mind*.

REFERENCES

Perls, Fritz (1973), *The Gestalt Approach and Eye Witness to Therapy* (Ben Lomand, CA: Science and Behavior Books).

Polster, E. and Polster, M. (1973), *Gestalt Therapy Integrated* (New York: Brunner/Mazel).

Ram Dass (1971), *Be Here Now* (San Cristobal, NM: Lama Foundation).

Wilber, Ken (1979), *No Boundary* (Los Angeles, CA: Center Publications).

Wilber, Ken (1980), *The Atman Project: A Transpersonal View of Human Development* (Wheaton, IL: Theosophical Publishing House).